£6

D0271436

DEATH
ON THE ROCK

DEATH
ON THE ROCK

AND OTHER STORIES

Roger Bolton

W H ALLEN
optomen

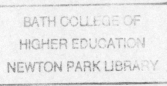
A WH Allen/Optomen Book

First published in Great Britain 1990
by WH Allen & Co Plc
Sekforde House
175/9 St John Street
London EC1V 4LL

Cataloguing in Publication Data
available on request from the British Library

ISBN 1 85227 163 9

Printed and bound in Great Britain by
Mackays of Chatham PLC, Chatham, Kent

For my children,

Alexander, Giles, Olivia and Jessica.

CONTENTS

ACKNOWLEDGEMENTS

I owe a great deal to the many journalists I've worked with, to the man who got me started in broadcasting, Patrick Mullins, and to Thames Television, the IBA, and the NUJ, who enabled me to stay in broadcasting.

I'd like to thank all of those who gave generously of their time to discuss the issues dealt with in this book. For reasons of confidentiality I cannot mention them, but they range from an occupant of No. 10 Downing Street, to a member of the Horse Race Betting Levy Board. Jeremy Paxman kindly read parts of the transcript and helped remove excessive moments of self-righteousness. Peter Smith, the Thames lawyer, has, I hope, kept me out of the libel courts. My secretary, Nicola Austin, was the calm, efficient organiser of the operation, employing the eloquent pause or raised eyebrow when I wrote something more than usually stupid. Thank you to Derek Wyatt who suggested I write the book, and to my wife Julia who, though delivering our baby in the middle of it, never complained about the nappies I missed changing.

Finally, thanks to Julian Manyon, Chris Oxley, Alison Cahn and Eamon Hardy, my *Death on the Rock* team. As I wrote to them when the Inquiry was about to start and no silver linings were apparent, "I can't think of a better group of journalists with whom to go on trial."

This is what I think happened.

BBC ABBREVIATIONS

DG	Director General
A/DG	Assistant Director General
MD Tel.	Managing Director, Television
MDR	Managing Director, Radio
DNCA	Director of News and Current Affairs
DP Tel.	Director of Programmes, Television
DPR	Director of Programmes, Radio
D. Pers.	Director of Personnel
DPA	Director of Public Affairs
CNI	Controller, Northern Ireland
HNPC	Head of Network Production Centre
HOB	Head of Broadcasting
ENCAR	Editor of News Current Affairs, Radio
HCAP Tel.	Head of Current Affairs Programmes, Television

1

BLACK FRIDAY

Friday, 23 September 1988 looked like being a wonderful sunny day, ideal for my first five-a-side game of the new season. *This Week* was safely back on the air with two good stories, and more in the bank. It was the beginning of my third year as Editor, longer than I'd lasted in any previous editor's job.

This Week occupies one large overcrowded room and a separate office for the Editor. My staff had glamour, foreign travel and expenses; I had a table, a few chairs and relative privacy if not sound proofing. I flicked through that morning's papers switched on the television set and dialled up the Oracle headlines. Nothing special.

I poured a cup of coffee and went through my in-tray, leaning back in my chair. The changing of an Oracle headline caught my eye. "Gibraltar: The Inquest". I sat up straight and stared, feeling sick. "Key Gibraltar witness admits lying." I dialled the report. "Kenneth Asquez, one of the key witnesses in the Thames Television documentary, *Death on the Rock*, about the Gibraltar shootings, today retracted his evidence in court and said he had been pressurised into making his original statement and offered money."

The office felt very quiet, and a slow silence enveloped me. In a crisis I always become very calm, perhaps unnaturally so. It's very useful in the sort of television I am involved in, frequently live and often controversial.

But this was more than a crisis, this was a disaster. Our programme was on trial at the Inquest and the team with it. I knew

[1]

how jubilant the Ministry of Defence and the Foreign Office would be at this turn of events. But the report simply wasn't true. We never offer money to witnesses: that would be a self-destructive thing to do. We could be accused of "buying them". In fact that was what we were being accused of, I suddenly realised.

Funny, I used to love Fridays. *This Week* transmits on a Thursday so the next day is one of relaxation and usually one of pleasure. Even if the previous day's programme wasn't up to scratch it is over and, ever the optimist, I believe next week will be better. And if the programme was good, the reviews may well say so, and so may colleagues in the corridor. My ego is never so sated that further reassurance is unwelcome.

And then there is five-a-side football. When I turned forty I thought team games had gone forever. I hadn't had much time for them in the last twenty years given the irregular days and hours I had worked. Suddenly at forty-two I had managed to inveigle myself into the South Bank game mainly run by London Weekend Television. Once upon a time David Frost used to play, stepping out of his chauffeur-driven Rolls immaculately dressed, if a little shaky round the stomach. Melvyn Bragg is alleged to have broken his leg in one rumbustious game. These gods of an earlier age had long gone, leaving their panting breath on the wind. Today's stars include the all-white John Birt, Deputy Director General of the BBC, a methodical player of carefully woven patterns and Greg Dyke, Director of Programmes at LWT, an all-action knees-and-elbows type, full of irrepressible energy and self-confidence. John's warming up exercises were elaborate and painstaking. I used to smile at them until I got a groin strain. Not for John the long-range shot, the lone dribble or the dummy, rather the careful build up with plenty of people behind the ball.

Friday was a day I didn't have to wear a suit, could come to work a little later and leave a little earlier, with a bit of time to doodle around the library or an exhibition. I might even have a banana milkshake from McDonald's across the Euston Road from Thames Television.

The past season had brought quite a few headlines, not least with our *Death on the Rock* programme, about the shooting of IRA terrorists in Gibraltar. The Inquest into these deaths had been going on for some days and the findings, so far, confirmed a great deal of what we had alleged in our programme. Today a key witness whom we had discovered, Carmen Proetta, was to give evidence.

I had left Warren Street tube station and crossed the Euston Road, passing groups of teenagers who seem prepared to wait for hours, regardless of the weather, in order to see the occasional pop star or DJ going into Capital Radio, whose offices are next to Thames Television.

Roger Wakefield was the security man on duty at the studios. He was Chairman of his local Conservative party and had a great sense of humour, continually urging me to acknowledge the existence of the Supreme Being, Margaret Thatcher. I told him we often invited her to be interviewed on the programme but she rarely accepted our invitation.

I went up to the fourth floor and then turned right down the long corridor which at first looks like the interior of a Holiday Inn, with thick carpeting and long ceilings and disguised lighting. This is where the boardroom is located. Further along through another pair of fire doors the corridor becomes as uninviting as any other in a sixties tower block. Little did I know what was in store.

I grabbed hold of my producer, Chris Oxley, and my researcher Alison Cahn, both of whom had worked on the Gibraltar programme. "What does it mean?" I asked them rather stupidly. They were white with shock. Why was Kenneth Asquez lying now about the statement he had given us?

The phone rang. It was the Thames Press Office. Had we heard? We had. They were receiving calls already, what could they say? I said I'd ring back shortly, and immediately I pulled my boss, Barrie Sales, out of the Executive Directors meeting that was being held as usual on Friday. Barrie is Deputy Director of Programmes and Controller of News and Current Affairs. He is a very shrewd judge of events and not prone to exaggeration. He rather underplays everything. "It's a f . . . . . g disaster," he said.

We looked at each other. We knew we had to respond to the story quickly or be swept away. Where was Julian?

Julian Manyon, the *Death on the Rock* reporter, was in court when

[3]

Asquez changed his evidence, but he had not gone there to hear Asquez or expecting trouble. He had just finished a story about General Noriega for me and was itching to get down for the Inquest just to see how things were going. At first, in my usual miserly way, I had refused to finance the trip but I had second thoughts when we heard stories that Carmen Proetta was refusing to testify.

It was yet another lie from "official sources" and we were getting used to these. The pressure on Mrs. Proetta had been intense. The *Mail on Sunday* had carried an "exclusive" story on 29 May under the headline "Carmen says 'No.'" The paper said, "Government sources in London have now revealed that Mrs. Proetta, a court interpreter, is refusing to repeat her story in court."

There was no truth to this rumour but it would have been hardly surprising if Carmen had begun to crack under pressure. Julian quickly discovered that, in fact, she had been given the choice of two days on which to give evidence and she had chosen the later one. She would appear in court, despite the best efforts of "official sources" and their allies in the press, to put her off.

After her interview with us was transmitted, Carmen was libelled appallingly. Led by the *Sun*, Britain's tabloids said she was a whore, a brothel keeper, and fanatically anti-British. She was pestered day and night by reporters. Her friends and colleagues were approached in the attempt to discover some dirt in her background. Her young daughter was even intercepted on the way to school and pressed to inform on her mother. She had received threatening and obscene phone calls and many of her neighbours had sent her to Coventry. It was a steep price for telling the truth. She, like the other witnesses, had received no money for doing so.

When her dog mysteriously disappeared it was pretty much the last straw – but she intended to testify, and stick to her story. Still, it would do no harm for Julian to demonstrate that she wasn't on her own so, late Thursday, he flew to Malaga in southern Spain and drove from there to the villa outside Gibraltar where Carmen was staying. Next morning, reassured, he drove onto the Rock to meet the lawyer who had worked for us during the filming, Chris Finch. Amnesty International had subsequently given his name to Paddy McGrory, who represented the dead IRA families and needed legal assistance on the Rock. Finch had agreed to help on the "taxi rank"

[4]

principle, and because he was concerned about his own discoveries regarding the shootings.

It was only at the last minute that Julian learned that Asquez was going to appear in the coroner's court that morning. Why? Finch told him. Although Asquez had asked us to keep his identity a secret he had written his eye-witness statement in his own hand but unsigned. It was a shocking account of how he had seen a British soldier "finishing off" a terrorist on the ground.

The police had interviewed Chris Finch regarding his own involvement in our programme and he had given them the anonymous statement and they had quickly worked out, or been tipped off, that it had been written by Kenneth Asquez. Now he was being brought to testify.

What would he say? Finch had no idea but no lesser light than the former Chief Minister of Gibraltar, Sir Joshua Hassan, was going to represent Asquez.

Julian smelled trouble. Why would Hassan represent a twenty-year-old bank clerk? He and Finch quickly finished the coffee they had been drinking in a café near the court and hurried to the Inquest deep in discussion. They hardly noticed the television cameraman filming them.

To enter the courtroom Julian had first to be accredited, so that by the time he squeezed into the back of the small crowded room Kenneth Asquez had already started giving his testimony.

Asquez spoke so softly, and in such a confused manner, that it was hard to understand him. However, it seemed that he was withdrawing his statement and was now alleging that he had been pressurised into it by a Major Randall, and that Randall had offered him money to make his original statement. The coroner cross-examined him:

CORONER: To whom did you give this [the *Death on the Rock*] statement?

ASQUEZ: To Bob Randall. At the time I was under pressure. He kept phoning me every day . . .

CORONER: Was this statement true, or parts of it correct and parts of it not true?

[5]

ASQUEZ: At the moment I'm a bit confused, because my mind is not clear.

Pressed further Asquez claimed he had invented the details of his statement from information he'd read in the press and heard in the street. The coroner was perplexed.

CORONER: The trouble is, Mr. Asquez, that this question of the beret, the ID card, and the words to the effect, "Stop, it's OK, it's the police," have only, to my understanding, come out for the first time in this court subsequent to the time that you made the statement. Can you try to explain a little further?

[Our programme had not revealed the details in the statement referred to by the coroner.]

ASQUEZ: No. I said before, I'm a bit confused. My thoughts are vague from that time.

The coroner shrugged and turned to counsel. Mr. Hucker, QC for the soldiers, pursued Asquez further and under cross-examination the young man claimed that Major Randall "had indicated that there might be something in it for me" were he willing to make a statement.

At no time did Asquez actually say that he was offered a sum of money, but he said he was told by Randall that "they were willing to make payments".

Hadn't he made up the original statement, Mr. Hucker asked? "I think so," said the twenty-year-old bank clerk. But he denied that Major Randall had helped him in any way with his statement, and admitted that he had never been given any money.

By the time Paddy McGrory stood up to represent the families of the dead, many journalists had left the court and the wires were humming with what soon became front page news.

McGrory pointed out that in addition to his own handwritten statement, Asquez had gone to see Christopher Finch and had given him an account of what had happened, although he then refused to sign the statement Finch wrote. In it he he had claimed to be "very scared for my own safety" in view of what he had seen.

McGrory pushed Asquez on the details of the alleged "finishing off" of one of the terrorists.

MCGRORY: Of all the people now present in this room, only you know whether you made it up or not, and what you are saying. There are eleven of your fellow citizens of Gibraltar, tell them whether it's true or not?

ASQUEZ: I can't say "yes" or "no". I was probably still confused.

Later Asquez said he had told lies.

MCGRORY: So without being offered an exact amount of money, are you telling the gentlemen of the jury that you're such a man as would make up a story that a man – and we now know who he was – committed murder?

ASQUEZ: No. I wrote that down to get these people off my back.

MCGRORY: Because you didn't want to be involved?

ASQUEZ: Not involved; I didn't want to be pestered.

The pestering according to Asquez had consisted of a number of telephone calls. At the end of his testimony Asquez apologised to the court. "I would like to say once again that I am sorry that I have put everyone through this ordeal."

"Yes, all right," said the coroner.

Julian had slipped away from the court when McGrory began his questioning. A newspaper wrote that he held his head in his hands on hearing Asquez's testimony. This was a lie, a colourful fabrication, by the London office, to the court correspondent's original copy.

Julian raced round to Chris Finch's office to avoid journalists and to call me in London. It was clear that we had to find Major Randall.

[7]

Julian Manyon can find anyone, given a telephone and sixty minutes. I suggested he try to find Randall in thirty.

Back in my office in London, Barrie and I set about drafting a press statement. I had learned from painful experience that unless you get your denial in quickly you're sunk. But we didn't have a verbatim transcript of what had been said. We had only the press summary and were groping in the dark. Consequently our statement didn't do much good. The tide was overwhelming us.

Then ITN rang. Would anyone from Thames appear on their lunchtime news? I said I would. I was the Editor, and the project had been my idea. I could hardly stand aside and put my team in the firing line. The only trouble was I had never met Major Randall nor had I been to Gibraltar. Never mind, I would just have to busk it. The phone rang again. This time it was BBC radio. Yes, I would do interviews for them as well, but after ITN.

Alison Cahn, our *Death on the Rock* researcher, ordered a car to take us to the ITN studios in Wells Street. I realised suddenly that with my long hair, drooping moustache and a green sweater on I could be mistaken for a member of Sinn Fein. One of my reporters, Denis Tuohy, offered me his shirt and tie. He is a few inches smaller than me but a tight fitting jacket and a colour clash would be preferable to the relaxed alternative. I set off with Alison pumping her for information in the car, and wondering all the while if in future the editors of television current affairs programmes would have to submit to studio auditions before being appointed.

At ITN I was led quickly into the studio. The presenter Jon Snow, like all news presenters, was too busy with last minute checks to do more than say hello.

Within moments the countdown started; there was no rehearsal. Fortunately I worked out where to look and tried to remember to appear serious and attentive but not fidget or look down. I had no idea what my item contained.

The news programme led with the Gibraltar story. I saw film of Julian walking along the street with Chris Finch, heard of Asquez's alleged retraction, and saw his words written on the screen. Government officials had insisted that they would not comment until the Inquest had been concluded but they could not resist the opportunity to kick us. ITN reported the Home Office saying,

"This is an object lesson to all broadcasters to beware of accepting evidence at face value."

It was no surprise to me that the news report was followed by an interview (taped before I reached the studio) with Michael Mates MP. Michael was a former soldier who had served in Northern Ireland, and, as Chairman of the Commons Defence Committee, he could always be relied upon to defend the MoD against journalists.

He was scathing and triumphant. He said that he wasn't surprised by the day's events. "I never thought the programme [*Death on the Rock*] was trying to get at the truth," he said, "it was trying to make a sensational story." He went on to pass judgement on the still incomplete Inquest.

I was surprised and gratified when Jon Snow asked Mr. Mates whether he wasn't doing what he had accused us of doing, passing a verdict before the inquest had heard all the evidence. The MP was not amused.

"What is unhelpful is to have garish stories hyped up by a television unit in this case simply trying to prejudice a matter and make a point, but the media is free to make a fool of itself and it seems as though on this occasion it has."

Having put Michael Mates on the spot Jon Snow proceeded to do the same to me. I couldn't help admiring his professionalism at the same time as I parried his questions.

"Mr. Bolton, the allegation is then that Mr. Asquez was pressured by a Major Randall who was in your employ."

"Well, Major Randall did not pressure anyone and he was not in our employ. We did try to get at the truth and we did not come to a judgement."

I went on to point out that the programme had ended not with a verdict but with an eminent QC's suggestion that a judicial enquiry be held. Furthermore, would much of the evidence have come out had we not made our programme?

Jon Snow was not to be deflected. "What then was your relationship with Major Randall?"

I explained that Major Randall had shot the video film of the aftermath of the shootings which all the news organisations had shown. When buying this material from him he had mentioned to

[9]

us that there were a number of witnesses to the shootings. Asquez, who was one of them, had given us a written statement via Randall and had then made another to our lawyer, but he had refused to meet us face to face.

"Would you then be in a position to say whether Major Randall had put pressure on Mr. Asquez to give this statement?"

It was a very shrewd question. I didn't know. I'd never met Major Randall. (Where was he, why wasn't he denying all this?)

"Well we don't know exactly what went on between Major Randall and the witness," I replied. "But – this is another element that needs to be stressed – Major Randall has not had his opportunity to put his side of the case. Certainly we are not in the business of paying witnesses and we did not pressurise or ask for pressure to be brought upon this man."

Snow persisted: "So you deny that there was any offer of money to Asquez directly or indirectly?"

(I didn't know the answer to that. I simply had to put my trust in my journalists. I couldn't equivocate.)

"Yes." I replied.

I then repeated the point that had so intrigued the coroner. Where had the remarkable details in Asquez's statement come from, since they had only been revealed by him at the Inquest?

The interview ended. Jon Snow went on to his next item and I sat back, feeling exhausted. I had given some hostages to fortune. If pressure or money had been offered, unknown to my team, I was sunk.

When the programme ended I was hustled into an office where an ITN film camera team and reporter wanted to repeat the interview for splicing into later bulletins. That done, Alison and I returned to Thames where Julian was talking on the phone to Barrie Sales. Barrie had been monitoring the news programmes and was dismayed: "We just can't get our side of the story across."

As soon as we walked into the Thames reception we were told that a BBC film crew was waiting for me in the boardroom. I sat down and chatted to the sympathetic reporter. "It must be terrible," he said, offering sympathy. It certainly was. He smiled kindly. "OK, turn over," he told the cameraman. He turned back to me. "Are you going to resign?"

Back in Gibraltar, Julian Manyon was still trying to locate Major Randall. It became apparent that the Major was on holiday, so Julian rang all the travel agents on the Rock to find out who had made Randall's holiday arrangements. Before long he tracked the Major's agents and went round to their office to persuade them to give him Randall's itinerary. They wouldn't budge but Manyon is a remarkably persistent man. Eventually they agreed to cooperate if Julian could get a letter from Christopher Finch's office authorising them to do so. Back went *This Week*'s reporter to the lawyer's office, then back again to the travel agent, where he was finally given it. At long last we knew that Major Randall was travelling with his wife and teenage son in the United States. Their tour included visits to New York, Philadelphia, Washington, Orlando and Miami. At last we had the names of the hotels at which he would be staying and the telephone numbers.

When we finally talked to Bob Randall on the phone in the early hours of Saturday morning he was flabbergasted and angered by Asquez's statement, which he categorically denied. He also revealed that he had checked with the Gibraltar police before leaving. They had known what Asquez planned to say, yet had told Randall not to bother to stay for the Inquest but to go and enjoy himself. Very strange; but the Major didn't see why he should interrupt his holiday. It was a trip of a lifetime, costing well over three thousand pounds, and his wife in particular had been looking forward to it for years.

Of course, Randall hadn't seen the British television news or read the newspaper headlines as we had. Friday's *Evening Standard* read, "I lied for TV's *Death on the Rock*." Barrie Sales, Chris Oxley, Alison Cahn and I had spent the rest of Friday on the phone trying to get our message across, but evidently without much success.

I was particularly angry with BBC *Newsnight*'s coverage and rang the deputy editor Nigel Chapman to tell him. I instantly regretted doing so. Nigel had once worked for me in the BBC and he stoutly defended his programme as I would have done in his place. But *Newsnight* seemed to me to be simply accepting the Government's version of events, as had the BBC's *Nine O'Clock News*. To my, not entirely unbiased, mind the ITN and Channel 4 news reporting had been vastly better and adopted a more sceptical and objective tone. "Why did you say Asquez 'admitted' he lied," I asked Nigel. "To say 'admitted' implies that you agree that he lied on our programme. He may just as well be lying now. You don't know. I don't know. You should say, 'Asquez *says* he told lies'."

Nigel grunted and said I might have a point and that he would consider it.

Not much sleep was had that night. I was up early and drove round to the nearest newsagent to get all of the Saturday papers. I read them and had my own version of morning sickness. The *Daily Mail* had "Lies on the Rock." "I told lie after lie," said the *Sun*'s headline. It ran the photo of Bob Randall with a caption "Major Bob the TV pest." Its editorial column was headed "Thames TV in the dock" and referred to our "infamous programme" which had "virtually accused our security men of murder and then went on to find them guilty". The editorial concluded, "What does Thames TV intend to do about everyone involved in this disgraceful programme? And what does the Independent Broadcasting Authority, the guardian of the public interest, intend to do about Thames TV?"

Perhaps Thames and the IBA could have shrugged this off but *The Times* asked the same questions in a long leader headlined "Serious Questions". It went on to say that the only way the whole story could be told ". . . is if Thames Television mount the severest internal inquiry of its own."

"A company sensitive to the concerns of its audience should be prepared to do so before any such action is requested by the IBA. Failing that the IBA should conduct its own inquiry."

Barrie Sales and I argued that nothing should be done until the end of the Inquest when all the evidence had been heard, or at least until Major Randall had been given an opportunity to put his side of the case. Agreeing to an Inquiry so quickly would be seen as a confession of guilt, we thought. It was to no avail. The IBA had already been on to Thames, and Sir Ian Trethowan the Chairman, and Richard Dunn the Managing Director decided jointly that there would have to be an Inquiry, or there would be one imposed on them. Barrie and I were not consulted and the news was given to the press by Saturday lunchtime. I knew how the *Sunday Times* would react. They had fiercely attacked our programme when first transmitted, calling it a "TV Lie". Sure enough, their front page story on Sunday 25 September 1988 read, "Thames set up inquest on TV lies."

The Government, which had consistently said it would not comment on the Gibraltar shootings until the Inquest had brought in its verdict, was unable to turn down the opportunity presented to it. George Younger, the Defence Secretary, told the *Sunday Times*, "I have not had an opportunity to study the evidence in detail, but when I have done so I shall be in touch with the Home Secretary, whose responsibility this area is, to see what further action, if any, should be taken."

This was a pretty direct threat, but the Defence Secretary had not finished. Major Randall was about to be found guilty in his absence. "As far as I can see," George Younger went on, "the programme people are saying that they did not pressure the witness. But this seems to gloss over the fact that it was an agent of theirs who did so."

There was one ray of hope on that Saturday. By its final edition the *Daily Telegraph* had managed to get hold of Major Randall and carried his denial. And all its editions contained a profile of the Major which ought to have given our assailants pause for thought.

It revealed that Major Robert Randall was a retired career soldier, a leading local football and boxing referee and president and chairman of Gibraltar's junior football league. His father was secretary of Gibraltar's Football Association and is commemorated by a trophy, the Randall Cup, played for in an annual match between Gibraltar and British Service teams. One of his sons is an officer in the Gibraltar Regiment, and was on a course at Sandhurst at the time of the Inquest. Was this the sort of man who would pressurise Kenneth Asquez to lie about British soldiers, to accuse them falsely of shooting an unarmed Irishman in the back and of finishing him off on the ground?

Chris Oxley and Julian had argued from the beginning that Chris should get on a plane for the States and get an affidavit from Bob Randall, who still didn't seem to understand the magnitude of the situation. I hesitated for twenty-four hours, partly because I didn't want to pressure Bob Randall to speak – I thought it would be better if he did it of his own free will – and partly because, absurdly, I was worried about the cost. The Saturday papers and the decision to hold an Inquiry made my mind up for me and Chris flew off.

The Sunday morning papers made me feel sick again. They were awful. That evening Julian flew back from Spain as there was nothing else he could do there. On the way home from the airport he stopped at my house in west London and we had a drink.

We were pretty much in despair. We hadn't lost faith in Bob Randall or in our programme but we were losing too much ground. No one wanted to listen to our side of the story. Before leaving Gibraltar Julian had talked with Paddy McGrory, the lawyer for the families, who waxed philosophically about the events of the last few days. "Don't worry, Julian," he said, "the truth usually comes out eventually."

Julian and I suspected it would come out far too late to save us. Even some of our friends and colleagues were criticising our use of Asquez's testimony. I thought my head would have to roll, but I was damned if we would go down without a bloody great fight. I was furious that witnesses who had spoken to us in good faith and with considerable courage, should be libelled and grossly abused. If we didn't stand up for them, and for our programme, who would?

Monday morning indicated just how tough the job of turning things round would be. The *Guardian* editorial spoke of "the somewhat murky role played by Major Bob Randall." Hadn't they seen the Major's denial? I rang the *Guardian* and eventually got through to the leader writer concerned – didn't he know Randall had completely denied Asquez's allegations? Er no. Well shouldn't he have checked with the Major before condemning him? The writer explained that he had penned his editorial that Sunday morning on the train to the Labour Party Conference in Blackpool, from the Sunday papers spread before him. I hung up before I lost my temper.

I walked into work. Even friendly faces seemed to look away. Animated conversations lapsed into embarrassed silences as I went past. I walked into the office and sat down.

The papers were now saying that investigative journalism was on trial, that its future in television depended on the result of the Inquiry, as did the future of the IBA and of Thames itself. It was a very very hot kitchen to be in.

How on earth had I ended up in it?

2

GROWING UP SLOWLY

My fascination with Ireland had begun when I was quite young, though it was the literature and landscape that captured me rather than politics.

My first memory of Ireland is of a holiday spent there in 1957. I was eleven years old and had taken a week off primary school to join my parents in Ballycastle, County Antrim, for an early summer holiday. Travelling across on the ferry from Stranraer to Larne I wore my new grammar school blazer which I was not yet entitled to wear. I looked around nervously in case anyone saw and reported me to the headmaster of Carlisle Grammar School. When I wasn't worrying about that I was thinking of a ferry on the same route which my parents had kindly told me sank in a gale shortly after the war with few survivors.

We travelled on by bus to Ballymena where we waited for another bus to take us to our destination. Dad bought a paper. The front page was full of a trial that was going on in which a local business man was accused of embezzlement. "Do you think he'll be found guilty?" my father said to a local man who was waiting beside. "Oh no," said the man jovially, "he's got a lot of good friends around here, he'll get off." And he did. While we were staying in Ballycastle a local radio and television transmitter was blown up by the IRA. It was about all they did in the fifties and early sixties.

The beauty of the North Antrim coast and the mystery of the Giant's Causeway cast a spell on me. Long sandy beaches, the wind in the reeds, bare headlands, fleeting clouds, birds singing and the silence.

During the next few years I read a lot of Irish history and was proud, and a little amused, to discover that St. Patrick was in fact a Romano-Briton from Cumbria who had been kidnapped by the Vikings and taken to Ireland.

When I then discovered that Robert the Bruce was a Frenchman who owned more land in England than Scotland, and that St. George was Greek, I began to cast a sceptical eye on nationalism.

By the time I reached the sixth form a wave of CND activity had spread throughout the school, and some very attractive badges could be worn if one joined, but I didn't have the faith – indeed I found faith deserting me altogether.

My parents were evangelical Christians and Sunday papers were not allowed in our house, until I pointed out to my father that it was the Monday papers he shouldn't take as they were written and printed on Sunday. Faced with the prospect of two days without papers he capitulated.

At one time I thought of entering the ministry and went on a course for potential ordinands at Rydal Water in the Lake District. Being so close to nature and to Wordsworth it was ideal for the job but I couldn't overcome the problem of suffering, or quite reconcile two of the Church of England's Thirty-nine Articles which deal with predestination and free will.

Our local curate Eric Pratt thought he had solved the dilemma. I was a rather troublesome member of the church youth club, always asking awkward questions, and I kept on about what I saw as the contradiction between these two Articles. Finally he thought he had the answer.

"Now, Roger, imagine that you are going down a corridor which has many doors leading off from it. Christ is behind only one of those doors, you are free to close whichever door you like, but whichever one it is Christ will be behind it."

It sounded profound – for a moment. I was also exposed to the emotional pressure of Billy Graham's "Youth for Christ" rallies. Many in my church believed that an emotional conversion was necessary. One had to know the time and place when you took God into your heart. A local lay preacher told us his conversion happened while he was standing on a soapbox in Sheffield.

One Sunday afternoon I had a really good try at it. The sun was intermittently shining from behind the clouds and its rays were pouring out like a William Blake picture. I ran along the road holding my breath until I was dizzy, gazing all the time at the sun's rays, shouting to myself "I believe, I believe, I'm converted." However, when I stopped for breath nothing had changed, and it began drizzling.

Perhaps doubting my spiritual state I was taken to the "Youth for Christ" rallies. We stood in the darkness surrounded by pools of light around us listening to emotional hymns. We were asked to go up on the stage and sign a card saying we had given our lives to God. "You have only three verses left to take Christ into your heart." I stayed still. "You have only two verses left. You know you have sinned and the Day of Judgement is coming." People on either side of me began to move. "Only one verse left." "Lord of my Life I come," sang the congregation. My body began to move but my heart did not. I sat down.

I had the same problem with the Campaign for Nuclear Disarmament. I loved the people, I admired their principles; but I couldn't order my mind to stop asking awkward questions.

This was almost entirely due to my parents' conflicting attitudes. The poverty of her family, brought on by the death of her father when she was twelve, prevented my mother from going on to higher education. Regretting what she had missed she wanted me to go to university; and to this end she encouraged me to read and to question everything.

My father, on the other hand, had a simple faith. He had joined the Peace Pledge Union in the thirties and was a devoted admirer of the Reverend Dick Sheppard who ran it. There were to be no more wars and he would not fight.

But when he and my mother went on a walking tour of Germany in 1937 it seemed transparently obvious to them that a war was coming and that the Jews in Germany were in great danger. When war was declared my father, though too old to be drafted, volunteered.

Later my mother would say they had had the worst of both worlds. By being pacifists they had failed to oppose Hitler's aggression early enough to avert the necessity of a world war. It was a war in which they lost many friends, including some young apprentices who worked in my father's small joinery business.

[17]

Even so my parents retained their faith in God but in an increasingly liberal way. Since my father would never condemn anyone to Hell he couldn't really believe that God would do so either. His was a God of love and a Christianity not only of faith but also of good works.

He was also an undertaker. In my teens I often acted as a funeral bearer for him. I was overwhelmed by the beauty of the Prayer Book and impressed by the comfort which faith and the burial service brought to the bereaved.

When I met the Protestants of Northern Ireland I felt I knew them very well, and was tickled to discover that many of the families "planted" in Ulster in the seventeenth century had in fact come from my Border area. But we had links with the South as well. I had sometimes wondered why my father was so fond of Count John McCormack's songs. My father himself had a lovely tenor voice and sang Victorian Irish ballads with great feeling. It transpired that like his father he had been baptised a Roman Catholic. But while living near Preston in Lancashire, my grandfather had committed the unforgivable sin of marrying a Protestant. Since this made both my grandparents outcasts in their communities they walked the ninety miles north to Carlisle to start afresh, where my grandmother proved herself to be a tough customer, rearing nine children who were baptised as Roman Catholics, but were brought up as Protestants. It didn't "take" with them all.

At Liverpool University I read Yeats and Joyce and spent the summer after graduation driving around Ireland visiting Stephen D's Martello Tower and bowing to the tombstone under Ben Bulben.

> Cast a cold eye on Life, on Death,
> Horseman Pass By!

That was in 1967, the year before the Troubles began again, and the year I joined the BBC as a general trainee, having been selected by a former colonial civil servant, Patrick Mullins, to go before the final multi membered Board of the Good and Great. I think that year they decided they couldn't select all Oxbridge candidates, so I crept in on the back of the Beatles.

In many ways it would have been better if I had first joined the

Thomson organisation as an editorial trainee, the job I turned down to go to the BBC. That way I would have had a crash course in the realities of local newspapers, births, deaths, and marriages, and the limitations and frailties of human nature and human organisations. Instead I moved heart and soul into the BBC and found a new religion, committed to the unvarnished truth and with a dazzling range of opportunities.

Before long I was attached to *The Question Why?* with Malcolm Muggeridge, whom I admired but who also rather angered me. He kept disparaging television but kept appearing on it, rather like Robin Day. The cheques were not returned. Malcolm called himself a pianist in a brothel. What did that make the members of the production team? Soon I had moved on to the Current Affairs Department then run by John Grist.

He had insisted on seeing me personally before deciding I could be attached to his department, so I approached his office with some trepidation, feverishly thinking of all the most difficult questions he might put.

I need not have worried. Grist was in ruminative mood. He asked hardly a question. After an hour of his reflections on the lack of historical knowledge in his producers, and the problems he was having with his daughter (was he seeking advice? from me?), I left his office bewildered but happy and was dispatched downstairs to *The Money Programme*, where I sat with nothing to do until some-one summoned me back upstairs to play Scrabble.

I was losing badly, when an extraordinary figure entered. It was Barbara Maxwell, now the greatly respected producer of *Question Time*, then a young and clearly impatient secretary. She wore a mini skirt that was little wider than a belt, and her flame coloured hair poured down over her wildly extravagant bosom. She told me of the *24 Hours* Editor, Derick Amoore who shot at photographs with an air pistol in his office, and of a *Panorama* producer who was having an affair with an African princess. Were they all like this?

Shortly afterwards while walking down the hospitality corridor I heard violent noises. Peter Ibbotson was smashing a chair on to the head of Richard Kershaw.

But *The Money Programme* turned out to be relatively respectable and I soon got down to the serious business of making economic reports. In those days the attraction of the programme was that it defined the approach to a subject but never limited the subject matter. Thus I could examine the fortunes of Workington Football Club as long as I opened its financial books, and I could film the beautiful starlet Julie Edge in a variety of revealing poses providing I used it to illustrate the economics of the film industry. Difficult but not impossible.

We also reported on the great new plans for expanding steel production and the bright future of shipbuilding.

I was not in a position to report on the Civil Rights marches in Northern Ireland in 1968 but by the early seventies I was examining the economic difficulties of both the North and South, or rather providing the pictures while Alan Watson and Francis Hope did so; and I met Brian Faulkner, later to become Prime Minister of Northern Ireland, then Minister of Commerce explaining how damaging "local difficulties" were to the business of getting firms to come to the North. It was very important, he said, that we painted a "positive image" of Ulster. Jobs depended upon it.

In the South we soon discovered that few were interested in reunification, it was a distant aspiration. What mattered there too were jobs and the standard of living. How could they stop so many young people leaving? We were welcomed wherever we went until one Sunday in Dublin when we came back to our hotel and were told we should leave immediately. The Government interviews planned for the following day had been cancelled without explanation. There was angry silence all around us.

It was 30 January 1972, "Bloody Sunday", the day British paratroopers shot dead thirteen civilians during a Civil Rights march in Derry. We left. The following day the British Embassy building in Dublin was burned down. To my regret I never worked with Francis Hope again. A fine poet and critic with a remarkable wit and intellect, he was killed in the Paris Air Crash of 1974.

When we returned to the BBC TV's Current Affairs Department at Lime Grove, a fierce row was still going on between the Corporation and the Government over a studio programme, *The Question of Ulster*. It was the first time I had observed a confrontation between the broadcasters and Whitehall, and it caused what the

BBC Chairman, Lord Hill, described as "a storm of a severity unprecedented in my experience".

The producer of this straightforward programme was Dick Francis, later the BBC's Controller in Northern Ireland, and then Director of News and Current Affairs.

Dick had majored in big studio specials and had masterminded the BBC's coverage of the American space missions in his role as Editor, Special Projects. He had done this brilliantly, but at the expense of importing a number of Americanisms into his vocabulary. Instead of "yes" or "no" it was "affirmative" or "negative" and a telephone call became a "two-way audio interchange".

Now he planned a three-hour programme, *The Question of Ulster – an Inquiry into the Future*. Taking part would be eight leading Protestant and Catholic political figures, not the IRA or Loyalist paramilitaries. Lord Devlin was to lead a distinguished three-man panel which would question each of the eight, who in turn could call their own expert witnesses.

As if to minimise controversy the programme was to begin with the views of the British Government and Opposition. It would be "a long cool programme of talk, not action," said the producer, "which would do something to complement the day-to-day newsfilm of violence and disorder."

If Mr. Heath's Government had its way it would do nothing at all. On 13 December the Home Secretary, Reginald Maudling, summoned the Chairman and the Director General of the BBC to see him. Maudling was an easy-going man but on this occasion, according to the *Daily Telegraph*, "Maudling blew his top." The Northern Ireland Prime Minister, Brian Faulkner, had led Stormont's opposition to the programme because it would contain only one official Unionist. Now the Home Secretary said he was seriously worried about what he regarded as a potentially dangerous programme.

The *Daily Telegraph* as usual came to the Government's aid. "It is scarcely surprising that some Ministers and Conservative MPs believe there are no limits to the irresponsibility of the Corporation," it said.

For the first time I witnessed that fundamental clash of principle between a government which believes it has the right to determine what is in the national interest and a broadcasting authority which feels that its role in a democracy is to report, to inform, and to represent the wide range of opinion existing in the country.

There followed a game of cat and mouse. The Corporation modified its programme proposal to give more emphasis to the "special position of the majority party in Ulster". The British and Stormont Governments then said they would boycott the programme, thus hoping to put an end to it. The BBC Governors decided that without an official Unionist appearing the programme could not go ahead, but Dick Francis and his team, working through Christmas and the New Year, found such a person in the nick of time, the MP John Maginnis.

The Home Secretary was left to decide whether he would use his ultimate weapon, Clause 13 (4) of the BBC's Charter which permits the minister responsible for broadcasting to order the BBC not to transmit specific material. According to some reports the BBC Chairman told the Home Secretary that if the ban was used the BBC would make it very public indeed.

Maudling held back but the day before the programme he issued an unprecedented public rebuke to the former Conservative minister, then BBC Chairman, Lord Hill. "I believe that this programme, in the form in which it has been devised, can do no good, and could do serious harm."

Robin Day had been asked to present the programme which would have been an ideal vehicle for his considerable talents. Faced with the Government's attitude, however, he pulled out and his place was taken by Ludovic Kennedy.

The programme went ahead and it would be difficult to think of a more sober and non-controversial contribution to the Northern Ireland Debate.

Lord Caradon, one of the tribunal members on the programme, summed up with the words, "We have not done much damage tonight. We may have been dull but we have not been dangerous."

A letter written to *The Times* agreed and quoted Sir Thomas Browne. "This is the dormitive I take to bed ward; I need no other laudanum to make me sleep."

All this cut little ice in Whitehall where, according to the *Guardian*, it was argued "with the utmost vehemence that the impact of

the programme threatened to create an attitude of despair and
indifference among the British public, and to feed the view that
British troops should be withdrawn."

For twenty years many parts of Whitehall, Westminster and
Downing Street have held unswervingly to that view.

Across on ITV they were having their problems as well. In
November 1971 *World In Action* had made a programme called
South of the Border, showing how the troubles in the North were
building up pressures in the South of Ireland. Those interviewed
included Sean MacStiofain, the Provisional IRA's chief of staff and
Ruari O'Bradaigh, its president, as well as Dublin politicians who
were hostile to the IRA. The Chairman of the Independent Television Authority, former Labour minister Lord Aylestone, felt it
was "aiding and abetting the enemy" and the ITA banned it.

Despite making controversial programmes, the independent
television companies somehow seemed to attract less odium than
the BBC, perhaps because there were so many of them and only
one BBC, or perhaps it was because of the word British in the
Corporation's title. It was the national instrument of broadcasting,
but what was the nation, or nations, it represented? The Troubles
raised a question about the very structure of the United Kingdom.
Could the UK deal with questions about its own integrity in the
same way as it dealt with more peripheral matters? Free speech
was coming under the most fierce examination.

I continued on *The Money Programme* until 1973 when I moved to
Panorama as a producer and a year later found myself close to the
border in South Armagh with Michael Charlton. We were making
a film called *Bandit Country* and it was an eye-opening experience. I
had become accustomed to army roadblocks between Aldergrove
Airport and the centre of Belfast and had once counted seven of
them as I drove to the Harland and Wolf Shipyards. Now in the
south of Ulster I was at more roadblocks, only these were operated
by another army, the Provisional IRA. On one occasion, as I was
driving along with an army intelligence officer in civilian clothes as
my guide, we came up against yet another IRA car check. Fortunately my companion saw it early and had me quickly reverse
and drive away.

In order to reach Crossmaglen we had to fly in by helicopter, landing in the forecourt of a police station by now protected like Fort Knox. I was determined to get the best pictures of an army patrol in this most republican of villages, and that meant getting ahead of the patrol. They opened the heavily guarded gate briefly to let us out and we tried to saunter as casually as possible with our camera equipment very very visible. Moments later the patrol dashed out and took shelter before moving off, each member covering the other. We squatted down by a bicycle until I remembered reading of one which had been booby trapped and which had blown up a squaddie. Everything was potentially dangerous. Did the pram contain a baby or a bomb? Was the parked car primed to explode as the soldiers went past? I did the patrol once. Nineteen and twenty-year-olds were doing it twice a day.

Through the depressing council house estate we went, back to the main square and then suddenly the soldiers were off, back into the police station. We stood in an eerie silence. What was the purpose of the patrol, this risking of life over and over again? Never did the British army look more like an occupying force, as they passed sign after sign supporting the IRA. We went into the hotel and were served by a jovial barman, who must have seen a dozen film crews. He chatted about the latest football news and some rich piece of gossip. It seemed most odd that no off-duty British soldier could drop in and join the conversation.

As I moved from republican bar to army mess, I found it difficult not to feel that stupid, naive, liberal, rather English response – "Look, if we just all sat down and talked about this I'm sure we would see each other's point of view."

By 1974, the Army had no illusions about there being a military solution to the Troubles. They were just holding the ring, and perfecting a lot of anti-terrorist techniques. They knew they were in for a very long haul.

Throughout the seventies television programmes in Ireland were banned, altered or postponed. For example, in 1973 the unique and admittedly awkward Kenneth Griffith made a brilliant and committed film about Michael Collins, the IRA leader in the war against Britain in 1920 and a signatory of the treaty which led to the Civil War in which he died. Sir Lew Grade, ATV's Managing Director, banned it and even Griffith did not have access to his own film. Griffith's previous film had been on Cecil Rhodes, but that was about another continent and had been transmitted.

Then in August 1977 Peter Taylor, an outstanding reporter on Irish affairs, made a film which he described as "an alternative diary" of the Queen's Jubilee visit to Northern Ireland. He pointed his cameras away from the cheering, flag-waving Protestant crowds to the silent, angry Catholic streets. The IBA took exception to several sections of the film and banned it with two minutes to go before transmission. The film eventually did go out, with some small alterations, two weeks after the visit when its topicality was somewhat reduced.

Over at the BBC Keith Kyle was investigating some extremely serious allegations that Bernard O'Connor, a Catholic school-master, had been illtreated by the RUC at Castlereagh. The film was checked and rechecked before transmission. Its allegations were well founded, however, as in July 1980 O'Connor won five thousand pounds in compensation as exemplary damages for mal-treatment.

Nevertheless, at the time the stance of the BBC was heavily attacked by the RUC, who said that "the fear here is that terrorists might seize on this as provocation to kill more policemen". At the House of Commons a dozen Tory MPs launched a heated attack at a private meeting on 7 March 1977 when they faced Dick Francis, then still the BBC's Controller in Northern Ireland.

Particularly critical was the Tory Opposition spokesperson for Northern Ireland, Airey Neave, who launched a campaign against the BBC, protesting to the Chairman and going on to make a speech in which he accused the BBC of undermining the propaganda war and helping terrorism.

We are losing the propaganda war in Northern Ireland. [he said] The security forces may make arrests, but skilful propaganda is as lethal as a gun or a bomb. A review of present attitudes to media freedom is needed therefore, to take account of a desperate emergency. Some of the media deny that we are really at war with terrorism. Some of their actions actually stimulate the hardcore terrorist mentality. The BBC, in particular, pronounce on the security situation with studied grandi-

loquence and ignore the true dangers . . . This *Tonight* programme has had the most damaging effects on morale in the
RUC. In justifying it on grounds of "impartiality", the BBC have
given the impression that they are not really on the side of the
civil power in Northern Ireland.

Neave called for a review of media guidelines.

Eleven days after the *Tonight* programme, an eighteen-year-old
constable was shot dead in Fermanagh by the Provisional IRA. Police
Federation Chairman Alan Wright immediately blamed this on the
programme. "BBC blamed for police killing," said the *Guardian*. The
Mirror had "Trial by TV: BBC accused." But the *Daily Express* rose to
the challenge of such competition. Its huge headline read "Murder by
TV." This was shooting the messenger with a vengeance.

Some time later it was officially confirmed that there had been
inhuman and degrading treatment at Castlereagh.

Airey Neave was the authentic voice of Thatcherism and her
most valued political adviser and colleague. It was he who had
urged her to stand against Ted Heath for the Party leadership in
1975 and had run her campaign brilliantly. Heath retiring after the
first ballot, several other contenders came into the second, and we
thought it would be a good idea to get them all into the studio for a
special *Panorama* programme. All, including Mrs. Thatcher,
agreed. I was to produce the programme and in the beginning it
seemed to be quite straightforward. Jim Prior, John Peyton, and Sir
Geoffrey Howe were to be recorded first. Then William Whitelaw
and Mrs. Thatcher separately, a little later. Whereas the men
behaved in the traditional Conservative manner, their female
opponent started to use her elbows.

To be fair, she had an extremely punishing schedule. Apart from
bidding for the leadership she was also, as a Conservative Treasury
spokesperson, fighting the new Finance Bill through committee,
often going into the early hours. This gave her an increased profile
but also much additional strain.

Both candidates were down to speak at the Young Conservatives
Conference in Eastbourne, which should have been in Whitelaw's
favour as the YCs were, on the whole, supporters of his candi-
dature. He was to speak on devolution, a rather dull subject.

Should he make an election call to arms, a statement of his personal philosophy? He thought that would be ungentlemanly and suggested to the Thatcher camp that neither candidate use the occasion as a campaign opportunity. They agreed.

Whitelaw then went through a boring question-and-answer session, while Mrs. Thatcher turned aside from her speech on the Economy and gave a five-minute political credo. This produced a sixty-seven-second count of applause and the first kiss of the day for the Chairman. Not content with that, Mrs. Thatcher arranged a photocall on the beach front at Eastbourne and, when Willie appeared, kissed him on the cheek for the cameras. Whitelaw looked embarrassed, Thatcher regal. Forty love.

By now she was so far ahead of the others that only a disaster could prevent her election. Her campaigners decided to play safe and Gordon Reece, her television adviser, told her to pull out. Reece thought another bonus would be that, as the other four male candidates would look much alike, it would be Hamlet without the Prince – or rather Princess.

According to Michael Cockerell in his excellent book *Live from Number 10*, "Her campaign manager's line to the press was that she objected to the format of the programme. As it was proposed to pre-record the interview, Mrs. Thatcher would not have the opportunity to reply to any criticism of her policy her rivals might make." The *Daily Telegraph* reported "Many of her friends consider that she was perfectly right to show the BBC that politicians are not at its beck and call."

The problem for Mrs. Thatcher was that she had given me her word that she would appear. To her credit she phoned me herself on the Sunday evening to tell me she would not be appearing. It was the first of three phone calls over the twenty-four hours before the Monday evening's programme.

She began by saying that pre-recording was unfair. She was the leading candidate, the others could, perhaps would, criticise her but although her interview was to be transmitted last she couldn't reply as it was pre-recorded. I promised to think about that and ring her back, after having discussed her views with my Editor.

We talked again the next morning. Yes we would interview Mrs. Thatcher live but we would ask her not to comment on the other interviews unless they contained specific criticism of her, otherwise those who were pre-recorded would be at a disadvantage. There was a pause. "No, I'm sorry Mr. Bolton, that's not good enough." We argued back and forward for the next half hour as I tried to counter each of her concerns and complaints. I gently pointed out that if she didn't appear I would have to explain to the audience the precise circumstances of her withdrawal. She suddenly got very angry, "I know the Copyright Law, Mr. Bolton." I didn't; what did she mean? Eventually she said she would have to think about what I'd said and ring me back again. There was now only a few hours left before the recording and live transmission.

In the *Panorama* office at Lime Grove we were all on edge. Brian Wenham, the Head of TV Current Affairs appeared and together with the Editor, Frank Smith, discussed what we could do. Mrs. Thatcher was the star attraction, it would be a big let-down if she pulled out; on the other hand if she was to be the next Conservative leader the BBC would not wish to start off its relationship with her on the wrong foot. "But she gave me her word," I said, rather indignant that politicians should be behaving like politicians and rather worried that my boss would think I'd cocked it up.

I fiddled with a piece of paper and tried to draw caricatures of the leadership candidates. I dared not go to lunch in case she called back and instead drank cup after cup of the chicory-tasting liquid which the BBC canteen called coffee.

At around 3 p.m. the call finally came. "Mr. Bolton," the woman on the other end was sobbing, "I'm sorry I can't take part in your programme. I agree you have been straightforward with me but . . . I'm sorry." I was so taken aback I hardly said anything other than to thank her for calling back. I put down the phone. Why had she been crying? Was it the strain of the last few days or did she really hate going back on her word?

Whatever the reason I now had to tell the other candidates. The three also rans were not much affected. Sir Geoffrey and Messrs. Prior and Peyton knew they were outsiders anyway, simply putting down markers for future jobs. Willie Whitelaw could be different. It appeared to be neck and neck between him and Mrs. Thatcher.

I met him coming along the corridor with his campaign "minder",

Michael Mates. When I outlined what had happened Mates was angry, but not surprised. The midnight meetings he had attended with Willie Whitelaw had had their share of tears and anger.

The candidate himself paused, should he pull out too? "Oh well," he said smiling ruefully, "I've agreed to it so let's get on."

It was not the most exciting edition of *Panorama*, and next day Mrs. Thatcher had a handsome overall majority.

Over the next few years I saw a lot of Gordon Reece, as I tended to produce most of the major political interviews for *Panorama* and later, as Editor of *Tonight*, *Panorama* and *Nationwide*, arranged Prime Ministerial interviews.

Gordon was an extremely attractive and engaging man, with a quick wit. On one occasion he invited me to his club and as we sat down beneath horse prints he offered me champagne and orange. His taste for champagne seemed to be unquenchable, and was the cause of some comment when he resided at Conservative Central Office. On his arrival the expense account expanded. "Never mind," someone said, "if you've got a Rolls Royce you have to treat it like a Rolls Royce." His reputation as a media guru soared. Under his tutelage Mrs. Thatcher's hair, teeth, and voice all changed. Although he obviously admired her greatly and owed his position and influence only to her he was capable of being quite tough when required. "Now Margaret," he would say, when she was becoming unreasonable.

Mrs. Thatcher never liked giving television interviews. "I hate them, I hate them, I hate them," she said, and would always be in a nervous and tetchy mood beforehand. If they went well the sun came out, she was relaxed and amusing, and would even partake of a little whisky, before gradually telling us all what we should think.

But although Gordon was so charming I was rather shocked by his strategy. In my rather naive way I thought Prime Ministers and Leaders of the Opposition had a responsibility to put themselves up to tough interviewing on a regular basis. And that meant Robin Day or David Dimbleby on *Panorama*.

Gordon Reece's analysis was rather different. He was interested in two things, the size of the audience and the image of Mrs. Thatcher that would be presented.

Accordingly she began to give interviews to the tabloid newspapers as frequently as to the broadsheets, and Jimmy Young on Radio 2 and television chat show hosts saw rather more of her than *Panorama* did.

When she finally appeared on our programme Gordon was rarely concerned with the content. He would ask for the coloured lights on the background of the set to be changed. Hard masculine desks would be frowned at. He wanted relaxed chairs and flowers. Once Mrs. Thatcher became Prime Minister he would try and ensure that she was interviewed at No. 10, with the trappings of Premiership, and flowers, all around her.

In 1977 I left *Panorama* to produce two programmes on the Soviet military build-up with Lord Chalfont, later to be one of my fiercest critics, with an attitude over coverage of Ireland and national security matters totally opposed to mine. I've always liked Alun, a remarkably charming man whose arrogance is laced with irony and self-deprecation, and whose violent speeches are undercut by a personal gentleness. The programmes were called *The Writing on the Wall* and, since there was a Soviet military build-up and Alun's commentary was more factual than polemical, we got on well. Even Clive James, not Chalfont's keenest admirer, thought it was quite good. He wrote in the *Observer*. "He [Chalfont] came out of this programme sounding more authoritative than you might have expected . . . he kept himself under tight rein."

After that I moved to *Tonight*, a nightly programme, as deputy to the Editor, Mike Townson. I commissioned a film which featured back-to-camera and silhouetted interviews, written statements by people too scared to talk openly and affidavits about intimidation and violent threats. A powerful establishment figure lobbied the BBC Chairman about it and there was much coming and going. Eventually it was transmitted and won a Royal Television Society Journalism award.

It was not about Ireland however. Called *The Didcot Dossier* it concerned the blacking of inland container terminals by the dockers' union, the Transport and General Workers' Union, and the strong arm methods some of its members were using. I suspect it was regarded as anti-Government propaganda.

In May 1978 Thames Television's chequebook came out and

summoned Mike Townson, my *Tonight* Editor, to the Euston Road. The day after his appointment a large number of *Tonight* employees posed for a farewell photograph, lined up in a queue outside Thames studios, awaiting a call. In fact hardly anyone left. We were all young and enthusiastic and five nights of live television was a lot to give up. Still, Mike was a considerable loss both as an Editor and as the subject of much amazement. He had taken the programme by the scruff of the neck, and by working five seventeen-hour days imbued it with great energy, grafting tabloid style and values on to broadsheet journalism. "Listen, cock," he would say, "this is a *New Society* piece, what it needs is a *News of the World* intro." Quite a few times we found ourselves with the reverse situation.

On one occasion he decided on a Thursday to present the programme from Rhodesia the next Monday. "Off we go cock," he said to me. I explained all the reasons why it didn't make sense. Ian Smith was unlikely to do an interview, the studio facilities were limited and we would have to take all the film to South Africa for processing. We didn't have South African visas etc., etc. "OK cock, let's go." We went.

Mike was hardly the last word in sartorial elegance. Considerably overweight, with cigaratte ash forever scattered upon his shoulders, he was always losing buttons in the most embarrassing places. A suit and he were strangers. On this occasion he outdid himself, arriving at Heathrow on the Friday morning with, instead of a suitcase, a cardboard box tied up with string.

I settled in beside him for the flight, cuttings at the ready, prepared to talk all the way to Johannesburg where we would change planes for Salisbury. Perhaps anticipating this, Mike went to sleep immediately. He slept all the way to South Africa, throughout the transit stop, and all the way to Rhodesia. Because of the danger of being shot at, the plane came in very low and I was convinced we had clipped the top of some trees, but Mike's eyes opened only when the plane stopped and he jumped up, clutching his cardboard and string and exited the plane.

Needless to say we worked nonstop for 48 hours, Mike leaving the presenter Donald McCormick and me, with 12 hours to go, in order to edit in Johannesburg the material already shot. Donald and I began that final morning at 5.30 filming in a bus of black workers en route to the capital, finally interviewed Ian Smith around 10 a.m., and then set out for the airport shooting three pieces to camera in different locations en route.

We jumped on the lunchtime plane which managed to be hit by lightning on take-off in a sudden drenching storm. When we reached Johannesburg and the South African Broadcasting Corporation studios we found Mike in front of a battery of video machines so up to date we had never seen them before. Mike looked totally at home, cigarette in mouth, ash on sleeve, buttons on the floor. "Give me the material, cock," he said and set about carving up what we'd shot. For a man whose grasp of world geography was somewhat shaky he had a remarkable grasp of how to structure a programme.

Some hours later the programme was sent back by satellite and appeared to be well received. We decided to go for a meal, keen to continue our discussions about the possibility of an internal settlement in Rhodesia. Mike declined and went to bed. "Listen, cock," he said, "it's all transistory [sic]."

The following day we flew back in time for Mike to edit the next edition of the programme and to collect his wages from the cash office. Whereas we were paid monthly by cheque, Mike insisted in being paid weekly in cash. Even in the BBC an Editor's salary looked pretty outstanding as it was counted out in pound notes. It was great fun being his deputy and I think we made a good team.

Because Mike left *Tonight* at twenty-four hours' notice I took over as acting Editor and must have done reasonably well, despite being scared stiff, because I was given the job permanently a month later.

The range of the programme was so wide that almost all our interests could be reflected in it. The Friday edition was only seen in London and the South East, and as I thought the News and Current Affairs coverage of the Arts was minimal, I turned that programme into *Tonight in Town*, a weekly what's on. I soon found a young producer who had a remarkable flair for such a programme and immense technical wizardry. He was Tom Gutteridge, later to make himself extremely well known and well off with *01-For London* and other projects produced by his independent company Mentorn. I pinched Valerie Singleton from *Blue*

Peter via *Nationwide,* and was delighted to see how well she did, particularly with the Arts.

There was also room for sport, social issues, films, even for my childhood hero Roy Rogers, as well as for the main coverage of news and politics. Late night on Thursday was a smashing time to be transmitting, particularly when the Government had only a slim majority, change was in the air, and one had Robin Day to ask the questions. It was bliss, but it was short lived. Before I had even been offered the job, and unknown to me, it had been decided to end the programme in the summer of 1979. Late night news and current affairs coverage would be switched to BBC-2, freeing late night on BBC-1 for five editions of *Parkinson.* The latter disaster was avoided but the demise of *Tonight* was not.

Before we left, however, I had managed to arrange for Robin Day what he called "My night of shame, which I've regretted for ten years."

3

ROBIN DAY'S NIGHT OF SHAME

As the Labour Government of James Callaghan drew to a close in the late seventies the arguments between broadcasters and politicians over Northern Ireland intensified. Once more, over on ITV, Peter Taylor and *This Week* were in the thick of it.

In October 1977 Taylor investigated ten cases of alleged ill-treatment of people held by the RUC for interrogation. The RUC refused to cooperate or to be interviewed but the IBA, the Independent Broadcasting Authority, insisted that they be represented. Then, the day before transmission, the Chief Constable, Sir Kenneth Newman, offered a five-minute statement to camera but insisted that no one be allowed to ask questions afterwards. David Elstein, the Editor of *This Week*, was ordered by his Head of Current Affairs, Peter Pagnamenta, to accept, otherwise the programme would not have gone out.

Having secured that advantage Newman then mounted a propaganda offensive. A few hours before transmission he issued a statement putting the RUC on special alert. "It is feared that terrorists could use the occasion as an attempt to 'justify' attacks against police officers and all members of the RUC have been advised to take every precaution for their safety."

The *Daily Telegraph* obliged again. Its leader was headlined "Lethal Television", and went on, "If the IBA will not stop this homicidal irresponsibility, the Government must step in." The *Daily Express* offered a "Death sentence by TV" warning. The attention once more was focused on the reaction of British politicians rather than on the disturbing allegations themselves.

The Northern Irish office then issued an unprecedented personal attack.

It is significant that the producers and the reporter of this programme have produced three programmes in quick succession which have concentrated on presenting the blackest possible picture of events in Northern Ireland.

After the last programme on prisons, a prison officer who appeared on the programme was murdered, and last night's programme may well place police officers, who deserve all support, at even further risk. That is not what one expects of responsible commentators.

Roy Mason, the Secretary of State for Northern Ireland, wrote a letter of complaint to the IBA, Sir Kenneth Newman complained to the IBA's Chairman Lady Plowden, and Opposition spokesperson Airey Neave accused Thames of providing "just the propaganda tonic needed to revive the flagging spirits of terrorism."

David Elstein was told to "lay off Northern Ireland" and to use another reporter, but eight months later *This Week* returned to the torture issue.

Amnesty had published a report in June 1978, more than a year after the *Tonight* programme on Bernard O'Connor. It concluded, "Maltreatment has taken place with sufficient frequency to warrant a public inquiry to investigate it." The report was due to be published on Tuesday, 13 June but over a week earlier it was leaked to the *Guardian* and we on *Tonight* quoted extensively from it. Thames TV's *This Week* planned to do the same. Their film consisted of five minutes of interviews with Catholic doctors, who had attended some prisoners, and further interviews with the Reverend Ian Paisley and a leading Protestant who both spoke up for the police. The film was to be followed by a studio discussion involving Enoch Powell, John Taylor and Patrick Duffy, all Westminster MPs.

The IBA banned the programme without seeing it, saying that discussion of the report should be postponed until it was published. Embarrassingly for the IBA, Roy Mason made a statement about the report in the House of Commons on the day transmission was planned. Thames Management, Unions, and many newspapers criticised the IBA. Perhaps it made a refreshing change for the Association to be bashed by some people other than Roy Mason and Airey Neave.

The *This Week* programme found its way to Lime Grove where parts of it were transmitted in the *Nationwide* programme. The Director of Programmes at Thames at the time was Jeremy Isaacs, and it was thought he smiled benignly on the "publicising" of ITV material. In fact he had personally authorised the handing over of the material to the BBC.

By the following summer Isaacs had left Thames, "half-resigning, half being pushed" and *This Week* was replaced by *TV Eye*. David Elstein was shunted into documentaries before going independent. Within eighteen months Peter Taylor was gone too. Fortunately for me he joined *Panorama* of which I was then Editor. Things quietened down in ITV, for a while, but at the BBC the temperature was also in the nineties, for the second Battle of Culloden had been fought.

In the autumn of 1976, the BBC had opened its new studio complex in Belfast and, to celebrate, hosted a dinner for thirty people at the luxurious Culloden Hotel just outside Belfast. Most of the BBC Top Brass were present including the Chairman of the Governors, Sir Michael Swann, his deputy Mark Bonham Carter, six other Governors and Dick Francis, Northern Ireland Controller. There was an impressive number of others present including the Lord Chief Justice, the Commander of Land Forces and the Chief Constable. The main guest of honour was the Northern Ireland Secretary Roy Mason. This small, pugnacious pipe-smoking Yorkshireman revelled in the job, determined to show how tough he was. He identified closely with the armed forces and thought a military victory was on the cards.

As was customary Michael Swann asked Mason to say a few words. It had been a friendly, relaxed, even celebratory occasion, but not for much longer. Roy Mason had been sitting next to the BBC Governor, and poet Roy Fuller. Both men reminisced about their north country upbringing, but when the Northern Ireland Secretary got to his feet his mood changed alarmingly.

He delivered what one present called "a tirade". According to the *Daily Mail* he said "the BBC was disloyal, supported the rebels, purveyed their propaganda and refused to accept the advice of the Northern Ireland office on what news to carry." He described the BBC's coverage of the North as "quite appalling" and then issued a stark threat saying that he was "involved in decisions about the BBC's charter and income, and that was something for you all to ponder."

He concluded with the proposition that there should be a three-month blackout on reporting paramilitaries. He was enthusiastically supported by the Commander Land Forces and by the Lord Chief Justice Sir Robert Lowry who told the Governors that the BBC should remember "what is good for the country."

As he left the dinner he was reported as saying "If any of this ever gets in the papers, I'll have the lot of you."

The BBC Handbook for 1978 described this event as a "long and frank talk". One BBC man did however come out of this with his position enhanced. Richard Francis, the Northern Ireland Controller, made an extremely skilful speech, acknowledging the problems and sympathising with Roy Mason's predicament, but without giving an inch on the principles of the BBC's coverage. The Governors were much impressed and soon after he became Director of News and Current Affairs.

As a way of reducing the heat, the BBC said it would re-examine its editorial policy for the province. Having done so it reaffirmed that original policy. "Once again, in no spirit of self-satisfaction or complacency, we came to the conclusion that the only justifiable policy was one of open reporting within the law and the constitution."

A year later, in December 1977, the balloon went up again. The *Tonight* programme, of which I was then Deputy Editor, transmitted a report by a young news reporter based in Northern Ireland, Jeremy Paxman. It was an end of the year analysis of the IRA. It traced the splits among Republicans and the emergence of the Irish National Liberation Army from the "Official" IRA who had previously separated from the Provisionals. There were interviews with the Presidents of Provisional and Official Sinn Fein, Ruairi O Bradaigh and Thomas MacGiolla, and also with the former Provisional IRA chief of staff, Sean MacStiofain.

It was hardly supportive of militant Republicanism. Paxman stated at one stage:

"There comes a point in an apparently interminable war, when the guerrilla army, far from being defenders of the people, come to be seen as their oppressors. There are many who believe the IRA is now at that stage."

The Times agreed that "the overall tone of the programme was far from sympathetic." No matter.

Roy Mason tried to stop the programme, writing to the BBC Chairman Sir Michael Swann, "expressing profound concern at the Corporation's intention to screen interviews with members of the Republican movement."

The Conservative Northern Ireland spokesperson Airey Neave was quick to follow suit and the following day released the text of a letter to the BBC's Director General Ian Trethowan.

He said the programme "was nothing less than a Party Political Broadcast on behalf of the IRA. . .

"I am obliged to ask the question: do the BBC want to prolong the 'armed struggle', in Northern Ireland? . . . The terrorists are using your Corporation for their own propaganda."

Roy Mason spoke out again on the same day. "I am appalled that the BBC should have deliberately provided a platform for the views described in the programme as responsible for organising violence in Northern Ireland."

The *Daily Express* obliged again, "Terror gets a free plug" was one of its headlines. The *Sunday Express* picked up the theme, "is it not a howling scandal that the BBC . . . should give thirty-five minutes of free publicity to the skulking killers of the IRA?"

Watching this remorseless attack I thought it was quite remarkable that politicians, who often complain that interviewers are too aggressive and prevent them getting their points across, should assume that any appearance by a militant Republican is free propaganda, or a platform. Do they think that these people are much more adept than they are, or that what the paramilitaries have to say is overwhelmingly seductive?

I believed then, and believe now, that if the interviewer is thorough and determined (and an interviewer would be an idiot if he or she wasn't in these circumstances) then the usual result of these interviews is to reveal the true nature of the interviewee and his activities. Since these frequently involve killing or supporting the killing and maiming of innocent people, albeit "by mistake" or as an "unfortunate by-product", such interviews are usually damaging to the paramilitaries.

Opponents of such interviews then reply, why would terrorists and their supporters give interviews if it wasn't to their advantage? People give interviews for all sorts of reasons, and frequently misjudge their impact. Perhaps they do feel it draws attention to their presence, but they do this by bombings and shootings anyway. The militant Republicans have to win hearts and minds if they are to achieve their aims. Is this likely to be prevented by enabling them to avoid challenge and scrutiny and to perpetuate myth and romance?

Equally if it is to be maintained that change is brought about by the ballot box and that we are a civilised state with high standards, we must not deny elected representatives a voice, whoever they are, or allow those high standards to be reduced under provocation. That way the state is in danger of becoming what those who wish to overthrow it says it already is, a tyranny, which can only be changed by force.

These beliefs underpinned our decision to interview an INLA spokesman.

THE INLA INTERVIEW

When James Callaghan's Government lost a crucial vote on devolution in March 1979 he had no alternative but to go to the country. We had little doubt that he would be defeated since the country had just been through the "Winter of Discontent". Callaghan thought so as well, and remarked to one of his closest advisers, Professor Bernard Donaghue, that there was taking place one of those significant shifts in public opinion which occurs once in every generation and it was shifting against the Labour Party and towards the Tories.

Given the excitement of the Election, and the severe economic problems that had helped bring it about, I didn't give any time to thinking about the changes in policy that Airey Neave might introduce as the new Northern Ireland Secretary.

The so-called Irish National Liberation Army clearly had, because on 31 March, almost before the Election campaign began, it planted a bomb on the underneath of Mr. Neave's car, probably when it was parked outside his London flat. The bomb did not explode however until Mr. Neave collected his car from the underground car park at the Houses of Parliament. As he drove up the ramp into the open air it went off, killing him almost instantly.

It was a devastating blow to Mrs. Thatcher, who had leant heavily on Airey Neave both in the leadership campaign and in the four years of opposition. He had guided her through a number of unfamiliar areas and helped protect her against a largely unsympathetic Shadow Cabinet. She knew that if she came to power she would be in a minority in her own Cabinet on a large number of issues. Now after the hard slog of opposition, and just when she needed him most, he was literally blown away. It was an extraordinarily cruel blow, but with typical courage and determination she carried on to become the first woman Prime Minister.

If anything could have confirmed her in her hatred of militant Republicanism it was Airey Neave's assassination, and she could not understand why broadcasters did not see the position as clearly as she did.

One of her closest advisers put her view this way when I talked to him recently.

> The media have got to decide, not to put too fine a point on it, whether they are going to join the human race or not, whether they are part of society or whether they stand outside and do what the hell they like . . . My view is they have to live within the law and one of the consequences is that you don't consort with terrorists *at all*. You have no bloody truck with them.
>
> Broadcasters must not give them airtime in a way which lends them a legitimacy. You do actually have faith in the institutions of society and you have to be a citizen first and a journalist second.

[40]

He went on, "She thinks you are all bloody brittle. You stand outside looking in and commenting, and you've never done anything constructive in your bloody lives."

We, on the other hand, did not see ourselves as agents of the State. Our job was to ask what, why and how, to give the public in a democracy the information to which it is entitled. Put another way, our job was not to further government policy but to report the facts, to get at the truth. Collisions were inevitable, the one over the *Tonight* INLA interview bloodier than anything that had gone before.

A recapitulation of the rows with Government over Irish matters gives the impression that all we ever wanted to do was make programmes about the paramilitaries but this wasn't the case. On a daily programme, like Tonight, we did many many stories about other aspects of Ireland, some political, like coverage of the Peace People, some social, some artistic, some sporting, and including series such as Bernard Falk walking the hills of Antrim. But the central problem remained and we determined to address it again.

Toward the end of the series I thought it was time to have another look at the IRA. As Humphrey Atkins, the Northern Ireland Secretary put it, "The first six months of this year [1979] have shown a marked increase in the level of terrorism and have demonstrated that we are up against a more professional enemy." I sent David Lomax and Mike Dutfield to Northern Ireland to see what sort of programme might be made.

They came to the conclusion that there was not a lot more to be said at the moment about the IRA but they had discovered quite a lot about the shadowy group who rather grandly called themselves the INLA, the Irish National Liberation Army. They were a relatively new phenomenom and not a great deal was known about them, indeed due to some oversight, they were not yet a proscribed organisation, despite killing Airey Neave. My team reckoned it might be possible to get an interview with one of their representatives, should they try? Non-journalists may wonder how it is possible to get in contact with paramilitaries in Northern Ireland. Well, as every journalist working there knows, including those working for *The Times* and *Daily Telegraph*, *Daily Mail* and *Daily Express*, all you have to do is seek out members of the political parties which are their "front", explain what you want, let them know where you are staying, and wait for the phone call. Whether the call comes and whether they will meet you is another matter.

Should we try to do such an interview? It was now over three months since Airey Neave's assassination, long enough I thought for such enquiries to be made. I had two main considerations. First, would an interview add something to our knowledge of the situation in Northern Ireland? I thought it would. Secondly, how much of a risk were David and Mike taking with their own safety?

I had no doubt about their courage. David Lomax had flown into some of the nastiest situations and talked to some of the nastiest people around. On one occasion he flew with producer Jack Salt-man to interview Idi Amin at the height of his infamy, when bodies were strewn throughout Uganda and in particular around Amin's prisons. Sitting with this terrifying man David quite bluntly put to him all the appalling stories which were circulating about him, and he did not stop when the bodyguards audibly slipped the safety catches off their rifles. When Jack Saltman got up at one point, in between changing the film magazine, to talk to the President he found himself suddenly lifted into the air by the gigantic Head of Amin's bodyguards. "Don't you ever come between me and the President," said the goon, depositing Jack back on the floor behind him.

The camera reloaded, David asked the next question. "Why did you have Archbishop Luwum murdered?" (Even watching the film in the cutting room, with both men safely out of Uganda, I shivered for them.) "It was a motor accident," replied Amin sweetly. "Yes," said David, "the Archbishop also had a large number of bullet holes in him put there by your soldiers."

David Lomax and Mike Dutfield were to continue working together in the world's troublespots until some years later, when they had to spend ten hours lying in a gutter of a country road being shot at by some Lebanese. The sound recordist lying with them was hit in his leg which lay a few inches from Mike's head. The problem with that conflict was that no one knew where the front line was and you simply couldn't calculate the risks. After that they decided to take a break.

I consulted Dick Francis, the new Director of News and Current

Affairs about the INLA interview. Could we see whether such an interview was possible? I was given the go-ahead and David and Mike confirmed that they thought it could be done. I then went back to Dick, could we do the interview? He agreed but made it clear that didn't mean it would automatically be transmitted. He would need to see it first.

The *Tonight* team went to Dublin, made themselves known, and waited.

Then as David told the television audience when the interview was transmitted:

In Dublin a man calling himself Mr. Gray gave us telephone instructions to go to a series of different hotels. The trail led eventually to a room which we found had been booked in my name in an hotel on the outskirts of the city. There we met two men wearing wigs, dark glasses and false moustaches. They also wore surgical rubber gloves and had strange bulges in the pockets of their anoraks.

When the film was brought back Dick and I looked at it and decided that it needed to be broken up and put into context. We also thought that it would be helped by being followed by a discussion chaired by Robin Day. Robin appeared on *Tonight* every Thursday in some sort of political item. Postponing the programme until then was to have one damaging consequence, however. It appeared to some people that as this was the last *Tonight* programme, we were trying to go out with a bang. In fact the feature had been originally planned for the week before.

When Dick was happy with the interview and when we had sounded out Gerry Fitt, the Social Democratic and Labour Party MP, and the Unionist MP, the Reverend Robert Bradford, I rang Robin to ask him to chair the discussion.

He was not happy, although I do not remember him being quite as appalled as he says he was in his recent autobiography *The Grand Inquisitor*. Certainly he never raised the matter with me in the weeks, months, and years afterwards. Perhaps he thought there was no point and had given up with me.

In his book Robin wrote that this interview "probably did more than any other to bring the BBC into disrepute". When I briefed him about the proposed discussion Robin writes, "I was appalled. I could scarcely believe what I had heard." Robin had been a barrister with Airey Neave in the same chambers at the Bar – 5 King's Bench Walk, where Margaret Thatcher had been a pupil. He had admired, as I had, Neave's remarkable exploits in the Second World War, when he had been much decorated and had escaped from Colditz. "All these personal details flashed through my mind. . . I felt sick with revulsion." Robin wrote.

With his usual fairness and accuracy Robin gives an accurate account of our conversations. He did not doubt that the interview was tough and challenging, as he knew and respected David Lomax. "What horrified me," he wrote, "was that a self-proclaimed terrorist was to appear, anonymously and in disguise, on BBC Television to offer his justification for a foul murder, the murder moreover of a member of Parliament in the precincts of the House of Commons."

Robin, who I always thought of as more of a lawyer by instinct than a journalist, made his views clear. I expressed mine which were that the interview revealed the poverty of the terrorist thinking and its curious Marxist cocktail of beliefs. At its simplest the public had a right to know why Airey Neave had been killed.

Robin was most unhappy. However he also respected the editorial hierarchy and as the interview had been passed for transmission he could only pull out, as I said he was free to do, or take part. He told me that he would chair the discussion only if there was no objection to him asking Gerry Fitt and Robert Bradford whether the BBC had been right to transmit the INLA interview they would have just seen. I, of course, agreed.

One of the saddening aspects of my work with Robin is that, because of my many arguments with him, he probably never understood how much I respected him. He was a meticulous professional, a brilliant cross-examiner, and one of the few good things about the demise of *Tonight* is that it resulted in Robin having his own show, *Question Time*.

Regretting his decision to take part in the INLA programme Robin wrote in his memoirs that "the day after the programme I felt, and still feel, ashamed for not withdrawing, which I had been free to do."

Having secured Robin's agreement to chair the discussion I turned my thoughts to Neave's widow. How would she feel if she was suddenly confronted on television by a man representing the organisation who had killed her husband? We needed to warn her, and I asked the producer, Michael Dutfield, to do so. He thought for a while and decided it would be better if Lady Neave was told by a friend rather than by a telephone call.

So, at seven o'clock that evening he telephoned the Chief Whip's office at the House of Lords hoping to contact Baroness Young, a close friend of Lady Neave, to ask her to inform the widow. At the time Baroness Young was on the floor of the House so Dutfield left a message. He then telephoned a senior Conservative Party information officer and asked him how else he could get a message to Lady Neave. The only suggestion was that we continue to try and contact Baroness Young. We did so but failed again to get through.

Finally Mike contacted Mrs. Thatcher's office at the House of Commons, where he was told that a message would be passed on to Lady Neave, to warn her about the programme. In fact No. 10 talked to Lady Neave's family who decided not to tell her until after the broadcast as she rarely, if ever, watched television. As luck would have it Lady Neave *did* watch that night while at a bridge party, and caught the trailer for the programme at the end of the *Nine O'Clock News*. Thus warned, she watched the programme.

Back in Lime Grove earlier that same evening I had returned to my office towards 7.30 to find Dick Francis on the phone to the Director General Ian Trethowan who was in an hotel in Norwich, getting changed before receiving an honorary degree at the University of East Anglia. He still had doubts and Dick was trying to allay them. I was worried that if Trethowan said no I might have an empty programme with nothing to put in its place.

Besides we had been through a detailed and lengthy process of consultation and the project had been authorised at every stage. Why the hold up now? Eventually the DG gave his final agreement, and Dick and I heaved sighs of relief. Now there was just the programme to get through. I stood in the studio gallery as the countdown to the last transmission of *Tonight* began. (As always I'd had to pop out to the lavatory with barely two minutes to go.)

The opening titles ran and I felt the familiar feeling of sickness and excitement as I stood in the dark and the presenters took over.

David Lomax introduced his interview, explaining the circumstances in which it had been shot, and the history of the INLA. It was a tough, challenging interview and a transcript of it is reprinted at the end of this book.

The questions went remorselessly on.

How did they finance themselves?
What were 'selective appropriations' – bank robberies?
Didn't they have very very little support?
Did they expect to bomb one million Protestants into a United Ireland?
Above all why did they murder Airey Neave?
What did the murder of Airey Neave achieve except widespread revulsion in Britain and a determination that no one should be able to get his own way in a democracy by force?

When the INLA spokesman claimed that Airey Neave supported torture, David Lomax made clear in a studio link that the survivor of Colditz, who himself suffered at the hands of the Nazis, was well known as an opponent of torture in any form and was committed to political equality in Northern Ireland. The interview lasted around twelve and a half minutes and afterwards a grim faced Robin Day asked Gerry Fitt and Robert Bradford to comment on the interview. They both condemned it. Robin asked whether it would have inflamed Protestant opinion in Northern Ireland. Gerry Fitt thought it would. Robert Bradford argued it would only reinforce Protestant determination.

The discussion then moved on to questions of future policy towards terrorism in Northern Ireland. Inevitably the Catholic and the Protestant could not agree. It was a sombre occasion. Robin concluded, "I regret to say that once again one can see no optimism in anything either of you say."

(Two and a half years later on Saturday, 14 November, 1981 five Provisionals walked into a community centre in Finghay in south-west Belfast where Robert Bradford was holding a surgery and shot him dead. A caretaker who was in the way also died.)

Immediately after the INLA interview in 1979 there was very little reaction to the programme – eighty-seven telephone calls to the BBC and fifteen letters. As Dick Francis pointed out this was "fewer protests than have been received about the use of a four-letter word on a misplaced piece of satire."

When the row took off almost a week later the BBC commissioned its Broadcasting Research Department to carry out a detailed investigation of the effects of the terrorist interview on the audience and their opinions, and to determine whether the audience felt it was right or wrong to broadcast the item and their reasons why.

A sample of two hundred and seven people, typical of the *Tonight* audience, was selected in seven cities of mainland Britain. The fieldwork was carried out in August and September 1979, with the result that three-quarters of the people viewing a recording of the programme, and completing the questionnaires, did so shortly after the Mountbatten and Warrenpoint murders of August that year.

The results showed that four-fifths of those questioned felt the BBC was right to broadcast the item, and most of those questioned claimed to be more hostile towards the INLA and the IRA, and more sympathetic to the security forces, as a consequence of watching the interview.

Those who favoured our decision to broadcast the programme said that people needed to be informed about the situation in Northern Ireland, but the item showed what the Government and the Army were up against, and that viewers were capable of making up their own minds.

Judging by this audience reaction we had clearly made the right editorial decision. But there was another, rather different, audience in Westminster and it was outraged. Humphrey Atkins, the Northern Ireland secretary, had complained about the programme the next day, but apart from that there was silence from Westminster and Whitehall for almost a week. On the following Monday evening the Director General Ian Trethowan was at the Commons and he had detected virtually no unhappiness.

Then the storm broke, set off by a letter to the *Daily Telegraph* from Airey Neave's widow. She wrote, "The terrorist was given ample scope to besmirch the memory of my husband." In fact we had deliberately written a script which had gone out of its way to contradict the terrorist's allegations, but Lady Neave's comments were entirely understandable. She went on "the decision to transmit the interview betrayed the traditional standards of British broadcasting."

The following day the *Daily Telegraph* editorial was headed "Forum for Murderers" and accused us of committing "at the very least, an extreme and repulsive error of taste", and of failing to show "the smallest regard for either the feelings or the interests of the nation."

Mrs. Thatcher found it inexplicable. She asked the Home Office on a visit there "What are we going to do about the BBC?" She revealed her anger about the interview in Parliament, "I was appalled it was ever transmitted and I believe it reflects gravely on the judgement of the BBC and those responsible." She told the Commons that the Attorney-General Sir Michael Havers would consider whether legal action could be taken against the BBC. Merlyn Rees, Labour's Shadow Home Secretary, backed her up saying the BBC had made "a grave error".

Faced with the cross party assault the papers followed suit. "Maggie blasts BBC" said the *Evening Standard*, the *Daily Mirror* had "Terror Quiz at BBC" and the *Daily Mail* "Appalling error by BBC".

The BBC defended us robustly. Richard Francis told a Broadcasting Press Guild lunch that the BBC had a clear duty to inform the public about groups whose aims were to undermine our democracy.

The BBC had shown only three interviews with members of illegal Irish terrorist organisations on the Network over the past decade. "By and large I think we have tended to do too little", Francis said.

Later Trethowan acknowledged that he had misjudged the emotional impact of the interview. As he wrote it in his autobiography *Split Screen*. "It was not only the Prime Minister's special feelings about the murder of her closest political associate, MPs of all parties had been affected by Airey Neave's death and there was a general feeling at Westminster, once the issue had been brought strongly to their attention, that it was too soon to broadcast such material, if indeed it should ever be broadcast." In the end, he concluded, the rational case for showing some controversial material can be "outweighed by a strong emotional hostility which negates the value of the material even on the broadcaster's terms."

Even Willie Whitelaw, the Home Secretary and a friend of broadcasting agreed. He told me recently "It was a really grave error not to tell her. [Airey Neave's widow.] All of us felt offended by the programme." A close Cabinet colleague from those years gave me a further reason why Mrs. Thatcher reacted as she did.

She was desperately affected by Airey Neave's death, desperately. And in a way this affected her whole thoughts on broadcasting coverage of Northern Ireland.

She had a mystical view of what he would do in Ireland, that he had actually been killed by the INLA because they thought he was going to do things in Ireland which would have been so successful it would have done a great deal of damage. I mean this is much too sophisticated a view for me. The INLA killed Airey Neave because he was a good catch to kill.

To my knowledge since the INLA interview there have been no interviews with members of proscribed organisations transmitted on any British channel.

Robin Day says that "Today, ten years later, it is rare to meet anyone in broadcasting circles who does not say that it was shameful to have transmitted the INLA interview. But if Roger Bolton has any regrets . . . [he] does not convey them." I do regret the distress caused to Airey Neave's family but I still think such interviews should be shown today.

As the BBC research showed, the viewing audiences are more mature than politicians believe. The public has a right to know what is happening in Northern Ireland, and what motivates those involved, including the paramilitaries. Such interviews should be rare, thorough and carefully placed in context but they should be done. The emotional reaction of politicans ought not to be the decisive factor. And, if we say we will not interview murderers we should apply that logic abroad as well as at home. Presumably this would have excluded TV interviews with Idi Amin and the late Mr. Begin, the former Israeli Prime Minister who was a founding member of the IRGUN. What should we do about Yassar Arafat today? The definitions of terrorist, freedom fighter, and guerrilla are complex ones.

And, while I do very much regret not having managed to alert Lady Neave, are we, by the same logic, obliged to warn, say, the Yorkshire Ripper's victims if his voice is to be broadcast or his face to appear? There cannot be one rule for the eminent and another for the person in the street.

Shortly after the Prime Minister's outburst, Commander Peter Duffy of the Anti-Terrorist Squad came to see us. We gave him what information we could about the circumstances under which the interview had taken place. David Lomax had warned the INLA before the interview was filmed that almost certainly the Special Branch would be interested in the interview and we would have to provide them with the information we possessed. In other words they had to be responsible for their own security.

The Squad also made clear that although they didn't want to 'trail' the BBC on such interviews, they would appreciate an opportunity to 'brief' those concerned about what to look out for. I politely declined the offer and Dick Francis was also firmly opposed to it. We could not become honorary members of the Special Branch.

All this meant that reporting on Ireland was going to get even tougher, but I was greatly cheered by the words of the Director General, Ian Trethowan, at a News and Current Affairs meeting on 17 July 1979.

There might be those who would be moved over the BBC's relationship with the Government, and such issues as the licence fee, to ask whether it was worth risking souring relations for such an interview, however justified the BBC believed it to be.

That is a dangerous insidious road to take. It would lead to a conscious or unconscious policy of 'playing safe' which, after a

time, would inevitably bring the realisation that the BBC had
shed something of crucial importance.

His thoughts have an extra resonance today. I was much
impressed and determined to take him at his word. . .

4

CARRICKMORE

An enormous number of initials crowded into the sixth floor suite of the BBC's Television Centre in Wood Lane. There was DNCA of course and ADNCA, CA to DG, Dep.EXSN, HCAP Tel., HSCAVR, CA to HCAMP and twenty-two other sets. Apart from Diana Rice of the Secretariat, who was minuting the meeting, the proud possessors of these initials were all men, sober-suited and extremely serious.

They were attending the weekly News and Current Affairs meeting of the BBC. Held alternately in Television Centre and Broadcasting House, it was the place where senior editors of radio and television met to discuss editorial policy.

It was 4 September, 1979, and normally the first meeting of the autumn would have been a relaxed occasion, a good opportunity to chat about holidays in Chiantishire, and long lunches in Languedoc, safe in the knowledge that the major job changes for that season had taken place. New people and programmes were in place including the latest Editor of *Panorama*, Roger Bolton.

The previous day I had given an interview to Penny Junor of the *Daily Mail* in which I had made it pretty clear what I was about. It was what I had told the BBC Board that had appointed me.

I want to do more programmes on domestic affairs. There has been a tendency to do overseas investigations because the pressures are fewer.

If you do a programme on Chile or the United States there are no pressure groups to create problems and no one who is going to be a friend of the management.

On the other hand, there are if you do a programme about British nuclear energy, the TUC, CBI, British Leyland or Northern Ireland.

So, although it is going to be more difficult, there are domestic affairs which ought to be looked into and I don't intend to be dissuaded. I think *Panorama* should lead public debate as opposed to reflecting it. This is one of the limitations of television. We look at issues when they become visual.

Take Northern Ireland. They shoot someone and we all rush out, but we don't look at that country before there is an incident or discuss the issues and debate alternative policies.

I had given a similar interview to Baz Bamigboye of the *Evening Standard*. I told him, "If the issues are sensitive there must be reasons for them. We'll be looking at the problems in Ireland, Official Secrets and the way some of the official institutions operate."

Bamigboye concluded "It looks as if Bolton's reign will be a controversial one."

There was already controversy enough for the News and Current Affairs meeting to discuss. On the previous Bank Holiday Monday the IRA had murdered Lord Mountbatten while he was on holiday in the West of Ireland. The explosion in his boat had killed not only Lord Louis but also one of his grandsons and a young friend, and injured several others. By any standards this was a cowardly and disgusting act. And at Warrenpoint on the border British soldiers had been blown up and killed by an IRA bomb.

For my first *Panorama* the previous day I had commissioned a quick reactive report about cross-border security followed by an interview with the Irish Taoiseach, Prime Minister, Jack Lynch.

The programme was called *The IRA's Open Door*. The biggest daily newspaper in Ireland, Dublin's *Irish Independent*, called it something else. "Trial by TV" read its banner headline. "A week of anti-Irish hysteria in the British media reached its climax last night when the BBC *Panorama* programme with a viewing public of millions put the Taoiseach in the dock over his security policies.

"It was seen in Britain as something tantamount to trial by television. Since the murder of Lord Mountbatten, the attacks on

[53]

Mr. Lynch in the British media have continued unabated – almost as if they were being orchestrated from Whitehall."

No matter that the programme had also featured former Garda detective, Tom Peters of Portlaoise, who had been blinded in an IRA booby trap explosion two years before. "I am living proof that the Gardai are not soft on the IRA", he told us. One of his colleagues had been blown to bits. "I abhor and detest the existence in this country of the Provisional IRA."

The News and Current Affairs meeting also heard about trouble on the other side of the border. There had been a Republican demonstration in Belfast at which arms had been brandished.

The RUC had interviewed the BBC reporter and film crew involved in a much more tenacious and determined manner than usual. They believed, erroneously, that the crew had prior knowledge of the incident.

The Director of News and Current Affairs, Dick Francis, ruminated about the events of the past week and the increased number of bullets flying in the direction of the messengers. These ruminations were meant to be read. The minutes of the meeting were sent all over the Corporation for guidance, though some cynics maintained that the lack of precision in some parts was due to a desire to create maximum room for manoeuvre for senior figures when trouble occurred. At that stage I would not have agreed, although it was said that the minutes were 'tidied up' to include remarks that senior figures wished they had made, or with emphasis subtly altered on occasion.

The pressure was already on. Dick Francis remarked with some irony that an interview in the *Irish Times* with a member of the Provisional IRA printed only days after the events of Bank Holiday had provoked none of the fuss which the *Tonight* interview with a representative of the INLA had set off. "One could imagine the uproar if the BBC had initiated it", he said. "Clearly the context for considering such interviews had changed. BBC policy however remained the same."

The Head of Television Current Affairs, John Gau, said it would be inconceivable if the BBC could not do now what the *Irish Times* and most of the national newspapers had done, because of this heightened sensitivity.

DNCA said that he would like to see a further approach explored: that of the BBC's journalists increasing their intelligence about how the IRA operated and thought, and the present feeling towards them in Republican areas.

I was not at the meeting but when I read the minutes I wondered how all this might affect a programme I was starting to make, for while the meeting was taking place, a *Panorama* team was flying to the United States to interview a prominent IRA defector on the run there, Peter McMullen. It was an interview authorised personally by Dick Francis.

A wider than usual gap was opening up between the journalists and the management and between management and Governors. I was about to fall down the crack.

When *Tonight* had come off the air, I had completed the emotional business of breaking up a team of young and idealistic people, and after surviving the usual all night party, I had gone off to the West Coast of the United States for a month. I knew editing *Panorama* would be tough and I felt exhausted from having worked five nights a week for a year and a half beginning at 9.30 each morning and ending around midnight.

I switched off and walked through Yosemite National Park, canoed down Russian River and watched the fog roll over Golden Gate Bridge. I did not spend time reflecting on how the BBC Governors would be reacting to the backwash of the INLA interview and the presence of an extremely unsympathetic Prime Minister with a safe working majority and a determination "to do something" about the BBC. I should have done so.

Unknown to me and my colleagues the goalposts were being dug up and moved a long way off and there was some doubt about when the next match would take place.

The majority of Governors had thought the INLA interview was a mistake and, although Ian Trethowan had defended its transmission in a letter to the *Daily Telegraph*, he admitted that the BBC had clearly misjudged the emotional impact of the interview.

The Chairman of the BBC Governors, Sir Michael (later Lord Swann) said the decision to show it had been taken "in the genuine belief that the public interest would be served by people in Britain being reminded of the intransigent and murderous nature of the problem." However, a number of Governors, led by George Howard, were determined that it should never happen again.

The pressure from No. 10 had been intense. Ian Trethowan spoke of "the bludgeoning" which the BBC and he personally had received going on for a fortnight.

"With the benefit of hindsight", he wondered, "was I wrong to allow the INLA interview to be broadcast? Almost certainly, yes."

Trethowan, an extremely subtle politician himself, tried to repair the damage. He assured the Governors that such an interview would not happen again for a very long time, if ever, and immediately after Mountbatten's murder he wrote to the Home Secretary, Willie Whitelaw, assuring him that the BBC planned no interviews with the IRA in the foreseeable future. "From now on, so far as Northern Ireland is concerned," he told senior colleagues, "we are in a different ball game."

It was a highly sensitive time. The BBC was fighting proposed cuts in the External Services, which are funded directly by the Foreign Office, and since the first licence fee negotiation with Mrs. Thatcher was coming up some caution was understandable, but there is never a convenient time for covering controversial Government issues. The timing is always wrong, there is always a reason to postpone and postpone and postpone.

Down in Lime Grove I didn't think these political considerations had much to do with me. That was the job of the management. I was a journalist. I proposed, they disposed. I didn't want the initiative and independence of my team to be stifled by self-censorship, and I had an overwhelming, perhaps obsessive, belief in the importance of the Northern Ireland question and the special nature of BBC journalism. We were set up to be independent of commercial and political pressures, to set standards, to tell the truth.

When the McMullen interview was brought back by reporter Jeremy Paxman and producer David Darlow, DNCA, the Head of Current Affairs John Gau, and I sat down and viewed the film. It was riveting. A genuine insider's view of how the IRA operated, which was far from the rosy-coloured, idealistic picture painted by its supporters, but which also revealed the extent of support for the organisation and the way in which idealists and young people, burning with resentment and looking for action, become involved.

[56]

Since McMullen had by then left the IRA and condemned its violence there seemed no problem about its transmission. I was still a little uneasy though. An interview was suitable for a magazine programme like *Tonight* but shouldn't *Panorama* be doing something more substantial? This was John Gau's view. He had been urging me to do a longer piece and discussed the need for this with the Controller of BBC-1, Bill Cotton.

Conditions had changed since the time at the start of the year when the IRA was thought to be in a state of decline. Warrenpoint, Lord Mountbatten's murder and the new evidence of McMullen, had shown the weakness of this analysis. The organisation was not going to fade away.

Dick Francis said this was exactly what *Panorama* should be looking at. A full in-depth analysis of the IRA, its history, beliefs, funding, organisation and present strengths. Go and do it, tell Cecil Taylor about it, and work to me directly.

Taylor was the Head of Programmes in Northern Ireland, a tough wily old bird, who had been Acting Controller for a while. He had wanted the permanent job himself and had been very disappointed when James Hawthorne had been appointed instead. He wanted to hold on to as many of the reins of power as possible, particularly the political ones.

On 14 September I sent John Gau a memo outlining the programme and then telephoned Cecil to tell him what we were proposing, and to indicate the lines of our thinking. He liked the idea, which didn't surprise me as we had discussed a similar venture for *Tonight* the previous June. It had not come off then. Taylor at once minuted both the Controller of Northern Ireland and his News Editor, Robin Walsh, about the "major proposal which is at the initial stage. He [Bolton] has put to DNCA, ADNCA and HCAP Tel. a proposal for a fifty minute programme which would look at the IRA over the past ten years and how it has changed philosophically and militarily. He has a November transmission in mind."

So we set off confident that everyone thought it was a good idea, and with no one raising any great concerns. There were so many weekly and nightly current affairs programmes that it would have been impossible for senior management to be personally involved in the detail, and to give the formal go ahead for each project. They devolved responsibility for individual decisions down, editors referred up, when they considered it necessary. The only specific prohibition was on interviews with terrorists. These required the Director General's personal authorisation, and at that stage I didn't have such an interview in mind.

After this universally warm reception to the idea it never occurred to me that the principle of doing such a programme at that time was in doubt. There was no mention of licence fees, or External Service cuts. No hand on the shoulder, rather a push in the back. Get on with it. So we did.

Jeremy Paxman was the obvious choice to make the programme. He was only twenty-nine, but was clearly becoming one of the outstanding reporters of his generation. After Cambridge, he had joined the Corporation as a news trainee and swiftly became a reporter in Northern Ireland. Three years there had given him clear insight into the problems and he had very good contacts. He was, as he is now, highly respected as a very intelligent, thoughtful man of great integrity. He had worked for me on *Tonight* where he had already made a programme on the IRA and I'd brought him with me to *Panorama*.

Unfortunately he wasn't free until the second week of October. Like most Editors taking over a current affairs series, I found the cupboard was bare. There were no films in the bank, it would take weeks of hole filling before all my new programme team joined me, and it would be near Christmas before well researched investigations could appear.

Critics and colleagues tend to watch the first programme of a new Editor's reign and make final judgements. Better to wait a few months. I certainly had an undistinguished start.

My deputy editor was away making a series of discussions with Shirley Williams and Jeremy himself was completing a programme in *The Bear Next Door* series about countries living next door to the Soviet Union.

In his absence I sent the producer off to research, telling him to keep BBC Belfast abreast of what we were about. David Darlow, now a distinguished film maker, was even then a grizzled veteran of current affairs, with a face that looked as though it had been chiselled in granite. Some thought he had a nerve and a sensibility to match. He certainly had guts and unlike many producers who professed the importance of Northern Ireland but kept leaping on planes for the United States, he was willing to have a go. Meanwhile I went back to the slot-filling, knowing that there was no intention of filming for at least a month.

Darlow didn't waste time. He soon gained the cooperation of the Army and the RUC, who promised briefings and facilities, and also established contact with Provisional Sinn Fein and the Officials. During those weeks in September he was in and out of BBC Northern Ireland using the office and talking to correspondents. He had a long chat with the News Editor and the highly respected political correspondent W. D. Flackes. Darlow told them that we hoped to interview the Provisional's leadership. Flackes thought it unlikely that Gerry Adams and the others would appear, since they had apparently refused all other interviews for some time.

Dick Francis, the Director of News and Current Affairs, also went across to Northern Ireland, although on other matters. Darlow had met him for a drink at the Europa Hotel, which changed its name almost as often as it was blown up, but which, after midnight, was the place journalists met each other and hammered their livers and their expenses. At that time Sinn Fein had said they would not cooperate as there had been what they called "a security leak". When David told Dick Francis this, Dick had been annoyed saying that "we must get these people on the screen more." The producer was even more annoyed because, while researching, he'd uncovered what we thought to be the first detailed inside account of how William Whitelaw, as Northern Ireland Secretary, had met the military and political leadership of the Provisional IRA on 7 July 1972 at a private house in Cheyne Walk, Chelsea, the London home of Paul Channon. We now knew all about the elaborate arrangements that had been made and could report the startling claim of the Provisionals that they had been allowed to keep their weapons during the visit. Darlow saw the filmic opportunities and I saw a good news story, that would illuminate the dilemma of how governments should deal with terrorists. Clearly this was developing into an important, if controversial, programme. Almost unnoticed by us callous young journalists, we had had our first bit of bad luck. The Director General Ian Trethowan had suddenly been taken ill. In fact he'd had a mild heart attack on the evening of 1 October 1979, while entertaining the Lord Mayor at Television Centre.

Although we didn't realise it at the time Trethowan (now Sir Ian and my chairman at Thames Television – make what allowances you think right) was about the best and shrewdest politician the BBC had ever had. The Conservatives thought him sympathetic to them, he was certainly centre right, and he had spent far more time outside the BBC than within it, largely as a Westminster political correspondent. Both these facts were positive virtues in their eyes. At such a sensitive moment the loss of his judgement and instincts was crucial, particularly as he was replaced by Gerry Mansell, his deputy. Gerry had been a lifelong BBC man, and was desperately disappointed not to have been made DG, but he led a life far removed from Lime Grove and political journalism, spent mainly in the more formal External Services at Bush House, and the bureaucracy at Broadcasting House. He was a man from another culture. We didn't speak the same language, or share some of the same assumptions. We were to have difficulty understanding one another.

By the beginning of October research was going well but I was getting worried because DNCA was not returning my phone calls and I couldn't fix a meeting to update him on the project. He was obviously a busy man, more so with Trethowan ill, but a penchant for travel also took him away frequently. I learned later that a great deal of his time had been spent organising a conference at Abingdon, to explore how press and broadcasting organisations should respond to acts of terrorism and revolution, and how far they should cooperate with the authorities in modifying their reportage to thwart the aims of terrorists. The Lords Goodman and Scarman were to be there as well as senior police officers, editors, lawyers and civil servants. But while they were playing out fictional scenarios we were trying to deal with a real one.

I finally caught up with Dick at the Labour Party Conference in early October but all we had time for was a brief chat, so when I found out that he was going to be at the Conservative Party Conference I arranged to meet him there on 10 October. The day before Jeremy Paxman had returned from holiday and flew straight to Northern Ireland to continue the research and talk to his friends in the newsroom. "I know what you are doing," said one of the senior newsmen with a grin. Given the sensitive nature of what they were doing Jeremy chose not to reveal too much.

At Blackpool, on 10 October, I watched the Labour Party beginning to tear itself apart after the Election defeat. I had seen enough of this political blood sport in 1971, after Labour's last defeat, and spent most of my time on BBC politics. Brian Wenham was there. He was now Controller of BBC-2, but for many years before had been my Head of Current Affairs. Brian has a political mind to match Machiavelli, Harold Wilson or anyone from Byzantium. I mentioned the project and my difficulties in getting Dick to focus on it: "Put everything down on paper and hand it to him here", said Wenham. I scribbled out yet another version of the proposal, the state of our research and our filming plans, handed it to one of the already overworked BBC Conference secretaries, and then went to see Dick. As it happened, he himself asked me for the latest plans on paper, so I popped back to the office, collected it and handed it to him personally.

In the memo I said I intended to start filming the historical sections of the programme the following week if possible. "I am looking for transmission on 19 November . . . Obviously I will not proceed with interviews with representatives of any illegal organisations without your approval."

What then took place was to be at the centre of the future disciplinary hearings which were to lead to me being dismissed as Editor of *Panorama*, before being reinstated.

I believe that Dick concluded the conversation by saying, "Fine, I'd better keep Gerry [Mansell] informed." As far as I was concerned the talk was not about whether or not the programme was "on", but about how to handle some of the delicate issues that might arise. We were two colleagues who saw eye to eye about the programme. Indeed, Dick had encouraged us in the venture, remarking once that Editors didn't put forward enough projects on Northern Ireland because they imagined the restrictions were greater than they were.

It was put to me later by the BBC that Dick Francis had added that the Board of Governors would have to be consulted and that Mr. Mansell would have to carry the Chairman with him. I never heard those words, had I done so I would have been an idiot to start filming anything.

What is not disputed is that despite my statement that I intended to start filming the following week, and that intended transmission was only five weeks away, Dick made no attempt to contact me for the next three weeks. By then we were unsuccessfully trying to put the lid on a No. 10 volcano.

After my meeting with DNCA I rang up Jeremy and David and authorised them to go ahead the following week and film the historical section of the programme up to 1970, including the split between the Official and Provisional Sinn Fein. The filming would take place in Dublin and from there on Friday, 12 October Paxman rang the BBC News Editor in Belfast saying that we were likely to start filming on the following Monday and indicated what that filming would be. Jeremy did not, as he wrote to me, "at any stage report to CNI [Controller Northern Ireland] since on all previous occasions when filming in Northern Ireland contact had been through local programme management (something I am sure both Head of Programmes NI and News Editor NI will confirm)."

I went back to my office in an Edwardian terraced house in Shepherd's Bush. With worn lino on the floor, curtains that were falling apart and an armchair with the stuffing coming out of it, it was not the most attractive place in which to work, and I would gladly have got away from it as much as possible. I had intended to fly to Belfast myself to chat to the Head of Programmes about the IRA programme a couple of weeks earlier, but a combination of the rather desperate empty vistas confronting me as I looked at my forward planning sheet and the fact that all current affairs editors were about to go to Northern Ireland on a military, police and political briefing trip kept me in Lime Grove. I would go in a couple of weeks' time and discuss the next, and I thought more difficult, section of the programme, post 1970. It was a bad mistake. I should not have relied on anyone else to pass on information, but gone regardless. I was naive. I thought that if there was trouble each editor would stand up and take responsibility for his team. I would protect my reporters, others would protect me. After all, everyone

thought the programme was a good idea, nobody had told us not
to go ahead. I thought the BBC was different from other organisations. I had only worked for, had only wanted to work for, the
Corporation. Its journalism was dedicated to discovering the facts,
to telling the truth fearlessly. Corporate self-interest wasn't
involved, was it?

5

"THE BBC MUST PUT ITS HOUSE IN ORDER"

Carrickmore, a village of some four hundred people, is in the heart of mid-Ulster, seventeen miles from the border, and one of the North's staunchest Republican areas. In 1979 I had never heard of it, neither had Jeremy Paxman nor David Darlow, as they finished filming the Dublin Post Office which had played an important role in the 1916 Uprising. They were due to travel to Belfast that afternoon, Wednesday, 17 October, and went back to their hotel to pack up. It was while they were packing up their gear, Darlow told me later, that the phone rang. On the other end was a man who knew a lot about them and the projected programme. This surprised neither Jeremy nor David. They had been to the offices of Provisional Sinn Fein in Dublin and had talked to several senior members of that legitimate political party. Dublin is a very small city if you are a British film crew. The caller said if they went to Carrickmore they would see something of considerable interest to them, but they must go now, immediately. He rang off.

Paxman and Darlow looked at each other. They decided they couldn't afford not to go. They had a shrewd suspicion that it would be some sort of military demonstration, perhaps a rocket launcher, but they knew that filming an event did not mean that the film would be transmitted. That would be an editorial decision back in London for BBC management. They were journalists on the ground, their job was to get the material from which to make a programme. A print journalist would take his pen and notebook, they took their camera equipment. Afterwards some Conservative politicians asked why the two journalists did not immediately ring the Garda, the Irish police. If they had done so then BBC journalists would have been seen as members of the security forces and their ability to report the situation in Ireland and elsewhere would have been seriously damaged, though the *Panorama* team might not have been around to notice.

When they reached the village nothing was happening. They drove down the main street and stopped at the far end. They waited a couple of minutes and discussed a little anxiously what they should do. Even though it was mid-afternoon it was getting overcast and dark. They decided to drive back through the village and then leave for Belfast. Their cameraman was Paul Berriff.

"All of a sudden, two men in hoods and carrying guns appeared about fifty yards away and started to walk away from us. I reached for my camera and started filming," he said. The team followed the men to a crossroads where four or five other men appeared. They stopped five cars saying "This is an IRA road check – can we see your driving licence?" Not one word passed between the IRA men and the crew. Surrounded by masked men carrying Armalites journalists tend not to argue too much. Altogether they saw about a dozen men armed with a mixture of modern and obsolete weapons, walking about the village.

The crew filmed for about ten minutes and then drove off, wondering what to make of it all. In one sense they were a bit disappointed. Such IRA roadblocks were not uncommon, it was not very special. I myself had been in one a couple of years earlier in South Armagh, and rather unpleasant it was, but I wasn't surprised.

Had it been set up especially for them? It was difficult to know whether or not the event had already been planned and they had simply been alerted, or whether the IRA had deliberately organised it to impress *Panorama*, hearing what the planned pro-gramme was about.

As they drove back the two *Panorama* men argued heatedly what should be done with the material. Should it be used at all? The danger was that the IRA might win either way. Transmit and there would be an unholy row. Fail to transmit and the cry of censorship would go up.

The fact however remained that the Provos had mounted the

operation in an area normally intensively patrolled and surveilled, well away from the border, only eleven miles from the nearest British Army base at Lisanelly Camp, Omagh, and only six miles from a joint RUC/UDR barracks in Pomeroy. It was a measure of the task still facing the security forces within the North ten years after the war against the IRA began.

It would be a difficult decision if and how the material should be used but planned transmission was well over a month away and that decision would clearly be one for senior BBC management not for them.

They drove on, managed to get lost, arrived in Belfast very late that night, and went straight to bed, exhausted. It had been a nerve racking day. In London, by contrast, I was beginning to relax a little. I had now got all my team on board and there were some good projects in the pipeline. We had just received some good reviews and that evening my team Carlisle United had won, a not too frequent occurrence. I went to bed happy.

7.45 a.m., Thursday, 18 October. The usual breakfast chaos, children getting up late, semi-conscious bodies bumping into each other in the hall. The phone rang. Even then I used to get a slightly sick sensation when I heard it, early morning and late at night. It usually meant one of my teams had a problem. More film, more money, more reassurance required.

It was David Darlow. As I fumbled for a pen to make a note he told me the broad outline of what had happened. At first I was a bit irritated, I'd told them just to film historical interviews and some external shots of key places in Dublin. On the other hand a moment's thought made me realise that I would have done the same thing. I thought the incident was mildly inconvenient, but not that remarkable, given the prevalence of such incidents and my own experience on the border. Had he talked to a BBC lawyer? He had. Just before phoning me he had called Glen del Medico of our legal department and told him of the incident and del Medico's advice had been that there was no need for us to report the incident to the police. Hmm, well, I tried to work out what to do next. "Make sure you tell BBC Northern Ireland", I said.

When I got into the office I called John Gau but discovered that he had just left for Northern Ireland. *Nationwide*, the BBC-1 early evening magazine programme, had been producing a week of programmes from Belfast and John had gone over to see the operation, encourage the team, and thank our colleagues over there. I tried to get hold of him a couple of times but failed and assumed that he would be briefed. He was returning the following morning and I fixed to see him to review the incident and the filming so far.

In Belfast, the *Panorama* team did some more filming of buildings and returned to their hotel for lunch. There was another phone call, this time from their army contact with whom they had been arranging to film troops on manoeuvres. He came straight to the point. There had been an incident the previous day at Carrickmore. A British film crew had been reported filming an IRA roadblock, was it them? Darlow confirmed that it was. "Oh dear," said the army man, "this will make future cooperation rather difficult."

Jeremy Paxman set off to see the BBC's News Editor, Robin Walsh, and ask his advice. Robin was tied up editing that night's local news programme and couldn't talk until after it had gone out. When it had done so they sat down over a drink and discussed the problems. Robin told him that he didn't need to do anything further about it. By now the security forces would be well aware of what had happened.

Robin then went off to the *Nationwide* party and joined up with John Gau. They were looking forward to celebrating a good week of programmes which had demonstrated how much more there was to Northern Ireland than the Troubles. The party was hosted by the new Controller, James Hawthorne, at his home. Seeing Walsh and Gau together, David Gilliland, the Chief Press Officer of the Northern Ireland Office, went over and asked them about what had happened at Carrickmore. Gilliland knew about the original project because he had been consulted by Jeremy Paxman. It would be a stupid journalist who did not drop in for a drink with David Gilliland when he was over. David seemed to know everyone, remember everything, and have been in his job since Stormont had been established in the twenties. As an Ulsterman he was not above expressing doubts with his eyebrows about the particular qualities of the politicians which Westminster sent over to govern him. He had a reputation for deviousness but for never lying. Not a bad combination of talents for a Government Press Officer.

John Gau was a little embarrassed, he didn't yet know of the incident. Robin Walsh deflected Gilliland and then filled John in. They agreed that the Head of Programmes, Cecil Taylor, should be told about the incident and Robin Walsh did so that evening. Neither Robin nor John thought of telling the Controller who was busy hosting the party. It would be for the Head of Programmes to do that as the next man in the chain of command. It is one of the abiding mysteries why he did not do so. It was to be fatal for John and myself.

The next day, Friday, 19 October, John flew back to London and I filled him in on everything I knew. That same day the film crew also returned to base. No further filming was planned for at least a couple of weeks as my producer was taking ten days' leave, and I was visiting Northern Ireland with other Editors, to be widely briefed on the present day security position.

I intended during the course of that visit, to consult with BBC Northern Ireland and after various briefings to decide how and when to proceed.

Meanwhile, John Gau and I went to see the BBC-1 Controller Bill Cotton, Alasdair Milne the Managing Director of BBC TV being abroad on business. Together with Bill we drafted a brief factual statement in the event of any Press enquiries, but it was never to be used. Thinking we had touched base with everyone, we relaxed and got on with making other programmes.

The young and ambitious journalists of Lime Grove could be forgiven for dreaming, in their wilder moments, that something might happen to the British Airways jet from London to Belfast on the morning of Wednesday, 24 October, 1979. It was carrying nearly all the management of Television Current Affairs Group, including the Editors of *Panorama*, *Newsweek* – Peter Ibbotson, and *Newsnight* – George Carey. Both were to follow me as Editors of *Panorama* and have their own sulphurous exchanges with Government; George over the Falklands and Peter over the alleged extreme right wing connections of some Conservative MPs. Also with us, bubbling with enthusiasm about everything, including the new extension to his train set, was Peter Snow, the former ITN Correspondent George had signed up for *Newsnight*. He too would feel the heat of the Downing Street flame-throwers during the Falklands.

[68]

Peter Snow and George had some time on their hands. Because of union difficulties their new programme had not been launched on time and it was to be many more weeks before it got on air. A large number of journalists were twiddling parts of their anatomy in frustration and boredom. George was managing to hold them together by such devices as making paper programmes. All would sit round one of the BBC's subterranean conference rooms as the scheduled hour of transmission came around. George would then cue presenters, interviewees, music, and a complete programme would go out – but only to those locked into the madness. The prospect of a trip to Northern Ireland must have been a relief.

At 12.30 we assembled in Room 528, the boardroom of Broadcasting House, Belfast, to meet twenty-five regional staff for drinks and lunch. It was a week after the *Panorama* team had set out for Carrickmore.

I took Cecil Taylor and Robin Walsh aside to talk about the IRA project and how we should proceed. As we were having an army briefing the following afternoon and dinner with the RUC after that, I was interested to know how they thought the security forces had reacted to the Carrickmore incident. "A bit irritated but nothing more." At the meeting Cecil made it clear that either he or Robin was the proper source of consultation on these matters. I had the impression that Taylor wanted to be seen as the man who, de facto, ran the BBC in Northern Ireland. Neither man seemed unduly concerned about the incident, or complained about lack of foreknowledge.

The following afternoon, Thursday, 26 October, we left BH in two cars for Army HQ at Lisburn, just south of Belfast. The Command Public Relations officer, Tony Brooks, was our host, and we were briefed by the Commander Land Forces, Major-General J. Glover, who was the Army No. 2 in Northern Ireland. We also met the General Officer Commanding (GOC), Lieutenant-General Sir Timothy Creasey.

Glover's briefing was superb. Clear, detailed, and remarkably frank. He quickly disabused any who thought that the IRA could be defeated by the military. Its activities could be contained, perhaps reduced a little, but that was it. He also provided some shrewd character studies of its leadership. Many were highly intelligent, highly disciplined and committed. I was much impressed, this seemed to reinforce the decision to make the programme. If only we could persuade Glover to appear in the film. (He refused, but did appear on a programme with Peter Taylor for the BBC, some eight years later. His message was as unpalatable to Westminster in 1988 as it would have been in 1979. When Peter Brook, the new Northern Ireland Secretary, made the same point in November 1989, there were widespread calls for his resignation.)

After popping back to BH to watch the evening news programmes we set off in the same two cars for the Royal Ulster Constabulary's Headquarters in Knock Road, Belfast. Our host was to be the Chief Constable, Sir Kenneth Newman, accompanied by four of his senior officers. Their names and responsibilities were not on the schedule, but were to be given to us privately, for obvious reasons. Cecil Taylor and Robin Walsh also joined us.

As we drove up the Knock Road in the dark and saw the lights of Belfast twinkling below us, like a quiet northern industrial seaport, I thought of the men we were about to meet. They lived behind barbed wire, forever varying their movements, and checking their cars. Inevitably they would develop great loyalty to one another and slowly become a little detached from the community they served. And what of their wives, left alone for long periods, worrying about their husbands' safety? And the future of their children? No wonder so many children left for the mainland, no wonder so many senior RUC men did the same on retirement, if they reached it.

At the dinner I talked to Bill McGookin, the RUC press man, about the filming. I think everyone at the dinner table was aware of the incident by the end of the meal, but it was not a major issue at the dinner, which was an harmonious occasion. I told McGookin that Jeremy Paxman would see him the following day to talk about future cooperation. Bill was friendly but firm. They couldn't give us any special facilities because of the incident.

I received the impression that a negotiation was being proposed. If we dropped the footage of Carrickmore, which was embarrassing for the security forces, we would get our facilities. I could see a long bargaining session ahead, but it required careful thought. I didn't propose to open negotiations over coffee.

The next morning, Friday, 26 October, we flew back to London. It had been a good trip. John Gau, his deputy Chris Capron, and I agreed it had reinforced the reasons for doing a programme, and we had strengthened our good relations with the brave people who ran the BBC Northern Ireland. However we were looking forward to some sleep. The late nights in the Europa Hotel with Robin Walsh would not wear off for a long time. There were a large number of drummers in my head as I climbed on to the early morning shuttle, and found myself sitting next to Ian Paisley. It would have been a good opportunity for a chat but I wasn't in the state for it. When I got back into the office I sent a memo to Cecil Taylor, confirming our latest plans and thoughts, and then went home to sleep.

I wouldn't have slept very well if I had known that the previous evening, while we had been at the RUC Headquarters in Belfast, the Controller of Northern Ireland was hosting a dinner party in Lockets, a Westminster restaurant popular with politicians and civil servants. The purpose was to improve relations in the province between the BBC and the Government, but Jimmy Hawthorne still didn't know about the Carrickmore incident.

James Hawthorne, a tall, bearded, native Ulsterman, had been away from the BBC for seven years, running Hong Kong's broadcasting service. While at the BBC he had worked in educational programmes and he was having some initial problems in establishing himself as Controller in succession to the popular current affairs professional, Dick Francis. Few of us journalists knew him and we tended to deal with Dick as the former CNI but also now in the more senior position of Director of News and Current Affairs, and on the BBC Board of Management.

Hawthorne set out to make his own contacts and the dinner at Lockets was to be part of the process. Unfortunately, the Secretary of State, Humphrey Atkins, had to cancel at the last minute. In his absence the main guest was Jim Hannigan, a very senior civil servant, who casually mentioned during the evening about *Panorama* "staging that IRA thing".

Hawthorne didn't know what he was talking about and said that he would surely have known about it because of the BBC's "reference up" procedures. Hannigan didn't believe him. After all his own press man, David Gilliland, had discussed the matter a week ago at the party in Hawthorne's house, with John Gau, the Head of Current Affairs. It was an uneasy moment.

Hawthorne returned to Belfast on Friday, met Jeremy Paxman and discovered what had happened. It was very embarrassing for him, but he decided to wait until Monday when his senior colleagues could meet him and advise what to do. Perhaps a brief investigation and a rap over the knuckles for whomever had kept him in the dark. He would make clear who was in charge.

The Government, however, decided to twist the knife in the exposed entrails of the Corporation. David Gilliland phoned the BBC's National Governor for Northern Ireland, Lady Faulkner, at the personal request of Humphrey Atkins, the Secretary of State. Lucy Faulkner is a kind, decent but extremely steely and determined woman, the widow of the province's former Unionist Prime Minister, Brian Faulkner. Through him she knew the civil servants and politicians intimately.

Gilliland said the Government were distressed and suspicious. He recounted Hawthorne's unsatisfactory responses at the Lockets dinner. Officials were angry about the takeover of the village and the fact that the crew had not immediately reported it to the security forces.

Lucy Faulkner was no unthinking defender of the BBC. She had experienced rows between her husband and the Corporation and had been appalled by the INLA interview. She saw herself as the guardian of the Northern Ireland public's interest. She phoned James Hawthorne on Sunday evening and asked what was going on. Sunday evening is a dreadful time in any BBC manager's life; the phone never stops ringing. The weekend ends almost before it begins.

At least the Controller was able to say that he now knew about the incident and promised he would make further enquiries on Monday. When he did so he found his colleagues knew of the project in outline and of the Carrickmore incident, but said they thought he was being consulted separately.

Hawthorne exploded. Embarrassed, angered and determined to show he was in charge, he fired off a broadside to Dick Francis, copied to John Gau, sending it by open BBC telex. As a result it was widely known around senior levels of the Corporation within hours.

Reading it now, over ten years later, one can still feel the pain and sympathise with its author's exposed position, but a telephone call would have been more sensible. The telex contained inaccuracies and was in part defamatory.

"It would appear," said Hawthorne, "that the NIO no longer sees much value in discussing matters of this kind with BBC management executives – considering my defence to Jim Hannigan, can you blame them? Lady Faulkner's dismay and embarrassment are at least as great as mine – i.e. extremely acute. And that is putting it mildly."

Rushing to judgement the Controller pointed an accusing finger at me. "It is inconceivable that Roger Bolton – the man who brought you the INLA affair – should not be aware of the paramount need for close and detailed consultation with the Northern Ireland management before embarking on a major Irish project."

The Controller concluded, "I now require a full report on everything that has happened so far in this matter and everything that is proposed, including a view of all the film shot at Carrickmore. Regardless of *Panorama*'s deadlines or commitments I shall want to see every item of the proposed programme before transmission and in sufficient time to allow for amendment or abandonment as appropriate. May I please have your support."

Dick Francis thought the time had come to refer matters up and together with Bill Cotton went to see the Acting Director General. They agreed to keep a close watch on the programme, which was still several weeks away from transmission, and Dick started to try and mend fences and bruised feelings.

That Monday, 29 October, *Panorama* transmitted a programme called "Fear of Freedom". In China a journalist had been jailed for questioning the legitimacy of the Communist government and its suppression of civil rights. We had obtained a transcript of the trial and from it had filmed a dramatisation of the events in Peking, together with a film report by Philip Short.

In Czechoslovakia six leading dissidents had just been jailed on charges of subversion, but their real crime had been to demand the human rights to which all signatories of the Helsinki Agreement are pledged. My reporter, Philip Tibenham, had obtained unique interviews with some of the defendants and their friends and relatives.

Both the Chinese and Czech embassies complained about the programme. Their usual charge, and that of the South African and Soviet Governments, was that our coverage of human rights issues was one-sided and hypocritical. What about Northern Ireland they would say – detention without trial, torture in prison? I replied that the BBC was different from their state media. We did report these matters. I redoubled my efforts to cover Northern Ireland, and to get the IRA programme back on the rails.

On Tuesday, 30 October, the day after Hawthorne's telex had burned its way across the Irish Sea, I attended the News and Current Affairs meeting as usual and met Robin Walsh, the Northern Ireland News Editor. We were both incredulous that the Head of Programmes, Northern Ireland, Cecil Taylor, hadn't told his Controller about Carrickmore. The following day John Gau, Jeremy Paxman and I had an informal chat with DNCA about the telex. We gave Dick a detailed list of what had been filmed and our future filming plans. There was no sense of crisis or great concern and for the following eight days there was silence. No enquiries, no suspension of research. David Darlow was due back from holiday to continue making the film. My programme team was finally together, *Panorama* was improving every week and morale was taking off.

Meanwhile, Mrs. Thatcher still knew nothing of what had happened, despite the fact that Humphrey Atkins had written to the Home Secretary, Willie Whitelaw, complaining about the incident. Neither told the Prime Minister. The bomb however was primed. It required only a spark to ignite it. Enter Ed Moloney.

Hibernian was a weekly magazine published in Dublin and had very good contacts with Republicans. Its edition of Thursday, 8 November, 1979 came out late the previous day. At the bottom of the front page was the helpful headline "Row Brews on Panorama/IRA Programme". It described the events that had happened at Carrickmore three weeks before and concluded, "the stage looks set for another rumpus between the Government and the BBC."

Moloney had gone to the village after hearing of the death of a

London man, called Peter Grogan, some twelve days after the incident filmed by my crew. There were allegations that he had died after having been interviewed by a British Army foot patrol in the street.

The evidence was inconclusive but Moloney heard stories of the area being saturated with troops and of helicopter patrols being drastically stepped up. The activity had started two days after the filming when three helicopters had landed foot patrols at different ends of the village and villagers had been questioned about the incident.

Moloney is a very good journalist and he soon had the full story, although he made it clear that "neither the BBC nor *Panorama* had foreknowledge of the Provo operation" and that the IRA patrol was between twelve and fifteen strong. There were wilder claims but Moloney dismissed them. He pointed out how embarrassing it was for the Army that the IRA could mount this sort of operation and, with his experience of the many earlier rows between the former Labour Northern Ireland Secretary, Roy Mason, and the BBC, concluded that we were in for another one.

The *Financial Times* picked up the story, and ran a small report in its Thursday morning edition. It was hardly noticed by the BBC governors as they met at Television Centre on the seventh floor. They were preoccupied with the problem of the licence fee.

For the first time in its history the BBC was in debt. Because both Labour and Conservative governments had delayed increasing the licence fee the BBC had been forced to borrow. It was £50 million in the red and even before the minimum lending rate went up three points to 17 per cent the previous week the Corporation was paying out nearly £500,000 a month in interest charges. "Money", the *Daily Telegraph* pointed out, "that we pay for programmes."

The Governors were hoping that the Home Secretary would redeem his promise to put the BBC back on a sound financial basis that morning at Cabinet. Mrs. Thatcher could not have been in a worse frame of mind.

Bernard Ingham had just taken over as her press secretary at No. 10. As usual he left his house in the Home Counties at 6.30 a.m. and drove in to Downing Street. While Mrs. Thatcher was listening to the *Today* programme on Radio 4 he summarised the papers for her. He pointed out the *Financial Times* cutting.

She was incandescent. "You must understand," one of her advisers told me some time later, repeating the views I had heard elsewhere, "Mrs. Thatcher believes you have to be for or against terrorism. A journalist is a member of the human race, some of them forget that, and a citizen first. You should have nothing to do with terrorists *at all*. And if you see a crime committed you should tell the authorities immediately. The whole thing was incomprehensible to her." When the Cabinet met, an official was dispatched to ring the BBC and find out what was going on. As all the members of the BBC's Board of Management were meeting with the Board of Governors a message was passed to the Chairman, Michael Swann. He was an extremely intelligent and astute University Vice-Chancellor, who had negotiated the student unrest of the sixties and seventies with great skill, but this was to be as difficult a problem to deal with as any he had faced previously.

The basic facts were quickly ascertained and members of the Management pointed out that journalists, faced with such a tip off, had little option but to follow it up. David Webster, the Director of Public Affairs was dispatched to prepare a statement while the Board considered other matters. He rang Lime Grove and asked John Gau for his thoughts. Gau rang me and I clattered up the lino covered stairs with a copy of the original press release we had prepared in the event of publicity.

Webster took it down, amended it a little and returned to the boardroom to have it authorised. The Governors were not happy. What about the Controller Northern Ireland not being informed? Others were not convinced about the need for journalists to act on such tip-offs. They were irritated at being caught unawares so soon after the INLA business. They wanted the statement toughened up. It was. Lucy Faulkner and George Howard, the plump, kaftan-wearing, fun-loving, great "commoner" and owner of Castle Howard, were particularly insistent that more should be done. Since Trethowan had authorised the INLA interview they had been obliged to bite their tongues, but the Carrickmore filming had been done without the approval of the Northern Ireland Controller. They were determined to show the BBC was not out of control, but in their control. Crucially Trethowan himself was still away sick, his authority and political astuteness missing.

The revised version was read to us in Lime Grove a few minutes before it was read to Downing Street and then distributed to the Press, who by this time were ringing up for the BBC's reaction to the *Financial Times* story.

As we listened our hearts dropped as we realised how inevitable disaster had become.

The statement had a long preamble, of the type loved by Governors and Management, but immediately thrown into the waste-paper basket by journalists as they went for the guts of the piece. The key passage read as follows:

> The Board of Governors have been informed by the Acting Director General of what would appear to be a clear breach of standing instructions in relation to filming in Ireland by a *Panorama* team. The Governors have asked the Acting Director General to complete his enquiries swiftly and report back to the board on action to be taken. In the meantime, there is no question of the projected programme being transmitted.

I couldn't believe it. The statement didn't make clear that the alleged breach of standing instructions related not to the filming at Carrickmore but to how much consultation had gone on with the Controller over the proposal for the programme. It didn't take a genius to see that it would be read as an admission that we had colluded with the IRA. John and I desperately tried to get the statement changed. The Governors refused to even consider it. Moreover we were not to speak to the Press at all and there were to be no further statements to anybody.

We sat with our heads in our hands. Where was Dick Francis, the journalists' champion? Why hadn't he explained the facts to the Governors, told them he had authorised, indeed commissioned, the project? Why hadn't he produced the press statement we'd agreed on a week before? The Governors should have stressed the fact that no film of Carrickmore had been transmitted, might never be transmitted.

Dick told me recently that he had tried to calm the Governors down and had undertaken to enquire into the affair, but that the Governors did not listen.

Things were even worse than we had imagined. The people who run the Republican Press Centre in Belfast are extremely sophisticated propagandists who attempt to manipulate the Press as does everyone involved in the Northern Ireland conflict. They had quickly worked out how Downing Street and the Press would react to the news so they lobbed in some more explosive. What staggered us as we read the tapes was how the Press Association could be so gullible. Their copy was headed "Stunt".

The London *Evening Standard* lapped it all up, and devoted its lunchtime edition front page to the story. The headline ran:

"Machine gun terrorists take over village – so *Panorama* can film them."

An even bigger headline followed:

"Fury over BBC's IRA 'Stunt'."

It reported the BBC's "admission" and went on,

The stunt was believed to have been set up on October 17th – the day a British soldier was shot and seriously wounded outside Springfield Road Barracks in Belfast.

Sources in Belfast said today that in the stunt all roads in and out of Carrickmore were sealed off by roadblocks manned by armed IRA volunteers.

Two M60 machine guns, RPG rocket propelled grenade launches and many Armalite rifles were brought into the village of 400 people for display in front of the camera.

Defensive positions were set up in the village and the main body of men drilled in the main street. The IRA stayed in "control" of Carrickmore for 3 hours in broad daylight after the Panorama film crew said they had enough footage. The Provisionals even offered to hold Carrickmore, 22 miles from the border, overnight if necessary.

This was of course absurd. The so called takeover and the filming had lasted between ten and fifteen minutes. No words were spoken between the film crew and the IRA. The crew only saw about twelve people armed with rifles not rocket launchers. And there were no blockades, only masked men asking to see driving licences.

Ironically the Army and the RUC were equally incensed by these reports as they knew they weren't true. The Army criticised the filming as "an appalling and disgraceful affront", but failed to get the report into perspective. The *Standard* was soon to have an even better headline.

In the House of Commons and the clubs of Whitehall, MPs frequently check the clattering new tape machines, particularly before Prime Minister's Question Time, which takes place on Tuesdays and Thursdays.

Our bad luck was holding, today was Thursday. What Tory MP could resist polishing a BBC ball and lobbing a full toss to the Prime Minister, in the sure and certain knowledge that it would be dispatched way over the boundary?

In the event, Ulster Unionist MP James Molyneaux got in first, urging Mrs. Thatcher to forward the names of those involved in "this most treasonable activity" to the Director of Public Prosecutions.

Mrs. Thatcher replied that was a matter for the DPP and the police. "It is not the first time I have had occasion to raise similar matters with the BBC", she told MPs. "Both the Home Secretary and I think it is about time they put their house in order." (It was not the phrase Mr. Whitelaw, the Home Secretary, would have used, but he had learned to ride these explosions.)

James Callaghan, the former Prime Minister and Opposition leader, stood up. He was not renowned as a defender of the Press, a believer of open government or a friend of the BBC. A former adviser to the Police Federation, he put the boot in mercilessly. "It is not the duty of the media to stage-manage news, but to report it." The whole affair was "distasteful and reprehensible".

It felt as if every phone in Lime Grove had a member of the Press on the end of it. The calls poured in, and we could say nothing, by order of the Governors. The row could hardly have been more ineptly handled by the BBC. While everyone who held a grudge against the Corporation put the boot in we were not allowed to defend ourselves.

It was like facing the West Indian fast bowling attack without bat, pads or a box, let alone a helmet or thigh protector.

By late afternoon, as the *Evening Standard* thudded on to Management's desk, there was general agreement that this silence was suicidal. It was being taken by everyone as an admission of guilt. But the Governors had now dispersed and their instructions had been categoric. Added to that there was an internal BBC press and publicity battle going on over who was to blame and who should handle the Press.

Alan Protheroe, the fiery Editor of Television News, had a very sensible idea. "Show the film," he said, "so that the public can see what actually happened, and how absurd the Press Association reports are." It would certainly have had people watching his news bulletin. That imaginative step was rejected.

By around 6 p.m., after the first editions had rolled off the press, the Management agreed to give the BBC Press Office an "off the record" briefing statement which could be used in answer to enquiries. It was far too late for next morning's newspapers. We were hammered.

The *Daily Telegraph* editorial was headed "Betraying Journalism". It referred to a "perverted exercise in journalistic enterprise." It went on, "A member of this newspaper who was guilty of anything resembling the conduct attributed to this *Panorama* team would be dismissed. If there are journalists in the media who positively want to be martyred in what is falsely described as the cause of 'editorial freedom' their wish should be promptly granted."

The *Daily Star* headline read "Field day for IRA thugs." "The fact that it happened while the Attorney-General is still studying reports of the notorious TV interview linked to the murder of Airey Neave is an outrage."

The *Sun* kept up the competition: "Within the Corporation there are clearly men either devoid of judgement, or else with a deliberate purpose to make mischief in Ireland. They must be uncovered and booted out."

I picked up the *Daily Express*. It was even worse if that was possible. Its opinion column was headed, "Close to Treason". It went on, "It was as if, during the Second World War, a BBC crew had gone to film the Nazis occupying the Channel Islands . . . Simply for the sake of some sensational film footage, the editor of the BBC's most distinguished current affairs programmes was prepared to endanger the lives of 400 villagers . . . The BBC only just escaped public prosecution a few months ago over the screening of an interview with the alleged assassin of Airey Neave. In the light of the warning they then received from the Prime Minister, their continued irresponsibility, their continued undermining of the Government's authority is beyond belief."

The *Daily Mail* can always be relied upon in these circumstances to deliver a conspiracy theory. In 1979 they did not have the outstanding talents of Paul Johnson to assist them in doing so. Instead, it was left to Roderick Gilchrist, the Entertainments Editor, and Nicholas Gordon.

Their article was headed "Just how much of what you see on TV *is* rigged?" It linked the Carrickmore affair with other allegations of stage-management in BBC documentaries and went on:

> It does, of course, all give credence to the allegations levelled at the BBC by politicians that inside the Television Centre there exists a small but efficient and dedicated cabal of Left-wing extremists who, by twisting the picture out of focus, are guilty of projecting propaganda.
>
> It is a most subtle fan of propaganda because it comes from within the most respected television company in the world – the BBC!

The *Daily Mail* article succinctly summarised what many politicians and members of the BBC Governors believed. Since there was no defence of the BBC journalists on that first crucial day of Parliamentary uproar, and all political parties joined in, even the usually liberal *Guardian* piled in, talking of *Panorama* being "lost in a mist". I drafted a letter to *The Times* and *Daily Telegraph* defending *Panorama*. It was sat upon by the BBC Press Office.

Although I had thought the Governors' statement was disastrous I still hadn't been prepared for the scale of the onslaught. I looked at my colleagues. I didn't know how they voted, or what their views about Ireland's future were. Mine were confused. I couldn't see how pulling the troops out would help, I thought it would very probably cause even greater conflict. I disliked the paramilitaries

intensely. However I'd been to Ireland frequently, and knew the
IRA wouldn't go away, and that they were supported, or at least
tolerated, by a significant minority of the Roman Catholic
population in the North. The British Army had told me that the
Provos could not be defeated militarily. Shouldn't the British
people know this? What united the journalists in Lime Grove was a
belief that they should, that we had a duty to report the facts and
try to understand how the situation had developed. We believed
ignorance and censorship often had fatal consequences.

I wondered what those national newspaper journalists who
actually worked in Northern Ireland thought when they read their
newspapers' editorials. Did their own editors not know how they
worked on the ground, how they met their "contacts", how they
were able to report what the paramilitaries thought? Perhaps
locked in their Fleet Street bunkers, wined and dined by Westminster and Whitehall the editors did not.

And yet could they be so ignorant? Newspapers seemed to be
quite happy to print interviews with IRA leaders and indeed to
show photos of IRA "stunts".

I didn't know whether to laugh or cry when I picked up the 16
November, 1979 edition of Sir James Goldsmith's *Now* magazine
and saw in its "Keynotes" section a colour photo of an IRA
roadblock. Sir James was not, even then, of the extreme left. The
article described what had happened a few days earlier when the
photographer, a German journalist and a man from the *Guardian*
had been taken by an Irish reporter to "bandit country" in South
Armagh. At the roadblock they had met a seven-man Provo patrol.

Now reported it was probably a publicity stunt, but they
published the details and the photograph.

Back in Ireland, Ed Moloney, who had written the original report
in *Hibernian*, told the *Guardian* "Half the things that are being
reported weren't in my piece . . . I'm a full-time journalist. I'm
really getting an insight into how awful they can be."

Meanwhile I had other things to think about. Two inquiries were
about to start.

Following the Prime Minister's statement in the House that
decisions about prosecution were a matter for the DPP and the
police, an inquiry was ordered by Sir Thomas Hetherington,

DEATH ON THE ROCK

Director of Public Prosecutions, at the request of Sir Michael Havers, the Attorney-General. It was stressed that Sir Michael had acted "within his own remit as a law officer", and not on the instructions of the Prime Minister or the Home Secretary. There are occasions when instructions aren't necessary. Sir Michael need never have come to Cabinet again had there been no inquiries. Once more Commander Peter Duffy of the Anti-Terrorist Squad headed down to Lime Grove.

Back at Broadcasting House, Dick Francis was appointed to head an inquiry into the project he himself had commissioned.

6

ON TRIAL

"You are an evil, vicious bastard, Bolton, I hope your friends in the IRA get you."

The hate mail had started to arrive. As usual it would be unsigned and often sections would be underscored in red ink. My secretary was only twenty-one and had never had to deal with this sort of abuse before. A lot of it was obscene and clearly the work of disturbed people. One day, however, we received a card from Belfast telling me that I had been found guilty by the Sons of Ulster and would be executed soon. No matter where I went, it said, I could not escape.

I was hardly the first person to receive this sort of stuff, but it did scare me, though I tried not to show it. My office in Lime Grove was in the front room of a terraced house facing directly on to the street, with no front garden. In the evening when it was dark and the lights were on I never used to pull the curtains. They never quite met each other anyway. Following the threats I took a safety pin and fixed the curtains together well before dark. I also started to look under my car.

Then the telephone at home started to make funny noises. I thought this was proof that it couldn't be tapped, for surely the bugging technology would have been more sophisticated. Still, if the DPP asks the Anti-Terrorist Squad to investigate you, it seems daft not to be discreet on the phone.

To some extent I was insulated from the pressures because I had the support of nearly all my staff and the journalists in Lime Grove. My seventy-year-old parents were not so fortunate. The local paper back in my home town, the *Cumberland News*, had reported the row in the usual local way.

"Carlisle-born journalist . . ." and later on ". . . Roger, whose parents still live on Dalston Road, Carlisle . . ." Soon my father and mother started to receive threatening calls. They didn't tell me at the time. If they had I don't know if I could have borne it.

On the day of the Commons row my first thought was to call and warn them. They had no knowledge of the dirty side of politics or the reality of reporting in Northern Ireland. How did they feel when they read their son was accused of treachery and treason in Parliament and when nearly all the papers were calling for his blood? They couldn't disguise their worry but they never wavered in their support. However the 300 miles between us never seemed longer. I couldn't get up to explain things to them.

They stopped reading the papers, and my father got used to the questions in the eyes of people at church and the bowling green, but he also got used to people saying that it would come out all right, and they had faith.

I didn't spend all my time worrying. I had a weekly programme going out which that week was dealing with the Government's new immigration laws and involved a sticky interview with a minister. I still had complete confidence in Dick Francis and senior colleagues. My job was to protect my journalists. After all I kept sending them to dangerous parts of the world to be shot at, so it seemed only right that when trouble at home occurred I should guard their backs.

I wrote to the Management taking responsibility for what had happened and making it clear that I thought Jeremy Paxman and David Darlow had had no alternative but to do what they did. Had I been consulted in advance I would have told them to go and report.

My worries were further allayed by a remarkably robust memo which I received from my Head of Current Affairs, John Gau. Reading it now it is easy to understand why John was so popular a leader to his troops.

He sent it to the Chairman, the Director General, the Director of

News and Current Affairs, and everyone who could possibly be involved in the BBC management.

As the man ultimately and proudly responsible for *Panorama*, I would like to say five things about the Carrickmore Incident.

1 I joined a BBC in the early sixties that was fiercely independent, journalistically courageous and steadfastly loyal to its staff, especially those under fire. The handling of the Carrickmore Incident seems to me to call these virtues into question. If the Corporation publicly suggests some of its staff have been acting irregularly, without itself supplying the context of the story, or letting those staff defend themselves, it ensures the maximum amount of bad publicity for itself as effectively as if it deliberately intended it.

2 As the person charged with ensuring that Standing Instructions are followed by my staff, I can say with complete confidence that there has been no "clear breach" of those instructions. The *Panorama* team acted in a proper journalistic way in response to an anonymous telephone call. Just as in similar circumstances BBC *News* did during the recent anti-internment rally in Belfast. Just as in similar circumstances the British Press and BBC *News* reacted to the flaunting by the IRA of their M60 machine gun. Had the *Panorama* team been able to telephone me in advance, I would certainly have sanctioned their following up the anonymous call. Suppose the IRA had been about to reveal a new weapon, like the Sam 7? They had a journalistic obligation to pursue the matter.

It is now evident that Controller, Northern Ireland was not fully in the picture. His subordinates certainly were and whether they are "nominees" or not as stated in Standing Instructions seems to me a moot point. Of course, I am sorry CNI heard about the Carrickmore Incident at party. So did I. It was embarrassing, but the imperatives of journalism sometimes cause embarrassment on these occasions. It is surely not a case for making an already restricted Standing Instructions even more so.

3 The reaction of politicians to a distorted story without benefit of a clarifying BBC statement was predictable. The false accusation of "stage-managing the news" by Mr. Callaghan, who himself has not been beyond orchestrating his own appearances, is sheer humbug. The proper BBC response to such hysteria is a firm and resolute reminder of our independence and journalistic integrity. The increase of appetite grows by what it feeds on. History tells us where appeasement leads.

4 The worst aspect of the whole affair is its affect on loyal staff doing a difficult job. Nobody likes filming in Northern Ireland. Indeed, Current Affairs is unable to get a BBC film crew to go at all. So to be publicly rebuked by one's masters, to see the facts of the case not being reported and then not to be allowed to defend oneself against distortion and slander, has a shattering effect on morale. It is difficult to see how I shall be able to get anyone in future to go to Northern Ireland, when he sees his colleagues stabbed in the back.

5 Finally, there is the question of reporting Northern Ireland and its troubles. Whatever else this furore achieves, it will effectively silence proper investigation of the IRA. Indeed, there are many who feel that is the reason for a great deal of the clamour. But if the journalistic independence of which the BBC has been justly proud, is to mean anything, it can only be right that a proper account of how a part of the UK has been in a state of near civil war for ten years be fully recorded.

I appreciate that there will now be an inquiry into the incident and I should like to point out that I take complete responsibility for everything done by my staff. If it is felt that disciplinary action should be taken, it should fall on me.

(John Gau)

In a sense the memo was to be his BBC epitaph. Not a bad one.

Another cause for reassurance was that Dick Francis was undertaking the inquiry. Together with Jeremy, David and John Gau I attended a preliminary inquiry in Dick's office. It seemed a bit of a formality as Dick was asking us questions to which he knew the answers as he had been briefed throughout.

I should have paid more notice to the *Financial Times* again. On 10 November, under a heading "The brick the BBC has dropped", Arthur Sandles wrote:

> It would be difficult to overstate the fury felt within the upper ranks of the BBC about the actions of its *Panorama* television crew in the village of Carrickmore, Co. Tyrone last month. For the Corporation the whole row could not have come at a worse time. Battling against external services cuts and fighting for the sort of increase in the licence fee which would enable it to compete to some extent with the recent ITV pay rises, the BBC now sees the rug pulled from under it – and it sees that damage to have been done from within.
>
> The more melodramatic voices within the Corporation feel that the Carrickmore affair could severely damage the BBC for a decade. The picture they paint is as follows: Government, angry at this latest turn of events, will be less than generous with its licence fee increase. The BBC after a difficult series of negotiations will settle its pay talks at a figure considerably below ITV's 45 per cent over two years. ITV 2 opens and the best BBC staff will leave en masse for the new channel.
>
> Going through this prospect yesterday, one BBC executive muttered wryly, "Well, they can take the *Panorama* team for a start."

The following day, Tuesday, 13 November, was my thirty-fourth birthday. It was a muted occasion. As I had worked the weekend to get the previous night's programme ready I had hoped to take the morning off. No chance.

Around the middle of the morning I received a call from the Acting Director General asking me to go and meet him at 2.15. He was taking over the Inquiry. As I was due to meet the Chairman of ICI at that time to discuss a *Panorama* project the interview was re-arranged for 4 p.m.

Gerry Mansell told me that he had received DNCA's report and was conducting further enquiries himself. He had been asked by the Chairman to report to the board that Thursday. This was not a formal interview but a discussion. When I talked to him for this book Gerry was very frank. "Basically my problem was that the Governors wanted heads on a plate, quickly." In 1979, he was more circumspect.

He said that he didn't want to dwell on the Carrickmore visit itself, but he was particularly concerned about the process of consultation in relation to the programme as a whole.

Alarm bells should have rung. If he wasn't interested in the incident itself and a scapegoat had to be found then it would be in the area of who told whom that the victim would be found. At that time I was somewhat naive and had not heard of the famous BBC adage, "Assistant Heads must roll".

I was relieved that Jeremy and David were in the clear but I also wanted to protect my colleagues in Northern Ireland and not drop them in it, so I was careful to offer facts not opinions. I soon realised that Gerry and I were having difficulty communicating.

He was from a different BBC, one where everything was put on paper and where you were a BBC employee first rather than a journalist. It also appeared to me that it wasn't a world that encompassed the Falls Road. His view was that Ian Trethowan had not run a tight enough ship and that it was naive to open your flank to the Government in the way we had. He interrogated me closely.

"Why didn't you obey the standing instruction that the Controller of Northern Ireland should be personally consulted about such projects?" I hadn't seen a standing instruction, I had just gone by custom and practice, and by what I'd been told by my Head of Group. Besides, CNI was frequently away on business and social occasions. The contact was always with his executives.

Mansell said "The mandatory system of reference upward must be understood and must work. On this occasion there was no opportunity to bring the concerns of the BBC as a whole into consideration, as there would be had CNI been consulted."

I started to get angry, but with some difficulty managed to control myself. I said some of CNI's remarks in his telex were defamatory and should be withdrawn. "Journalists in Lime Grove were left in real doubt about the Board's attitude to any activity by them in Northern Ireland. I feel let down by the Board's statement on 8 November which left me exposed to Press accusations of treason and treachery and of responsibility for putting the lives of 400 people at risk." The Acting DG replied that in the light of this incident and others the Board of Governors had felt itself let down. "It had faced a very loaded situation on 8 November and that situation would have been worse if it had not issued its statement." We didn't agree on that. I asked whether there had been concern about *Panorama* while I had been Editor. Mr. Mansell replied "No."

After an hour the interview came to a close. Mansell had been tough but fair. I asked what would be the next step. A/DG said he would present his report to the chairman and it would be for the governors to decide what happened next.

I asked if I could have a copy of DNCA's Report. No.

Back in Lime Grove I joined John Gau and other Editors for an end of the day drink while we watched *Nationwide*. What did he think would happen? John stretched out his not inconsiderable figure and put his feet up. "Oh, a reprimand, that's all," said John, "don't worry about it." So I didn't.

On Thursday 15 November around mid-afternoon, I received a phone call from Robin Scott's office asking me to come and see him at 6 p.m. I was not told what for. Robin Scott was deputy Managing Director of the Television Service and in charge in Alasdair Milne's absence. He was reputedly very attractive to ladies. He had written pop songs before becoming Controller of Radio 2 and then moving to television. He was called the white tornado for the perverse reason that although his hair was white he hardly seemed to move, but just appeared, like a Red Indian in moccasins. He was also bilingual in French.

He was in a friendly mood and offered me a drink. No one else was present. He handed me a letter asking me to attend a disciplinary hearing with A/DG the next day at 12 noon. He also handed me a photocopy of the procedures for disciplinary interviews. I asked whether I could have a copy, or see a copy, of A/DG's report to the Governors which presumably provided the basis for the interview. DMDTel. said he would see.

Almost as an afterthought he said I could have a witness with me if I wanted. We finished our drinks and exchanged television gossip before I left and went home. Standing on White City tube station waiting for the one in four trains which go to Ealing Broadway, I reflected on the conversation. It all seemed a bit of a ritual, really. Everyone knew we'd behaved quite normally and had the Carrickmore incident not become public then nothing would have happened other than a massaging of bruised feelings, and a sensible discussion of how, not whether, to proceed. There was only one troubling thought: where was Dick Francis?

The next day, Friday, 16 November, I went to my office as usual and got down to work. There was a knock on the door. In came Helen Jenkins, Father of the Lime Grove Chapel of the National Union of Journalists. She wanted to know what had happened. I filled her in and asked did she really think it was necessary to take a witness. "Too bloody right it's necessary" said Helen and arranged to come herself. She bore the scars of many disputes in newspapers and she didn't think the BBC Management was different from any other. "Oh, but it is", I told her. "The BBC is different." She snorted. "Make sure you ask for an adjournment if it gets difficult. We have to see what you're charged with and get a look at the reports that have been written." I thought she was overdoing it a bit but nodded agreement.

At 11.30, Robin Scott's car arrived and we climbed in beside him and drove up town to Broadcasting House. As I entered, John Gau was leaving by another door.

Gerry Mansell was sitting at the Director General's desk. He looked comfortable at it, and had a brisk businesslike air. Suddenly he and Robin Scott started to talk quickly to each other in French. Gerry was bilingual as well. I tried to make out what they were saying but a scraped O'level was no qualification to interpret.

At about 12.10 the interview got underway. Mr. Mansell said this was a formal occasion and Mr. Bolton would have the right of reply. He would inform Mr. Bolton of the conclusions he had reached resulting from his investigations. He had reported those conclusions to the Board in the form of a Confidential Board paper, available only to Governors. The Board had discussed the paper on the previous day (15 November) and what Mr. Mansell now had to say had been agreed with the Board.

(I later learned that as my interview was beginning No. 10 was being told what the results of that interview would be.)

I said I had had no opportunity to see the evidence leading to this interview. "Can I have a copy of your report to the Board?" "No." "Can I see DNCA, Dick Francis's report as there seems to be a conflict of evidence between DNCA and myself over whether, at that meeting at Blackpool, he had put the IRA project on hold?" I knew damn well he hadn't. "No."

(Ten years later, while preparing this book, Dick, now Sir Richard Francis, told me that my account was right.)

"Can I call witnesses?" "Not necessarily." This began to seem like a Kafkaesque nightmare. I said that where statements had been called into conflict I had a right to try and assess the evidence for myself. At present I could only comment on Mr. Mansell's conclusions and not on the basis for them.

We were soon banging backwards and forwards over the consultation question that we had dealt with exhaustively at our previous meetings, and about what Dick had said to me at Blackpool.

Mansell asked, "Did DNCA say to you 'I will have to talk to Gerry, who will have to carry the Chairman with him *and then discuss it further with you*'?" "I have no recollection of that and, if it was the case, why didn't Dick contact me again until three weeks afterwards? Why had he never complained to me that I had gone ahead without his agreement? Had Dick said those words it would have been suicidal of me to press on. I'm not that daft."

We returned to the matter of consultation with CNI. "As a senior BBC manager you have high responsibilities to the Corporation. You should have been aware of the delicate state of the BBC's relationship with Government." Inwardly I fumed. That's your job not mine, I thought. I'm a programme editor, a journalist. My responsibility is to the audience and to the facts.

The Acting Director General seemed to be coming to an end. We couldn't agree. We seemed to work in different organisations, with different practices, and different priorities.

Mansell said he accepted that I had told the truth and been very frank but he took a very stern view of my failure adequately to consult. "It has been said that the price of independence was external competence and that saying is very relevant in this case. I can therefore issue you with a formal reprimand for not having discharged your responsibility in this respect. Your Head of Department has been similarly admonished."

I thought it was over. Oh well, I thought, I suppose they had to do it to someone, but after the formal bit was completed couldn't we all just get together and try and stop this happening again? We'd invite Gerry down to Lime Grove to meet us and get him across to Northern Ireland. I checked that Jeremy Paxman and David Darlow were in the clear and that nothing would happen to them and then got back to the question that kept puzzling me.

How had Mr. Mansell reacted when Dick Francis first told him about the programme on 15 October, the day after Dick and I had met in Blackpool? The A/DG said his response had been to express grave doubts and to say that DNCA should not go ahead too quickly. That was the first I'd heard of it.

I got up to go but Gerry hadn't finished. "The whole matter has caused me great concern. I have now reached the conclusion that it is desirable from every point of view, including yours, that, as you have been in the firing line for some months, you should be moved to another sphere. A secondment to Secretariat will be a very valuable experience for you. After your long spell at Lime Grove and in television journalism it will provide you with a broadening experience and enable you to acquire more knowledge of how the BBC is run, and of BBC policy."

Mansell went on, "This is not a disciplinary move, but it is my firm decision that you should leave your present post as Editor of *Panorama*. The situation will be reviewed in about a year's time and I expect that, at a future date, you may well return to the television service in some other capacity."

The world stopped then went into slow motion.

I looked around; all was silent but Mansell's lips were still moving. What? Why? My eyes began to water. Oh God, Roger, don't cry now. I hadn't dreamed this would happen. I was like a child who feels a burning injustice has been done to him. Self-pity and anger mixed together.

I looked at the Head of Secretariat who was minuting the hearing in the corner. He was Patrick Mullins, the man who had recruited me to the BBC twelve years before. He was everything that gave the BBC a good name. A former colonial administrator, he looked

[93]

like a typical civil servant, but beneath the three-piece suit he was an independently minded man. He was my BBC Father Figure. Had I let him down? I now proceeded to insult him by accident.

"A secondment to Mr. Mullins' Department in these circumstances would be the BBC equivalent of Siberia," I said. "There is no guarantee that thereafter I will be allowed to return to television journalism at an editorial level. It will be seen by everyone that I was the guilty man of Carrickmore. The Press will make a ready connection between this enforced move and the Board of Governors' statement issued on 8 November that had led to me being accused of treachery, treason, and of putting 400 lives at risk. The Anti-Terrorist Squad is investigating me and now the BBC does this. And I haven't seen any of the evidence or been able to call any witnesses."

I repeated my request for the meeting to be adjourned.

Mr. Mansell said that the decision to move Mr. Bolton from the editorship of *Panorama* must stand and must take immediate effect. "From this afternoon?" "From now."

Helen Jenkins was calm and decisive. She pointed out that the relevant staff instruction over disciplinary hearings had not been complied with. A formal union request to see the evidence had been refused. The same inhibitions would handicap Mr. Bolton in any appeal hearing before the Chairman. Mr. Mansell replied that the BBC was acting entirely within its rights. Mr. Bolton was not being disciplined, the move would be good for him. ("Oh bloody hellfire, Gerry," I thought, "you can't say that with a straight face." – He could.)

"I've only been editor of *Panorama* for two and a half months, is it seriously thought that I already need a rest from the firing line? Won't this decision make all production staff reluctant to tackle any Northern Ireland issues?"

While I was still reeling from this, Helen Jenkins asked Mansell to identify the News and Current Affairs minute to which he had referred and which had the status of a staff instruction. It had formed the Appendix to the 1 October 1971 minutes. No wonder we hadn't seen it. In 1971 I had been a studio director.

I again asked for a further meeting, during the following week, at which I would be able to call witnesses. Mr. Mansell said Mr.

[94]

Bolton's move from *Panorama* could not be deferred. He could appeal to the Chairman, but Mr. Mansell's report to the Board must remain private. He would consider a resumption of the meeting. He was not opposed personally to an adjournment but he would have to check.

The interview was over. Sentence had been passed and carried out before the trial had been concluded.

As I was led in a daze down the long dark corridors of Broadcasting House I understood why George Orwell had used it as a model for the Ministry of Truth in *1984*.

We came out into the reception area and Sue Summers of the *Evening Standard* was waiting. She had the best BBC contacts of any print journalist and was a friend. She half rose but I was bustled passed her into a car and driven off to Lime Grove.

7

SACKED

Lime Grove was once as pleasant as the name suggests. Located a few streets west of the rustically named Shepherd's Bush Green it was the scene of one of Charles Dickens's charitable acts. Dickens shared with Gladstone an interest in young prostitutes and was determined to help these twelve- and thirteen-year-olds start a new life.

So he enlisted the enthusiastic support of the charitable banking heiress, Lady Angela Burdett Coutts, and bought a house in Lime Grove, then in the country. Vulnerable young girls from the East End were taken there, taught how to speak and dress, how to lay a table and make a curtsey, and then dispatched to the Colonies where they would become respectable married women.

Dickens laid himself open to the charge of setting up a house for prostitutes, a charge which slightly modernised, had been levelled at the BBC. The former Gainsborough Film Studios had been bought by the Corporation in 1950 as its Television Centre, and a number of the Edwardian terraced houses alongside had also been purchased. When the new Television Centre had opened in Wood Lane, half a mile north, the Current Affairs department had remained there, glorying in its isolation. Since there were few attractive places to go at lunchtime or in the early evening most staff used to stay on site talking among themselves. It built up a sense of cameraderie, and loyalty, some would say ignorance and arrogance.

John Gau had returned to Lime Grove half an hour or so before me. He walked along the ground floor corridor and entered S7, one of the hospitality rooms and scene of legendary rows, romances, and political skirmishes.

Every Friday lunchtime Current Affairs Editors would meet there for a plate of hot food and drink to talk about the week's programmes and pass on concerns and gossips to the Head of Group. Today they were apprehensive and subdued, waiting for the result of the disciplinary interviews.

John entered. The room fell quiet. He staggered forward clutching his bottom as if he'd just been beaten by the Headmaster. "Cor," he groaned. The place emptied with relief and John went on to detail what had happened, impersonating Gerry Mansell and the formal bureaucratic style which seemed a world away from Shepherd's Bush.

When I arrived some thirty minutes later I doubt that my colleagues expected such an amusing performance. I did take myself terribly seriously. But they weren't prepared for the ashen-faced figure who came in. There was silence. "I've been sacked," I said.

Fortunately Vincent Hanna was there. Although a reporter and not an editor he was also a national official of the National Union of Journalists and a lawyer by training. He maintained informal links with the BBC's Director of Personnel and he was quickly on the phone to point out that I was entitled to an adjournment, entitled to present evidence, and that pretty obviously sentence could not be passed until the hearing had been fully completed. He suspected that the BBC had tried to take me by surprise and move me to Secretariat before I realised what had happened. I was quickly reinstated pending the outcome of the adjourned hearing.

A cursory run through the proceeding convinced him that the Management had cocked up the disciplinary procedures and that I could sue them for constructive dismissal.

The last thing the BBC would want would be an Industrial Tribunal hearing at which the details of Senior Management performance and Government pressure would come out.

As a lawyer, now that we knew the precise standing instruction that had allegedly been broken, he soon got all of the Current Affairs minutes since 1971 showing how the original instruction had been modified. He had little difficulty in demonstrating that my interpretation of the instruction was a reasonable one and was the same as that held by all the other Editors in Lime Grove. Loyally they all wrote memos pointing this out. Indeed Hugh Williams, the Editor of *Nationwide*, wrote that when he had produced a week of editions of *Nationwide* from Northern Ireland the previous month, he had never met the Controller or dealt with him even on paper. It had all gone through his subordinates. Still, Broadcasting House would have expected Lime Grove to have acted in this defensive way. Some broader support was required and Chris Capron set out to get it.

Since John Gau had himself been disciplined it was thought inappropriate for him to organise my support. Instead his deputy Christopher Capron would do so.

Chris was an excellent choice. He was well known and loved throughout the Corporation, with a rather different background to most of his colleagues. He was a Northamptonshire squire with an estate in Southwick and a London home to boot. He was in his early forties, with a perennial boyish smile, had spent considerable time in radio at Broadcasting House, and played for the elite BBC cricket team, the Bushmen. He was transparently decent, pragmatic and more likely to be a Tory wet than anything else, although as with just about all my colleagues I never knew how he voted and would not have dreamed of asking. He was devoted to the concept of an independent BBC and had the added distinction of being about the only BBC producer whom Robin Day liked and respected.

Chris called a meeting in his office late that afternoon with senior colleagues from departments other than Current Affairs. They included the Editor of News and Current Affairs Radio, Peter Woon, and two colleagues from the Features and Science Departments at Kensington House, Paul Bonner and Desmond Wilcox. All agreed that I was being made a scapegoat but that something much more was at stake, namely the public's perception of the BBC's independence and very probably that independence itself.

Chris agreed to draw up a document the following day summarising their concerns and to take it round to each of them for signature on the Sunday before sending it off to the Acting Director General.

Meanwhile Vincent Hanna called a mandatory Current Affairs

NUJ Chapel meeting that Friday at 5 p.m. He outlined the situation and needed to use few of his considerable oratorical techniques. The chapel was unanimous in my support and authorised Vincent to call a strike if I wasn't reinstated. Lime Grove was abuzz with anger and indignation and united in seeing the BBC Management action as threatening the independence of BBC producers.

That night I went home exhausted. There had been the shock of my dismissal and then the emotional business of seeing everyone rally round in my defence. I felt sick with the sense of responsibility for what was happening, and for one of the only times in my life I couldn't sleep. I loved the BBC and hadn't counted on this crisis developing. In the privacy of my own bedroom I tried to be honest with myself. Could I have avoided all of this without giving up altogether the attempt to make a programme about the IRA? I couldn't see a way through which would avoid the most terrible damage to the only place I'd ever wanted to work and to the colleagues I liked and respected.

Could I have been much more formal in my dealings with BBC Northern Ireland or DNCA? That had never been the way we operated, was hardly practicable, and would have demonstrated a lack of trust in them. The whole thing was done on trust. Besides the project was supported by everyone and what had happened at Carrickmore wasn't that unusual. At least Jeremy Paxman and David Darlow were out of the firing line. And yet if only I'd flown to see the Controller . . . Even so programme-making would have ground to a halt if one had to go on getting signature and counter signature on programme proposals. Such a massive amount of output meant delegation was inevitable, with reference up only when necessary. It did however begin to occur to me that this system did allow Senior Management a way out. If there was no trouble reference up had worked properly. If there was – then they had not been sufficiently put in the picture. Assistant Heads must roll.

It seemed as if I had only just finally gone to sleep when the front doorbell rang, and rang, and rang. Short, sharp, insistent. I looked at my watch, it was 7.30. The milkman so soon?

I went downstairs bleary-eyed and opened the door. Flash! I hardly knew what had happened for a moment, and then I saw the press photographer's back going down the road. It was Saturday morning. It must have been the Sundays getting a photo. Buggers.

I went to make some tea, and on the way back picked up the papers which had just arrived. They had part of the story, all reporting that I was likely to be sacked, which explained the photographer.

An hour or so later the front doorbell rang again. This time it was a young woman. She smiled gently and was very sympathetic. "I'm terribly sorry to bother you, Mr. Bolton, but I'm sure you must be as appalled as I am at the Government's behaviour and the way you have been treated by the BBC. Would you like to give us your side of the story?"

I told her I really couldn't say anything, the situation was too delicate. Her mood changed, her face hardened. "Look, you're being very silly. My editor will just insist I stay here all day and follow you wherever you go so you might as well get it over with now." I shut the door, went upstairs and watched her through the curtains. After a while she began knocking on the neighbours' doors. Dog was eating dog.

The front doorbell rang again. This time it was a man in the traditionally grubby raincoat. I explained that I could say nothing and closed the door. It wouldn't shut. I looked down and true to cliché the thick-soled shoe was in the doorway. I kicked it out and slammed the door.

For the rest of the morning I stayed inside as a couple more reporters huddled together on the other side of the road. My neighbours and my children must have thought I was a criminal.

Eventually I decided to go into work to write out a detailed account of what had happened and to check on that Monday's programme. I went out the back way and drove the car out of the garage. There was no one around. When I reached Lime Grove, Vincent Hanna and Helen Jenkins were already hard at work preparing my defence, surrounded by documents. While I had been wallowing in self-pity they had been hard at work.

On Sunday, Chris Capron climbed into his car, with copies of the document he'd spent the previous day composing, and set off for a conference centre near Abingdon, where many of the leaders of the News and Current Affairs departments were taking part in

Dick Francis's conference on how the press and broadcasters should respond to acts of terrorism and revolution.

The document was addressed to the Acting Director General through the Managing Director of Television and the Director of News and Current Affairs.

Headed "*Panorama* on the IRA" it began:

> We understand that the disciplinary procedures involving Roger Bolton in connection with the above programme have now been adjourned until Tuesday. We are therefore writing to you to express our sincere hope that he will not be dismissed from his post as Editor of *Panorama*. We are very concerned about even the possibility of such an outcome and feel we should let you know the reasons for our concern.

There were three.

1 Our greatest fear is that a serious injustice may be done to Bolton . . . [he] was doing no more and no less than his predecessors on *Panorama* and the Editors of other Current Affairs features programmes have done over the years.
2 We are concerned about the reputation of the BBC's editorial independence . . . we find it difficult to believe that any formal inquiry at such a high level, let alone the subsequent formal disciplinary procedures, would have been undertaken but for the outcry in Parliament and the Press. We fear therefore that any severe disciplinary action taken against Bolton would be seen in many important circles as stemming from Government pressure. Rightly or wrongly our editorial independence would seem to be compromised.
3 Regrettably that might well be the view of many members of the BBC staff too. If Bolton were to be removed from his present post . . . they would be reluctant to undertake difficult assignments of a "sensitive" nature and our journalistic programmes would therefore serve the public interest less effectively.

The document was eventually signed by the Editor of News and Current Affairs Radio, Peter Woon; the Editor of Radio News, John Wilson; the Editor of Television News, Alan Protheroe; the Head of Talks and Features in the World Service, Bob Milne Tyte; the Head of General Features Television, Desmond Wilcox; the Head of Science Features Television, Paul Bonner; the Head of Special Current Affairs Unit Radio, Bernard Tate; the Head of Parliamentary Broadcasting and former Northern Ireland News Editor, Martin Wallace, and Chris Capron himself, the Assistant Head of Current Affairs Television.

It was a formidable list, comprising just about every senior BBC editorial figure connected with journalism. In addition Capron now had statements from himself, Paul Ellis the Editor of the *Money Programme* and Hugh Williams, the Editor of *Nationwide*, confirming that their interpretation of the rules was the same as mine. He had a similar memo from Brian Wenham, now Controller of BBC-2 but John Gau's predecessor as Head of Current Affairs Television. He could also allude to the unanimous NUJ motion in my support.

While Chris had no trouble in collecting the signatories in Abingdon he had great difficulty in getting hold of Dick Francis who was running the conference. This occasion was extremely important to Dick. As Director of News and Current Affairs, he had found that he had no staff of his own and no money. Those things belonged to the Managing Directors of Televison, Radio, and the External Services. He was in charge of policy. Consequently, he had flown here and there as a most assiduous attender of conferences. Now he had a most prestigious one of his own. No little local problems were going to disturb him. He ignored requests to come out and talk to Chris Capron. Eventually Alan Protheroe sent him a tart note telling him he would have no editors left if he didn't do so.

While fictitious scenarios were being played out in conference time ("You are an editor and you get a news flash of a siege. Whom do you contact first?") an equally dramatic scenario was unfolding in the real world. Francis had been angry to read of his local problems in that morning's newspapers. They detracted from his conference. He was even angrier when Chris Capron arrived and drew his phalanx of editors away from him. The Director of News and Current Affairs listened to what his Editors said but did not offer to do anything himself.

That night it seemed to those staying at the conference that a BBC civil war was imminent. On the following Monday I put out a *Panorama* programme on the American Presidential Campaign. I wondered whether my on screen credit of Editor would be my last.

In fact others were on the phone that weekend. At least one member of the Senior Management rang Gerry Mansell and told him that he had better reinstate me because if I was sacked, others higher up than I would have to go as the full details of who knew what came out.

My disciplinary interview was resumed on 20 November 1979. Vincent Hanna presented the case for the defence. He did so with a practised air, acknowledging the difficult situation Mr. Mansell was faced with, never for a moment questioning his good faith. Vincent handed Mansell a folder containing excerpts from News and Current Affairs minutes that bore on the question of the internal communication of programme intentions about Irish affairs. He then gave Mr. Mansell "some highlights" from his full documentary analysis of the minutes. It was a devastating case and Mansell had to grant "the dynamic nature of the process of creating policy".

Hanna also pointed out that DNCA had been continually informed, that he outranked CNI, and that therefore editorial control remained in London. Mr. Hanna pointed out that DNCA could of course have stopped the programme at any stage, if he had so wished.

Vincent concluded that if Mr. Mansell felt unable to change the decision about Mr. Bolton, he would have to raise some procedural points about how the investigation into this affair had been conducted. It was a delicate reference to a loaded revolver. Earlier, Mansell had been told by the BBC's own lawyers that the procedure had been completely cocked up and that any appeal would be successful.

Gerry Mansell said he would have to adjourn the meeting until 2.30 so that he could read the submission in detail.

The session closed with regret expressed on both sides that there had been a "leak" to the press about the interview with Mr. Bolton the previous Friday. It was an unreal moment, but a fitting end to a formal dance.

We adjourned to a pub and discussed what we would do if my dismissal were not rescinded. The NUJ would call a strike and I would refuse to go to the Secretariat and would sue the BBC for constructive dismissal. Terrible damage would be done to the BBC and I wouldn't get my job back. It was a dismal prospect but Vincent Hanna whistled throughout lunch. He had no worries about the outcome.

On resumption the Acting Director General confirmed my reprimand but reinstated me as Editor of *Panorama*. He begged me to raise my sights when dealing with such problems as Ireland and "to remember the wider interests of the BBC".

Honour was satisfied. Now the Acting Director General had to go and face the Governors while I had to go and face Commander Peter Duffy of the Anti-Terrorist Squad.

Why did Gerry Mansell change his mind? Was it the new evidence that was presented, suspicions about whether some other key figures in the incident had been telling the truth, or a straightforward pragmatic political decision about what would cause the least damage to the Corporation? He told me in 1989 that it was because of Vincent Hanna's paper which had greatly impressed him.

The Board of Governors were not best pleased by the events of the previous week when they met on 22 November; no heads were offered to them, but they had no alternative but to accept the Acting Director General's decision. They vented their anger.

"Staff working at Lime Grove were under the impression that they had no corporate editorial ties" . . . The Board was aware of "a frame of mind in the Television Service which rejected or shrugged off criticism, especially when it came from what some senior people called 'the Regent Street Branch'. This must change." (The Regent Street Branch was of course Broadcasting House.)

Communications between management and staff had to be improved and between different members of management.

"The Television Service needed an Editor News and Current

Affairs Television, on Mr. Milne's staff but with a strong editorial link with Mr. Francis."

The failure to implement this was to be a bone of contention between the future Director General Alasdair Milne and the Governors. He believed he should devise his own management structure. They didn't believe he was in charge. The chasm widened.

The Governors took one final decision. "The programme on which Editor, *Panorama* was working when the Carrickmore incident took place must be abandoned. This did not rule out starting again from scratch *later on*. But a line must be drawn under the events of the past weeks, and that means scrapping the work done so far."

I knew nothing of this instruction but let things calm down for a couple of months. After the Christmas break, however, my conscience began to nag me about the project. The reasons for doing the programme seemed to me as valid as before. The public needed to know how the IRA thought and operated and what its real strength was. *Panorama* had the time and the resources to do such an investigation. How could I chuck it?

So, as Lime Grove's chief kamikaze pilot, I wrote to John Gau on 23 January 1980 relaunching the proposal. I carefully copied the memorandum to the Managing Director of Television, the Director of News and Current Affairs, the Controller of BBC-1 and the Controller of Northern Ireland.

On Friday, 1 February, John Gau phoned me up to report the contents of a memo from the newly returned Director General, Ian Trethowan, to Alasdair Milne. He had OK'd the project but the Carrickmore footage could not be used, nor could any of the interviews previously shot, and of course there could be no question of interviews with terrorists; not that I planned any.

I still thought we should go ahead, but Jeremy Paxman, my reporter, took a different view. He doubted whether we could get the interviews we needed as we would have to ask the same people to answer the same questions and they would point out that we already had their answers on film anyway. How could we explain not showing the Carrickmore footage? We would be open either to the charge of censorship or of having something to hide.

Although I disagreed with him I didn't for a moment question Jeremy's courage. In the course of his work for me he had been shot at and was to be under fire again. I couldn't give the project to someone else as it would seem to demonstrate a lack of confidence in him. So we let the project lapse, and sought different ways of dealing with the Northern Ireland problem.

When Ian Trethowan returned to duty he adopted a fairly robust attitude to what had occurred.

As he wrote in his autobiography *Split Screen*:

My own view is that the *Panorama* crew were naive to go to Carrickmore without further enquiry, and should have reported sooner to the authorities what they found there, but their behaviour could not justify the sensational response of the London papers, and of very senior politicians, and the rather febrile attitude of the BBC's Governors.

What cannot be said too often about this affair is that, when the balloon went up that Thursday morning, no film had been shown on television. It is one thing to complain about something which has been broadcast, but to condemn, and in such violent terms, the recording of a piece of film not one foot of which has been screened seemed a ludicrous over-reaction. This is the rock on which the BBC Governors should have stood.

The Government had not finished with us yet, however. Shortly after the uproar in the House of Commons, and Mrs. Thatcher's pointed nudge to the Director of Public Prosecutions, my old acquaintance Commander Peter Duffy of the Anti-Terrorist Squad had visited me in Lime Grove and taken away the film shot at Carrickmore. We had not heard anything from him since the previous summer when he had interviewed me and my *Tonight* team about the INLA film. His report about that had been sent to the DPP at the beginning of October, but we had heard nothing.

On 1 August 1980, Lady Airey, the widow of Airey Neave, made her way to the public gallery of the House of Commons to hear the Attorney-General, Sir Michael Havers, condemn members of the BBC staff who had interviewed Irish terrorists. Sir Michael said, "I profoundly disapprove of the conduct of the staff directly involved, which was, in my opinion, deplorable."

The Attorney-General had found us guilty of offences but had decided not to prosecute. This was extremely convenient for him as it dispensed with the boring necessity of a trial at which we would have been able to defend ourselves. He also told MPs that the Government would take a tougher line in future with media organisations which published interviews with terrorist organisations.

He repeated that he was satisfied that the BBC had committed an offence under Section II of the 1976 Prevention of Terrorism Act. It had been "very wrong" of the staff at the Carrickmore incident to have witnessed a terrorist act and not reported it. The BBC must have known they were being used for propaganda purposes.

Ivor Stanbrook, the Conservative MP for Orpington, joined in the denunciation. He objected to the BBC being let off "scot free" when a serious crime had been committed. He also referred to "some curious" items broadcasted, notably on the BBC's World Service, of IRA songs "which led one to believe some BBC staff are in active sympathy with the IRA."

Sir Michael said he had made it clear to the BBC that his decision not to prosecute did not mean that similar activities in future would not be treated as an offence.

"If similar incidents take place again I would take a stricter view, and those who had participated would be warned that, subject to the evidence and circumstances of the case, they risked criminal proceedings under the Prevention of Terrorism Act."

This was too much for the BBC Governors, now reinforced by the returned Director General, Ian Trethowan. Their sense of fair play was affronted by this sort of summary justice. Sir Michael Havers had written to them on 20 June 1980 expressing his views in ever more condemnatory language. Sir Michael Swann had replied robustly for the Governors but the correspondence had remained secret, although the BBC Chairman had ended his reply by saying "If you wish to make your letter public, we would intend to make our reply public also."

Well you couldn't go more public than issue a statement and hold a debate in the House of Commons, so the BBC published both letters. The Havers letter made me very angry indeed, for it said that the two incidents "constituted little more than propaganda exercises to which your staff have willingly given their support."

Fortunately it seemed to have made the BBC Chairman very angry as well. "We reject absolutely the suggestion that our staff willingly gave their support to any propaganda exercise by the IRA or INLA. Indeed, in the case of Carrickmore there was, in fact, no publication by the BBC."

They then went to the nub of the dilemma with which the Anti-Terrorism Law confronts the journalist. Referring to the Havers letter they said, "In your penultimate paragraph you say 'any interview with a person purporting to represent a terrorist organisation is potentially a source of information of the nature referred to in Section II of the Act arising not only from the actual contents of the interview but also from any negotiations leading up to and the actual arrangements for it.' This last phrase could be read as meaning that the public should be informed, at every turn, of the letter, phone calls or meetings with go-betweens which are, I have no doubt, necessary if a journalist is ever to acquire information from known or suspected terrorists. If this is really what the law says, then all reporting of who terrorists are and what they say, would, in practice, be halted abruptly."

The Attorney-General was determined to have the last word. On Monday, 4 August, in the House of Commons he said, "I regret the manner of the reply by the BBC in not accepting the law which is, I believe, absolutely clear on this point".

Reading these exchanges ten years later it is clear that journalists, particularly in the press, have interpreted the law in a different way to that of the Attorney-General. Indeed, the sober *Independent* newspaper published an interview with an unnamed IRA spokesman in 1987.

However as I pointed out in an earlier chapter, since 1980 there have been no interviews with IRA or INLA spokesmen on the BBC or ITV, although there are allegations that certain senior Sinn Fein leaders are in fact members of the IRA. Nor has there been much original film of the still continuing roadblocks. Instead the terrorist organisations have shot film, or videotape, themselves and put it into circulation. In a curious way this is thought to be more "respectable" as it does not involve direct contact between the terrorist organisation and the broadcaster. It is, however, much poorer journalism, because it is taking their own propaganda at face value, with no independent scrutiny – the very sin of which we had been accused.

When the Attorney-General was speaking in the Commons I was away on holiday. I was half-way through the standard two year stint for Editors on *Panorama* and I still hadn't done those programmes on the Security Services.

Indeed, on the day I had been sacked by Gerry Mansell from my job as Editor, before being reinstated, the Prime Minister was standing up in the House to make the astonishing statement that the former personal adviser on art to the Queen, Sir Anthony Blunt, was the "Fourth Man" in the Burgess and Maclean affair.

Moreover the day before the announcement the Secretary to the Cabinet, Sir Robert Armstrong had personally rung up Blunt's solicitor to give him twenty-four hours' notice of the statement being made. Not surprisingly Blunt had then disappeared, although he was to reappear later.

What was going on? We had also heard stories of an MI5 plot against Prime Minister Harold Wilson during his administration. It seemed a proper subject for *Panorama* to look at. Bloodied but unbowed we decided to have a go.

8

FROM PANORAMA TO NATIONWIDE

The Anthony Blunt business had set me thinking about the secret services, MI5 and MI6. It did seem as if the bigger the crime the smaller the sentence, or was it simply the "Old Boy" network looking after its own? I had met one or two former members and I had not been impressed by their political sophistication, or understanding of Labour politics. One former high-up figure, George Young, was so far out on the right that he found his natural home in the "Monday Club" which is perched perilously close to the outer edges of the Conservative Party. It seemed to me that he couldn't understand the difference between social democracy and communism. Were people like him under control or in control?

I didn't doubt for one moment the need for secret intelligence services, and of course I knew that details of the operations could not be revealed in public, but were they really accountable in our democratic society? Theoretically they were, via the Foreign Secretary and the Home Secretary, but was that sufficient in practice? I had been intrigued by the fact that you could pick up a telephone and dial the Central Intelligence Agency or the FBI in the United States, yet in Britain our intelligence services did not officially exist. And in America there is also a Senate intelligence oversight committee which seems to function well.

In view of the freedom the Secret Services are given to break the law it semed to me worth asking if they are clearly under control, and whether their members are selected from a wide ranging section of society and not a narrow elitist one. Surely Parliament should determine what "subversive" means, not someone like

George Young. Besides Chapman Pincher had written books about the Intelligence Services; why shouldn't television investigate the question of their accountability? The problem was that to persuade the audience that the question was worth asking we had to give details of how the Services operated and find some causes for concern. Whatever we did seemed likely to run the danger of breaking the Official Secrets Act but I felt sure that the accountability was a perfectly proper thing to examine.

Of course before we could decide whether or not it was possible to do a programme we needed to find out more about the Services and in particular try and find former members who would talk. So Tom Mangold the reporter, and John Penycate the producer, started to ring up people such as Sir Dick White and Sir Martin Furnival-Jones former Heads of the Services. It was a bit naive of us, for all the people we talked to checked back with base and it wasn't long before the BBC Director General Ian Trethowan received a telephone call from Whitehall asking what the hell was going on. Trethowan was understandably fed up that he hadn't been warned of our intentions, but I argued that I had to find out whether a programme was possible before proposing one.

There were many phone calls back and forward between the Director General and John Gau, Head of TV Current Affairs and my immediate boss, with Trethowan wondering whether the project should be cancelled and Gau arguing robustly that the question of accountability was a proper one. Eventually the DG said we could go ahead and make the programme but with no guarantee of transmission. We turned over some interesting, if relatively minor scandals about the way people were blacked from jobs because they were erroneously believed to be "unreliable", and we constructed a reasonable filmed debate about the accountability issue. It was hardly earth-shattering but at least it was something.

One or two funny things happened on the way to transmission, however. On one occasion my reporter, Tom Mangold, was summoned to see the DG and told something in confidence which he was not allowed to tell me, his Editor. This put me in a very difficult position, as it seemed to show a disturbing lack of trust. I decided to bite my tongue, however, and concentrated on getting something out. The final viewing of our film before transmission took place in Tin Pan Alley. We usually edited in-house but on this occasion we were using an outside film editor in Denmark Street. It lay next to St. Giles where felons were given water and a blessing on their way to execution at Tyburn (now Marble Arch). I felt sympathy with them as I turned past the sex shops and up the myriad sets of stairs to the viewing room at the top of the narrow late seventeenth century building.

Eventually the Director General arrived, together with his closest advisers and two people I'd never seen before and to whom I was not introduced. They did not look very happy or very welcoming but sat at the back of the room scribbling furiously. After the viewing, they all left without a word and we adjourned to Lime Grove to await the verdict. Around thirteen points of criticism were made, some minor, some significant, some plain daft. We accepted most of them but stuck in our heels about cutting two of the interviews. In the end we got our way and the programmes went out.

As usual on these occasions, when there is such a tussle, the expectations of the audience are raised unrealistically. The almost inevitable result on transmission is a cry of "What was all the fuss about". It happened this time. The knowledge that so much time and effort is going to be spent on difficult, often unrewarding, subject matter is enough to make many journalists simply refuse to get involved in the first place. It's much nicer to get on a plane to the sun instead. I was extremely fortunate that I had journalists prepared to have a go.

For me, the period of 1979 to 1981, when I was editing *Panorama*, was a golden time. I had the length of programme – fifty minutes – the staff, resources, and freedom, from undue ratings pressure, to explore basic and fundamental issues and to do original journalism. We could make our own agenda as well as follow the conventional one.

We established that Pakistan had obtained the capability to make nuclear weapons and discovered how that had been done. The programme, by reporter Philip Tibenham, and producer Chris Olgiatti, won a Royal Television Society Award. We did a similar report on Libya.

Peter Taylor and Jonathan Holmes examined the politics of

hunger: the way in which food aid to the Third World was often misused on arrival and rarely stretched out of the towns to the starved countryside.

One of my producers, David Graham, later a founding figure of Channel 4 and, as the boss of Diverse Productions, Mrs. Thatcher's favourite independent producer, spent six weeks on a council estate on Clydeside examining the real impact of unemployment. He was shocked by the poverty trap and the way everyone became involved in an underground culture of fiddling and the black market. It was to have a fundamental impact on his political thought.

As he wrote in *The New Enlightenment* which he co-authored with Peter Clarke, "the problem . . . was immobility. No one could go anywhere or leave the one place in Scotland where they were entitled to a council house . . . The Left was refusing to acknowledge the problem . . . that sent me off to look for other ideas . . . Now I have been lucky enough, with others, to explore the liberal revival all over the world and to speak to its best minds." He went on to say with a certainty I have rarely had about any political matter, "that we are looking at the greatest political shift of our century."

I was not concerned whether David's politics were left, right or anything else, only that his journalism was honest, factual and as objective as possible. It was, and he was a remarkable producer. I understood why he moved over to polemical journalism on Channel 4, but he was a loss to more straightforward investigative programmes.

One day I was stuck for a producer to go with Jeremy Paxman up the Khyber Pass to Afghanistan. As a child I had read *King of the Khyber Rifles* and would have done almost anything to get there myself, but as Editor I had to remain at base. So I turned to a researcher just twenty-three, not long out of university; who still wore pullovers and jackets that were too small for him, like a schoolboy who was undergoing a growth spurt. Could I really send him? Well he was a good friend of Jeremy's, and Paxman was capable of directing as well as reporting. I decided to give the young boy a chance.

So Robert Harris, now a distinguished author and political

columnist on the *Sunday Times*, got his plane ticket to Pakistan and sat beside the international jet-setting reporter as they drove towards the Afghan hills. On the first night they stopped at a small hotel. Robert unpacked his pyjamas, slippers and very English dressing-gown, put them on and wandered into his reporter's bedroom.

Paxman was laying out the mosquito net, khaki clothes and medical provisions that the experienced traveller evidently required. Robert slunk back out of the room and wondered what he had let himself in for. Needless to say he did an excellent job, but quickly decided that reporting was more glamorous and so became a reporter himself, with great success. He left his slippers behind.

When Reagan came to power in 1980 I popped over the water, listened to what the new incoming administration was saying and came back to commission another Tom Mangold programme called "The Rearming of America". It didn't take a genius to work out that the next thing to develop would be a widespread concern about the apparently increased danger of nuclear war. I therefore asked Paxman, Harris and David Darlow to examine the state of Britain's civil defence. As their film *If the Bomb Drops* showed, the preparations were hopelessly out of date, almost laughably so. The enterprising Mr. Darlow managed to obtain copies of the Government films that were to be transmitted on television in the event of a great military emergency. Called *Protect and Survive* they were supposed to be locked into safes at the BBC and ITV ready for the awful day.

I decided to run them in the programme without reference to anyone because it was clearly in the public interest to reveal how hopelessly antiquated these films were. I did not enquire as to copyright.

I impressed on the team, however, that the film must not be sensational and must not terrify the viewer. As I walked into the cutting room I said, rather peremptorily, "Right now, this better be relatively low key." I flicked the switch on the Steenbeck viewing machine and sat back. There then occurred the most terrifying re-creation of a nuclear explosion I have ever seen before or since. David Darlow clearly had the ambition, since fulfilled, to be a feature film director. "Right, that's out", I said. In fact, it was essential to point out the irrelevance of many of the civil defence instructions of the time and I placed it a little later in the film. Perhaps as a direct result of the programme, the Government promptly revised its civil defence publicity.

The Conservative Government seemed to be baffled as to how to deal with the CND campaign that was taking off with the setting up of peace camps at American cruise missile bases like Greenham Common. One day I got a call from the Ministry of Defence. The junior minister Peter Blaker wanted to have lunch with me. I thought this a little peculiar but agreed and found myself with the minister in a small private room of Lockets, the well-known but discreet Westminster restaurant where a few months earlier James Hawthorne had first heard of Carrickmore.

I was puzzled at first but it soon became clear that the Minister was asking my advice about how "we" could defeat the anti-nuclear campaign. I was bemused for two reasons; first because he assumed that as a BBC Editor I must be on the "right side" on matters of defence, and second because he expected me to advise him on a matter of public controversy. That wasn't my view of a BBC journalist's role at all. As it happened I did sadly agree with his view that nuclear weapons could not be disinvented and that they probably did help to keep the peace, but I wasn't about to tell him that or to help him achieve his personal political ends. I felt that would be an abuse of my position.

I felt that politicians and journalists have different jobs to do and while I respected and liked many MPs I tried to keep my distance from them for that reason. Indeed, in a somewhat priggish way I was shocked when Robin Day accepted a knighthood from the Government while still an active broadcaster, and I felt the same about Alastair Burnet. I understood the ruthless patronage of the newspapers by both Parties with knighthoods and peerages in abundance, but I thought we in television should steer clear of it. The knighting of Larry Lamb while Editor of the *Sun* put such things in perspective, I thought.

At the end of my first year, David Dimbleby, the finest broadcaster of his generation, joined me and we got on very well indeed. With other reporters like Richard Lindley, Fred Emery, and Michael Cockerell on board my job was a delight. I sent Michael off to make a film about the official Chinese government news agency which controlled information throughout that astonishing country. His programme the "Chinese News Machine" won another award.

When Chris Dunkley wrote in the *Financial Times*, "Three cheers for *Panorama* and Roger Bolton . . . they have rallied to the banner of the Fourth Estate to carry on the valuable tradition of scrutinising those who could acquire power via mystification, whether they be priests, politicians, doctors or spies," my cup was full.

It overflowed when the *Evening Standard* wrote "Under Editor Roger Bolton, *Panorama* has regained its ancient dominance in current affairs by rejecting the simplistic, sensational and parochial in favour of thoughtful, lucid and intelligent journalism."

However, there was one programme which caused me great heart-searching and also caused great distress to some viewers.

One of my producers was Dr. Anne Moir and she had discovered that, unknown to the public and without reference to religious leaders or, most importantly, to Parliament, the medical definition of death had been changed and a new concept called "brain death" introduced.

This development allowed still-living organs to be taken from the body of someone whose heart was still beating and transplanted in order to save the lives of others. Anne and Richard Lindley discovered that there were many doctors including two at Papworth Hospital who had doubts about the existing definition of brain death and the ethics of transplanting still-living organs. They were concerned that electrical activity was still going on in the brains of those who had already been diagnosed "brain dead" because the brain stem had ceased to function.

They were also worried about mistakes being made. This had occurred in the United States when people had recovered after being diagnosed as dead. In addition no proper study of the British criteria of brain death had been carried out. We felt it significant that Norway, which had the most stringent criteria including electro-encephalography (EEG) and the use of angiography, had the highest proportion of donors in Europe, indeed was an organ-exporting country. These additional safeguards seemed to give much greater confidence to the ordinary doctors involved in providing organs, and reassured the donors' families. Why weren't they in force here? These seemed to be important questions: literally of life and death. So we made a programme called "Transplants – Are the Donors Really Dead?"

When the British transplant establishment heard what we intended they attacked us and the BBC ferociously, in such an arrogant and emotional way that they almost guaranteed we would not concede their arguments. The programme went out and the doctors who were critical demanded a second programme which would give them the opportunity to criticise and contradict what we had said. At first our team was opposed to a second programme, believing it would appear that we had caved in and that each time we offended an establishment group it would demand a right of reply.

Although that was a danger, I decided a second programme was in order this time. The issue was important enough to merit further airing. Moreover, it was alleged that the number of transplants had dropped dramatically to about half the previous number as doctors, many of whom shared our reservations, became more reluctant to ask the families of potential donors for the organs of their deceased loved ones. Never an easy request to have to make. The numbers of transplants had, in fact, begun to decline from month to month even before our film. Even so, there was little change overall.

The second programme was taken out of our hands and produced by Christopher Capron, the Deputy Head of Current Affairs. In it, both medical sides to the debate, for this was a dispute within the medical profession, made their own film and debated in the studio. In the end both sides remained confident of their contrasting views and subsequently the definition of brain death was amended and extra safeguards were built into its diagnosis. There are still doctors who refuse to have anything to do with the concept and have deep ethical and religious objections to the process.

I was no stranger to these ethical dilemmas. As Editor of *Tonight* I had dropped a film about breast cancer because it was too depressingly honest about the low survival rates of those who had the disease at that time. What right did I have to take away hope? Yet if

[117]

society is to make a judgement about whether a form of expensive medical treatment is worthwhile it needs to have the facts about the survival rate. This is particularly true of transplant surgery. How do you measure success: six months, one year, five? And in the battle for scarce resources, in the ever expanding health care field, is money perhaps better spent on preventative medicine and less glamorous treatments which greatly enhance the lives of more people; for example on hip operations?

These were the unanswerable questions and dilemmas with which I had to deal. Nevertheless I cannot escape the fact that as a result of my editorial decision, the number of transplants may have declined temporarily, and some people may have died earlier than they would otherwise have done.

Conversely, as a result of the change in brain death criteria some lives may have been saved. The debate continues today.

In spite of these dilemmas, I loved editing *Panorama* and as the end of my statutory two years approached (how restrictive of the BBC to permit its editors so little continuity in their jobs) I was hoping for an unprecedented third year. It was not to be, perhaps to the relief of Senior BBC Management who were wondering how many more controversies they could stand in so short a period.

John Gau had left Lime Grove to become an independent producer. He had been the BBC Management's choice to succeed Bill Cotton as Controller of BBC-1. Normally that would have got him the job, but the new Chairman of the Governors, George Howard, had not forgotten Carrickmore and he blocked John's appointment. It was an ominous development and signalled the start of the increasing intervention by the Governors into what had been the provenance of Management. It led to friction and animosity. John decided to leave. If the DG and the Managing Director could not deliver now on a senior appointment then why should he believe they would do so in the future? It was a shrewd and not unprofitable decision. He joined the Board of Channel 4, to become a leading independent producer, the Chairman of the Royal Television Society (and CBE) before becoming the Director of Programmes of the five channels of British Satellite Broadcasting. It was a grievous loss for us and for BBC-1, however.

DEATH ON THE ROCK

Christopher Capron, his deputy, took over as Head of Current Affairs and turned his attention to revitalising the ailing BBC-1 early evening magazine *Nationwide*. It had been a marvellous success, but after ten years was inevitably showing its age, and was suffering from a not entirely deserved reputation for being more interested in skateboarding ducks than serious politics. Its Editor, Hugh Williams, had done a three-year stint and was moving off to be Assistant Head of the Music and Arts Department. His departure gave Chris an opportunity.

One Tuesday morning, I came into work in a jaunty frame of mind and clattered down the linoleum-covered stairs into my linoleum-covered office with its strictly functional BBC standard issue desk and chair. I felt *Panorama* was really humming along, the reviews had been good again, and I had a fresh series of fundamental questions I wanted to examine. Colleagues had warned me that I really ought to avoid controversy for a while and think of my future career. I hadn't much time for that sort of talk. I felt I would never have a better job in my life and it would be dishonest of me to think more of serving my future career interests than serving the public. And perhaps I thought I could do both.

My secretary stopped opening the latest complaint letters and told me Chris Capron wanted to see me as soon as possible. I went back upstairs and entered his office. I could see by the way he carefully closed the door, offered me a cup of coffee, and sat down opposite me and not behind his desk, that it was something out of the ordinary.

He came to the point. The early evening on BBC-1 was to be reorganised in a year's time. The *News* was to be followed by a serious network current affairs programme and then the local news magazines. I would become the Editor of the current affairs programme but in the meantime he wanted me to take over *Nationwide* and toughen it up so that it could gradually change into that new programme.

I was suspicious. Was this a way of getting me off *Panorama*? Chris swore this was not so. Why couldn't the major change be made this summer? Logistically impossible, said Chris. Well why not let me stay on *Panorama* for another year and let me take over then? Not on. That would have meant an interim editor for a year.

Besides the way things were going on *Nationwide* if it wasn't made more serious maybe current affairs would lose the early evening slot altogether and a much extended news would take over. We didn't want that. *Nationwide* still had a much bigger audience than *Panorama*, around seven to eight million, and it went five days a week. Didn't I have a responsibility to try and serve that audience with serious popular journalism? My vanity was aroused. Besides, said Chris, I was probably the only person who could persuade David Dimbleby to front such a programme, which was what the television service wanted. So much for their wanting me!

I needed a very good reason to turn down such a generous offer. What could I do, where would I go after a third year of *Panorama*, if I got it? Granada had talked to me about *World In Action* but I had often voiced my belief that the early evening audience could take more serious fare. I asked for time to think about it but in the end said yes.

My *Panorama* team gave me a fine send off and David Dimbleby in particular said how sorry he was we were parting. I didn't intend it to be for long.

But *Nationwide* already had Frank Bough, Sue Lawley and Sue Cook as presenters. How would I fit David in?

The *Daily Telegraph* gave me a rather different send off. The BBC had found itself in the middle of another controversy when it appeared that E. P. Thompson, the eminent historian and anti-nuclear campaigner, had been invited to deliver the Dimbleby Lecture. The official Corporation view was that Thompson had merely been "sounded out". That was not his impression, and when the BBC made it clear that someone else would be chosen he was angry, and many others with him. The *Telegraph* might have been expected to applaud the BBC's decision, but this was too good an opportunity to kick the Corporation when it was down. It attacked the root of the problem which it said was "the Dimbleby Lecture itself". It was a cruel, wounding attack, the more so for being laced with considerable wit.

"It [the Lecture] is a much-trumpeted event in which an audience of high minded and important people gather to hear the oft-aired views of one of their number, and be filmed doing it." If that was true one would have thought that a lecture by E. P. Thompson would have made a very refreshing change.

The editorial writer went on, "In short it is a deeply pompous occasion, pretending to a wisdom and authority it cannot reach. It seems an odd tribute to Richard Dimbleby, a popular and tubby commentator on public occasions, rather as if one had a Brian Johnston Memorial Symposium on Economics."

All good, if rough, knockabout fun, but the editorial didn't stop there.

"It is ironic that the BBC should be attacked in this way when many of its regular programmes (especially 'documentaries') are far more subversive than Mr. Thompson's thoughts on the Cold War. Hot on the heels of the lecture now comes the little item of news that Mr. Roger Bolton has been made editor of BBC 1's *Nationwide*. It was Mr. Bolton who arranged for IRA gunmen to take over the village of Carrickmore for the benefit of his cameras in 1979."

That was it. I had had enough of allegations that I was a subversive. Far from having planned the filming at Carrickmore I had not even known of it in advance, only learning of the incident the day after it occurred.

I decided to sue the newspaper otherwise every time my name was in the news these sorts of allegations would be made. The BBC agreed to assist me and there then took place the Dickensian-like snail's progress of libel litigation. Finally, the *Daily Telegraph* agreed to settle.

On 9 February 1984, the Press Association announced that "Television Editor Roger Bolton received 'substantial' undisclosed damages and his legal costs in the High Court, London today over an unfounded allegation in the *Daily Telegraph* that he had colluded with the IRA so as to film its gunmen on patrol." The next morning's copy of the newspaper carried a handsome apology. We could have gone to trial but I wanted an apology as soon and as fulsome as possible, but I was wrong to think that this would stop newspapers from libelling me again over Carrickmore.

Nationwide

Almost before I had settled down on *Nationwide* the Party Conferences were upon us. I thought of one small innovation. When I had run the nightly BBC election campaign programme in 1979 I had introduced a campaign diary where the gossip and cock-ups could be recorded. There had to be a smile somewhere. I thought we should do the same for the conferences and I had the ideal person in Glyn Worsnip to do it. Some rather po-faced people in the BBC and the political parties were rather put out but we pushed ahead.

It was always a pleasure going to Conferences not least because of the pleasure of watching Robin Day and Professor Mackenzie work together, and it was a privilege to have both work for me.

Hunched over the table with an important politican in his sights Robin was at his formidable best. The compromises and fudges of Conference resolutions were ruthlessly exposed under his brilliant cross-examinations. On one occasion his pursuit of John Nott was so remorseless that the then Defence Secretary took off his microphone, threw it down, and stormed out of the studio. The question Robin had asked was pretty inflamatory, however. Why should the public accept John Nott's assessment of defence requirements rather than that of a senior military figure, after all wasn't Nott a "here today, gone tomorrow" politician?

But Robin did not seem an entirely happy man. When you have wanted to be an MP all your life and failed to be elected, it must be galling to see your juniors – men who had been in short pants when you were already a well-known broadcaster – turn into ministers, and to have to show them respect if not actually defer to them. Leon Brittan was one case in point.

Robin hated travelling outside London and even when recording *Question Time* in the regions would often return by car to London the same night, if possible. He spent much of his time in Westminster and the Garrick Club and since the opinions of those he met there were not balanced by his own experiences on the ground I felt some of his views were insufficiently informed.

Robin had three topics of conversation: politics, sex and money; not necessarily in that order. And he certainly thought he didn't get enough of at least one of them – money. As a consequence perhaps he was not regarded as the most profligate of hosts.

One year, Brian Wenham, the Head of Current Affairs and a frequent sparring partner of Robin's, decided to make him aware of the fact that he was considered a little stingy. Brian told some of the other commentators and editors, like Alan Watson, to charge all their expense account meals in the hotel to Robin's bill. At the end of the Conference everyone assembled in reception to watch Robin settle his account. The explosion that ensued was relished for years.

Bob Mackenzie was more instantly lovable. He had a passion for politics and wanted to teach and communicate his enthusiasm. He was just as delighted to do three minutes for *Nationwide* as to do thirty minutes for a more serious programme. He kept telling other, more pompous presenters, "Look at the size of the audience".

Perhaps because he had another career as a professor at the London School of Economics, he was more relaxed about his appearances and was even glad to assist in the preparation of political items in which he didn't appear. He was best known of course for his "swingometer" and who doesn't mourn its replacement by endless graphic sequences!

We mourn him also. I had hoped to use Bob a great deal when editing *Nationwide* and he had talked enthusiastically about helping me harden up the programme. But when I went down to Brighton for one of the first Party Conferences after I became Editor I found him locked in his room. He was fatally ill and he knew it. He should never have come to the Conference but he couldn't stay away. Unfit to broadcast he spent the days in his hotel bedroom with a bottle of spirits trying to keep the pain away, following the proceedings by television. It was obvious he had to be got back to London and hospital immediately. I called one of the BBC cars and travelled back with him to his flat near Harrods. He sat in the front seat and, when he thought I couldn't see, his grey face grimaced with pain. It was reflected, however, via the wing mirror to where I was sitting. He wouldn't hear a word of pity and maintained the fiction of being just off colour throughout. A few days later he was dead. All that enthusiasm, laughter, and mischief, gone.

Moving into *Nationwide* without fresh resources or staff I encountered considerable resistance to what I was trying to do. Frank Bough thought he knew precisely how far you could and couldn't go in a hardening up process. He considered me daft, and he was a lot nearer the truth than I gave him credit for. At first, however, the strategic approach which Chris Capron had formulated to prepare the way for a full reorganisation of BBC-1 early evening programming seemed to be going to plan.

A conference was held for all the relevant BBC editorial staff involved at the Oakley Court Hotel by the Thames near Windsor. It was the location of several Hammer Horror films which in retrospect seems appropriate. Representatives of news, current affairs, and the regions all agreed to changes that moved the local news magazines from their scheduled time, after the news, to a later time, after the current affairs. This had been a matter of hot dispute. The new Director General, Alasdair Milne, was there and I watched his feet with fascination.

He clearly had the lowest boredom threshold of anyone I'd ever met. His hush-puppy shoes would move backwards and forwards at a gradually increasing pace until suddenly he would interject a brusque, often rude remark into the discussion. He would then laugh and half apologise before sitting back in his seat motionless. A couple of minutes later the leg would start swinging again and the process would be repeated.

Never mind. He supported our plans and with everyone else's agreement said they would happen. They didn't – at least not for two more years and after the débâcle of the *Sixty Minutes* programme which was to succeed *Nationwide* and which was to be stuck with the same schedule, news, regions, current affairs, rather than the new one proposed. I found it quite remarkable that a final decision could be taken by the DG and then gradually undermined in the subsequent months. How could one plan on this basis? I felt we were in a delicate position steering through those changes, and I'd much rather have run *Nationwide* under the old order, taking up the slack I'd found.

It was going wrong with David Dimbleby as well. Perhaps I had overpersuaded him for he had certainly had several reservations and insisted on several difficult conditions when presenting. He wanted a separate office of his own, whereas all the others mucked in together in a family atmosphere. I sympathised with this request as it was difficult to prepare interviews with the noise of the general office around him. Still this separated him from the others, as did his insistence that he would do only serious items and that he would do those in their entirety, not sharing with another presenter. Since the others were all of Sue Lawley's calibre I felt this was short-sighted. Also he only wanted to work six months of the year.

I felt David Dimbleby and Sue Lawley should be anybody's dream team, but I couldn't make it work. After six months, David decided not to renew his contract. He is the best presenter on television, one of the best interviewers and a maker of fine documentary series like "The White Tribe" and "An Ocean Apart", but I think he has not made the impact on broadcasting he could have made, because of his interest in extraneous things, like his newspaper group, and because of his reluctance to get involved in the *News* or popular programmes like *Nationwide*. As a friend and colleague, I can't help but regret this.

The death-blow to our plan to revitalise *Nationwide* was the advent of *Breakfast Time*. This venture became *the* priority and some of my best staff and resources were syphoned off to make it succeed. It certainly did, not least because of Frank Bough who had moved over to present it, and Ron Neil its Editor. Ron had been my deputy on *Tonight*, and *Breakfast Time* was his big opportunity. He produced it brilliantly and it had the most immaculate launch of a new programme I've ever seen. In my carping way, however, I did have reservations, doubtless fanned by my resentment at losing facilities.

I felt it was wrong for a publicly funded organisation to pitch programmes below those of its commercial rival, thus guaranteeing that that rival has to follow you downmarket. The Peter Jay *TV-am* may well have imploded anyway but the Anne Diamond and Roland Rat-like nature of its successor was made more likely by the sweaters and star gazers of *Breakfast Time*.

Some of the new technical equipment which we had to try out on air drove me to despair. The sound and picture of telecine machines would run at different speeds and in different directions. Since it was almost impossible to release *Nationwide* this happened with increasing frequency on air. I had always prided myself on being calm in a crisis but when I sat in my office on transmission and saw this sort of thing happening I lost control totally. I broke chairs and at one point simply climbed on to the roof and walked away. Eventually things quietened down and I simply played to *Nationwide*'s strengths.

Finding myself on a daily programme again was very exciting. On days when dramatic events occurred, like the shooting of President Sadat of Egypt, the programme was at its best and I felt I had something to contribute. My features on the failure of Soviet agriculture were not so successful. But I was able to expand our coverage of Ireland and one of my producers, Peter Weil, did four films about the work of the Northern Ireland Secretary, James Prior. With a magazine format we could cover a wide range of Irish matters, light-hearted and serious.

However, like all television news and current affairs editors the main problem I had to deal with between 1981 and 1983 was the Falklands War and its aftermath, including the Election.

9

THREE IRON LADIES AND
THE BELGRANO

The BBC was well aware that the Falklands War posed great difficulties for the Corporation in its coverage. In some ways they paralleled the problem of Suez in 1956.

Sir Anthony Eden during Suez, and Margaret Thatcher twenty-six years later, considered the country to be at war with our servicemen at risk: therefore the duty of broadcasters was to support Britain and maintain morale.

The broadcasters, on the other hand, deemed their job was to report the facts under the law, and to reflect the differing opinions in the country, and especially in Parliament. In the early days, according to the polls, a majority opposed military action although a majority also supported sending the Task Force. A quarter of the population disapproved of the Government's action throughout.

There were particular problems with the Falklands as war was never declared, and British journalists could enter and report from Argentina. No censorship laws were invoked and therefore broadcasters believed they had to continue reporting as before, bearing in mind the axiom that "In war truth is the first casualty". We all understood that it would be criminally irresponsible to reveal military details that would assist General Galtieri and his Junta and endanger British troops, but how could we not report the divided opinion in the country? This was not a war for national survival.

To Mrs. Thatcher the broadcasters' attitude was incomprehensible. Norman Tebbit, in his autobiography *Upwardly Mobile*, spells out the Thatcherite view of these matters and of the damage done to the relationship between the Government and the BBC. He wrote:

[127]

The unctuous "impartiality" of the BBC's editorialising was a source of grief and anger. Few of us directly concerned will ever forgive the phrase "the British authorities, if they are to be believed, say . . ." or the regular references to British and Argentinian forces rather than "our forces" and "enemy forces". The elaborate even-handedness jarred cruelly with those whose lives were at risk, those of us who took ultimate responsibility for committing our forces, knowing the human costs of what we had to do, and with the general public. Nor did the excuse that the Overseas Service broadcasts would lose credibility with their foreign listeners unless the BBC remained "impartial", hold water because it confused truth with impartiality and balance.

It was not impartiality that impelled Germans to risk punishment by tuning in to the BBC during the Second World War. For me the British Broadcasting Corporation might have better called itself the Stateless Persons Broadcasting Corporation for it certainly did not reflect the mood of the British people who finance it. The wounds inflicted by the BBC have still not healed.

Tebbit's view seems to be that the BBC should be like any other State broadcasting system and reflect the view of the Government, more SABC (South African Broadcasting Corporation) than BBC. Those of us brought up in the Corporation thought the BBC should be and was more than that. It was respected and admired throughout the world precisely because it was not the mouthpiece of the British Government. Its independence was sacred and had to be sustained especially when British interests were involved. The British public in particular had a right to the truth not propaganda. I subscribed to that view. Conflict was therefore inevitable. We were not going to fulfil the expectations of one MoD press officer aboard HMS *Hermes* who said to ITN reporter Michael Nicholson "You must have been told when you left you couldn't report bad news. You knew when you came you were expected to do a 1940 propaganda job."

Nationwide was given the remit of ensuring that it covered the rest of the news and wasn't overwhelmed by the Falklands campaign but *Newsnight* and *Panorama* were dominated by it. The nightly show's presenter, Peter Snow, was first into the firing line.

Shortly after the capture of South Georgia, Snow analysed the conflicting claims of the two sides. Peter was a most enthusiastic defence correspondent, indeed some people feel he is the most enthusiastic person they have ever met. He loves military matters, has thousands of toy soldiers of his own, and is widely admired within the MoD. The fact, therefore, that he was the subject of charges of treason is instructive of the tensions and differing perspectives of the time.

On *Newsnight* Peter Snow said, explaining why he on the whole accepted the British version of events, "We cannot demonstrate that the British have lied to us but the Argentinians clearly have. Unless the British are demonstrated either to be deceiving us, or to be concealing losses from us, we can only tend to give a lot more credence to their version of events."

The reaction was immediate. A Conservative MP, John Page, attacked *Newsnight*'s coverage as "totally offensive and almost treasonable." The Prime Minister conveyed her strong feelings in the House of Commons saying that many people were concerned that "the case for our British forces is not being put over fully and effectively." In which case, one was tempted to add, she should address those remarks to her own ministers and the MoD Press Office, which was hardly a state of the art operation. The Prime Minister went on. "I understand that we and the Argentines are almost being treated as equal." This gave great offence, she said.

Peter Snow's remarks were read to mean that the British might sometimes not tell the truth. How outrageous. But of course he was correct; governments sometimes do lie when involved in military activity and quite right, too, if it gives their armed forces an advantage and reduces casualties. The MoD did in fact lie during the Falklands Campaign. It was not, however, the broadcasters' job to lie. If they had done so, why would anyone believe them in the future? Reputation is a frail flower.

The pressure on the BBC increased early in May 1982 when what had been a rather exciting escapade began to become a serious and bloody business, with the sinking of the *Belgrano* and HMS *Sheffield*. Both BBC and ITN showed film from Argentina of the grieving relatives of the *Belgrano* dead, but it was the *British* Broadcast-

ing Corporation that felt the lash of the Conservative Party, MP
Robert Adley saying that the BBC was becoming "General Galtieri's fifth column in Britain".

George Carey had succeeded me as Editor of *Panorama* and he
was now being initiated into the delights of the job. George was
rather more diplomatic than I was, had great charm, a Jesuitical
training, and a news upbringing before editing the first joint news
and current affairs programme *Newsnight*. Previous *Panorama*s had
dealt with the military situation, now George felt he should explore
the possibilities of a peaceful solution.

The first element in the programme was an interview by Peter
Taylor with the Argentinian representative at the UN, probing his
position. This was followed by a report by Michael Cockerell on
parliamentary worries about a military solution which included
interviews with two Conservative MPs who were willing to
express publicly the doubts that perhaps twenty per cent of Tory
MPs had in private. Finally there was an interview by the *Panorama*
presenter Robert Kee, with Cecil Parkinson, a member of the War
Cabinet, to whom these concerns were put. To the broadcasters
this seemed a difficult but perfectly proper programme. After all,
reservations did exist and if a military solution was sought many
lives would be lost. Surely, it was legitimate to ask whether a
diplomatic solution was possible? Should the public be denied the
information on which to make that judgement?

Mrs. Thatcher was dressing for dinner when the programme
started. She slowly sat down and remained almost motionless
throughout. "She was transfixed" said her Press Secretary,
Bernard Ingham, who found it as unbelievable as did his mistress.
He believes that the BBC, funded by the licence fee, always has to
prove it is more independent than independent television. No. 10
thought the BBC was simply out of control. A close adviser in
Downing Street told me "Of course you report the war, but you
have regard to the fact of the society in which you live, and which
pays your licence fee." His contempt for people like myself was
considerable. "These editors who regard themselves as in a state of
pristine purity. What did I describe them as? These editors who
regard themselves as being white knights of unutterable veracity.
Tripe. Absolute codswallop. It's the biggest bloody fraud per-

petrated on the Advertising Standards Association. I mean for God's sake if you are so damned concerned about what the public should know, then be honest about the kind of things you do yourself."

He went on to describe the Prime Minister's feelings. "I think she does recognise that the media these days has its own peculiar set of values which I think is derived largely from the United States First Amendment. I firmly believe that Watergate has corrupted two generations of journalists, corrupted in the sense that they presume guilt regardless of the evidence."

With these sorts of feelings emanating from Downing Street, with a disaster in the Falklands a real possibility, and with it the fall of the Government that had allowed the Argentinian invasion to happen unobserved, it was not surprising that Tory backbenchers started to lose self-control. John Cole, the BBC's Political Editor, was advised by a Government whip to wear his steel helmet the day after the *Panorama* programme when he went into the MPs' lobby. An armoured personnel carrier would have been more appropriate.

At Prime Minister's *Question Time* Mrs. Sally Oppenheim, one of Mrs. Thatcher's former ministers, offered her former mistress an underarm ball to hit. Would Mrs. Thatcher like to comment on a programme which was "an odious and subversive travesty which dishonoured the right of freedom of speech in this country."

Apparently freedom of speech was only to be used in support of the military campaign, a novel concept.

The Prime Minister rose. "I share the deep concern that has been expressed on many sides particularly about the content of yesterday's *Panorama* programme. I know how strongly many people feel that the case for our country is not being put with sufficient vigour in certain – I don't say all – BBC programmes. The Chairman of the BBC has said in vigorous terms that the BBC is not neutral on this point and I hope his words will be heeded by the many who have the responsibility for standing up for the Task Force, our boys, our people, and the cause of democracy."

The Director General Designate, Alasdair Milne, was not surprised by this. "I always thought the Government would turn on us, once there were losses and they came under pressure. But it happened several days later than I expected."

As it happened I shared the majority view that, given that General Galtieri and his particularly nasty Junta had invaded the Falklands, a military campaign was probably the only way of dislodging the aggressors and that they should be dislodged. Whether we should have been in this situation is another matter. But my personal views were irrelevant. I felt we had to report all shades of opinion about the conflict, and never knowingly pass off propaganda as truth. If the Government had chosen to invoke censorship openly then at least the public would know what was happening, but we were not going to be party to a conspiracy against the public's right to know.

Such was the fury in the Conservative Party that the BBC Chairman, George Howard, and Alasdair Milne agreed to attend a meeting of the Tory Media Committee on 12 May. Over a hundred MPs packed into Committee Room 13 and Howard, a big man in every way, was sweating. Later the event was called the "ox-roasting", with George Howard the ox. He was no left-winger but a Whig grandee and was not used to the abuse he now faced from the self-made Thatcherites. Milne, who felt contempt for the hysteria, fared no better. "It was like being in the Star Chamber", he said. "When they got really angry they started waving their order papers and growling like dogs."

Winston Churchill, the grandson of the wartime leader, derided the BBC's claim that it was trying to live up to its World War II standards. Goebbel's propaganda machine, he said, had not been given equal time. This was an interesting statement as the people interviewed in the *Panorama* programme criticising the military option were fellow Conservative MPs of Churchill. Were they Nazis?

As the meeting ended a young Tory MP jabbed a finger at Howard. "You, sir, are a traitor." "Stuff you," said the BBC Chairman.

Afterwards the MPs gave a colourful account of their brave actions. "There was blood and entrails all over the place," one said. George Howard and Alasdair Milne slipped away to Willie Whitelaw's office for a drink. He was disgusted by the behaviour of his party, although he felt the meeting had had to happen to let off steam. Whitelaw, while a stalwart member of the War Cabinet and a holder of the Military Cross, understood and sympathised with the broadcaster's dilemma and he tended to shrug off these outbursts of emotion from his leader and some of his colleagues. He didn't think expressions like "putting their house in order" meant very much and anyway it wasn't for ministers to tell the BBC what to do with its staff.

He thought it was extremely difficult to handle a situation when you are actually at war, but not at war. As for the reference to the Nazis he pointed out that Kate Adie, the BBC reporter, couldn't have been in Berlin in the middle of the war, but she could be in Buenos Aires. And in his view there was no reason why she shouldn't be there.

Balancing Willie Whitelaw, however, was Norman Tebbit who differed violently from him and whom many thought had a BBC phobia. Perhaps it is significant that those who had actually fought in the Second World War and seen the true nature of warfare were more understanding of the broadcasters and less gung-ho about the whole business. They were not caught by surprise at the sinking of HMS *Sheffield* or the sufferings of the Welsh guardsmen. They were well aware that casualties were inevitable. It did not affect their support for the military operation but it made them rather more sober about the situation. I found this also true of the military commanders themselves.

Richard Francis, now the BBC's Managing Director of Radio, also found himself in trouble again. He had gone to Madrid to a conference of the International Press Institute. In the course of defending the BBC's coverage against charges of bias and national propaganda he remarked that "the widow of Portsmouth is no different from the widow at Buenos Aires." This eminently Christian remark did not go down well with that eminent organ the *Sun*. Its headline, after the *Belgrano* was sunk with the loss of hundreds of lives, was "Gotcha". Argies, in the *Sun*'s view, seemed to be a lesser breed of humanity.

On his return from America, the BBC's Director General, Ian Trethowan, was appalled to hear of the "blood on the floor" of Committee Room 13. He quickly arranged a further meeting with the Tory backbenchers, many of whom he had known from his years as a lobby correspondent and television interviewer. They thought he was "one of them" and without giving up any point of principle he argued that the BBC was not neutral, but was fulfilling its allotted function to the best of its ability. Things calmed down but Trethowan thought that the BBC's war coverage would have to take account of what had occurred and the heightened emotions that had been aroused in Parliament and in the country at large. He told the BBC's News and Current Affairs meeting on 18 May that the BBC's reporting had to be "sensitive to the emotional sensibilities of the public."

In his amusing, highly enjoyable but inaccurately titled book, *The Last Days of the Beeb*, Michael Leapman put it this way:

> It meant, in effect, that the BBC was not free to pursue a line that diverged to any significant degree from the jingoism that the Government's information machinery was encouraging. Its editorial independence could be exercised only within defined limits – and one of the factors that defined them was Parliament's responsibility for setting the licence fee.

I think this is a slight exaggeration, as opposition to the Government's policy in Parliament was not great. Even the Labour leader Michael Foot, a passionate member of CND, committed to significant reductions in defence expenditure, was firmly in support of the Falklands campaign. Galtieri was, after all, a military dictator of a vicious kind. Without significant debate in Parliament, debate in the media was never going to be very pronounced.

Back on *Nationwide* we felt free to report, but as we had no reporters with the Military Expedition (numbers had been strictly controlled by the Defence Ministry) our coverage was not significantly different from anybody else's. The only matter that caused me real concern was the blanket instruction not to interview war widows or parents of the war dead. This followed one or two rather insensitive "How do you feel" type of interviews, but could have been interpreted as a desire to turn the audience attention from the inevitable price of warfare. The BBC didn't operate by blanket instruction and I was able to get it changed, and we subsequently did interview relatives of those killed, with rather more sensitive questions.

Getting Galtieri

Over on ITV they seemed to be having a quieter time. ITN was certainly regarded by the Government as doing a good job, while some of us in the BBC wondered if they were not a little too gung-ho, with reporters rather too caught up in the excitement of it all. However, Current Affairs can usually be counted upon to upset the apple cart and so it proved. *TV Eye*, the successor to *This Week*, had sent Julian Manyon to Argentina. Julian was no stranger to difficult situations having begun his broadcasting career in his early twenties in Vietnam as a radio reporter. When the Viet Cong were about to take over Saigon, he had decided to stay on and report, a typically courageous decision.

In Argentina, however, his attempts to report came to a terrifying stop. At first he had a relatively easy time. He had been in a radio station when the news of the sinking of the *Belgrano* had come through, together with the details of the dreadful loss of life. People around him were in tears but they did not demonstrate any great anti-British feeling. Indeed, there has always been a large British society in Argentina and, in this war which was not a war, there was little hindrance of British journalists moving about.

One morning, however, he went with his crew, producer Norman Fenton, cameraman Ted Adcock and sound recordist Trefor Hunter, to the Foreign Ministry hoping to interview its Head. After a frustrating morning hanging about they were told to come back after lunch. They left the building and climbed into the two large American limousines they had hired to carry their equipment and set off down the avenue to the local hotel where they sometimes had lunch. They were relaxing and thinking about what they would eat when, within about a quarter of a mile from the Foreign Ministry, a car suddenly pulled out in front of the first limousine in which Julian and his producer were travelling. Julian got out, somewhat irritated, and started to move towards the obstruction.

Suddenly a man jumped out of the car in front, gun in hand. At the same moment, armed men came up from behind and the reporter saw that the two Thames cars were now sandwiched, unable to move. Norman Fenton, realising quickly what was happening, got out the other side of the car, and casually walked into the adjoining park and away to raise the alarm.

Neither Julian nor the rest of the team were so fortunate. Manyon was grabbed from behind and a silver automatic pistol pushed into his face. The men then pushed him down on to the floor of his car in front of the back seat, threw a cloth over him and held the pistol to his temple. The car drove off. Julian is over six feet tall and the gunman kept forcing his knees down as he lay face upwards in the bottom of the car. "I tried to see where we were going", he told me, "by squinting through a gap between the cloth and the back edge of the seat. I suddenly saw we were going past the airport. In my back pocket I had five hundred dollars in cash. I told the gunman about the money, asking them to let me out and I would leave the country immediately. I had no idea who or what they were, military police, soldiers, or just plain death squads."

The gunmen took the money out of Julian's pocket but drove on. They were holding leather thongs which prevented the door and windows being opened. They kicked Julian's knees again. Back in the second car Ted Adcock and Trefor Hunter were getting similar treatment.

About forty-five minutes out of Buenos Aires, well into the countryside, the cars stopped and all three members of the *TV Eye* team were put into the same car, which then drove on for a further thirty minutes before stopping at the edge of a ripe cornfield. It was suddenly very quiet.

Argentinian death squads have a justifiably appalling reputation. Manyon thought he was to become another of their statistics. The three Britons were hustled out of the car and guns in their backs pushed and prodded them into the middle of the field.

"We were told to take off our clothes, except for our underpants, and then to turn and walk away." As they did so they heard cocking of rifles, then silence. They waited for the gunfire. Suddenly they heard the screeching of car tyres and then the sound of the limousines driving off.

Three Britons were left, in the middle of a cornfield in the middle of Argentina, with only their underpants to cover them. Their clothes had gone the way of their money.

After a while a peasant on a tractor came by but he refused to stop and drove away as quickly as he could. Did he think they were British airmen who had landed secretly? Eventually a man in a van drove up and took them, still without clothes, to the local police station.

Julian tried to get the police to ring up the Interior Ministry in Buenos Aires where he was known to the Minister Colonel Alfred St. Jean. The police were very suspicious and it took Manyon three hours to persuade them to do so. Julian is so persistent they probably gave in out of sheer exhaustion. Norman Fenton had gone straight from the site of the kidnap to the Interior Ministry where St. Jean appeared genuinely concerned both for the team and for the reputation of his Government.

The Minister sent his own limousine to pick up the television team which greatly impressed the police who were holding them. They saluted as the three pairs of underpants climbed into the car and waved goodbye.

The driver had a message for them. After getting some clothes they were to go immediately to the Palace Casa Posada where St. Jean would be waiting for them. Norman Fenton had received the same message and had arranged for the ITN crew in Buenos Aires to accompany him, as all Thames equipment had been stolen along with everything else.

Julian expected simply to thank St. Jean, try and get a quick interview with him and then go back to his hotel, but St. Jean had a surprise waiting. Would the Thames crew like to meet the President, General Galtieri, who wished to express his personal concern about the incident?

After checking that the ITN crew were ready to film, Julian followed the Interior Minister down a long corridor into Galtieri's action room where a naval adjutant asked them to wait. Julian could hardly believe what was happening. Here was the British and Argentinian Armed Forces locked in conflict in the South Atlantic and he was in the military headquarters of the Argentinian President. The naval officer was trying to say something to him. "You know, once a year we have Navy day. We celebrate a great deal. It is very important to us." Julian looked puzzled. "Today is Navy Day. The General is celebrating." It suddenly dawned on Manyon that the adjutant was saying Galtieri was drunk, or at least merry.

Suddenly the doors opened into a large ballroom-like area and the Thames and ITN crews were moved forward to meet the President. The cameramen started filming, as arranged, and Julian seized this astonishing opportunity to talk to Mrs. Thatcher's Enemy No. 1. Manyon thought he might get a minute or so but in fact the interview lasted for six or seven minutes. After many protestations of concern by the General the meeting was over, and the team rushed back to satellite the material to London for that night's *TV Eye* and the *News at Ten*. It was an amazing coup, but the price in terms of nerves and clean underpants had been great.

Back in Downing Street, however, the Prime Minister and her War Cabinet were aghast at Thames's intention to transmit the interview. The Home Secretary was instructed to make the Government's views known to the Director General of the Independent Broadcasting Authority, Sir Brian Young, who then insisted on watching the interview in advance. He passed it for transmission with minimum amendments. Sir Ian Trethowan is reported by Michael Cockerell in his book, *Live from Number 10*, as saying that "The idea that the sight of Galtieri speaking could create a mass collapse of national morale was a great nonsense." Trethowan does think however that broadcasters were "Occasionally insensitive to the fearful pressures on those who had to make the crucial decisions, particularly the Prime Minister herself. But politicians in their turn showed an alarming lack of confidence in the emotional sturdiness of the public on whose behalf they claim to govern."

Transmission of the interview went off with little fuss or viewer reaction.

Some years later I talked to two of those intimately involved in Downing Street at that time. One, a member of the Cabinet, took a relaxed view of it all.

"The interview with Galtieri completely rebounded against him. There is always this assumption that the interview is always in the interests of the person giving it. It isn't, it isn't at all!"

The other, a close adviser, took the majority Tebbit line which I quoted earlier in this chapter. He referred to the news of the recapture of South Georgia. There was a discussion about how to release it, he told me, and finally it was decided that the Secretary of Defence should give the news to the waiting journalists outside in Downing Street. The Prime Minister would accompany him. As they left Bernard Ingham, her press secretary, warned both politicians that the first question they would be asked after the statement was "Will you declare war or do you regard yourself at war?" The adviser clearly thought such questioning would be contemptible.

Out went John Nott and Margaret Thatcher and made the statement. "And too bloody true," said the adviser. "The first question came in on cue. When are you going to declare war? I mean!" Mrs. Thatcher replied "Fancy asking a question like that at this time – rejoice, rejoice."

The adviser went on "I find it very difficult to differentiate between whether we were or were not at war when shells were flying and ships were being lost and Christ knows what was happening."

He expected broadcasters to speak on behalf of the Government; the broadcasters felt they should continue to report and try to keep their audience as informed as possible. We were not at war, no censorship had been invoked. National survival was not involved.

The other thing we had to bear in mind, of course, was that we were not dealing with a government of national emergency or a wartime coalition. This was a one party Government which would certainly use its military success for political advantage and to direct attention away from the disturbing question of how it had got into this mess in the first place.

That very independent Conservative MP, Julian Critchley, writing in his extremely witty book *Westminster Blues*, suggested an annual Galtieri award for services to the Conservative Party. Mrs. Thatcher was not slow to see the electoral advantages. She herself went on a highly publicised trip to the Falklands in 1983, and in a *Panorama* interview that year told Fred Emery, "Before we had the Falklands, people were always asking 'When are you going to make a U-turn?' We never get those questions now." She told an interviewer from American television that she applied exactly the same principles in the Falklands as she had to the economy. "People saw the kind of results it produced in the Falklands and I think they began to realise it was the right way to go at home as well. I think people like decisiveness, I think they like strong leadership."

The Belgrano Resurfaces

At *Nationwide* we had been untouched by Falklands controversy but out of the blue we became involved a year later during the 1983 General Election.

As part of its election coverage *Nationwide* traditionally invited the party leaders to appear individually in its "On the Spot" feature. This involved the leaders answering questions from viewers. In the past this had been a bit of a soft option as the viewers' questions were sent in by postcard and read by presenters who operated at the Jimmy Young end of the interviewing range. Their supplementaries were often soft lobs.

In 1983 I thought we should do things differently. I decided to ask the viewers to write in but then to invite into regional studios those whose questions we had selected so they could ask their own questions. However, this would still leave the advantage in the politicians' hands as they were experienced in television techniques and the audience was not. I, therefore, ensured that the questioners came into the regional studios early and had a full dress rehearsal on the afternoon of the programme. We urged them to ask supplementary questions and "to stick in there". In addition we had our own iron lady, Sue Lawley, to chair the proceedings. Sue had become an outstanding broadcaster and was already among the best political interviewers.

We did our first programme with three weeks to polling day. The interviewee was David Steel, the Liberal leader. He arrived early, went swiftly through a technical rehearsal and, being a former television presenter himself, felt quite at home. He spent the waiting period in the green room making arrangements to see his family during the hectic campaign, and in particular arranging for his son Billy to travel with him. I admired both his coolness and his sense of priorities. During the programme he was relaxed, reasonable and persuasive, but he still appeared like a supporting act.

Two weeks later it was the turn of Michael Foot, a likeable man fighting a disastrous election. He was more suited to Gladstone's Mid-Lothian campaign than to the television age. The programme went out "live" and he was late. I paced between the control room and the reception area trying to work out what to do if he didn't turn up. I always tried to plan for disaster but I couldn't think of anything on this occasion. The Labour leader had already missed the rehearsal period, and the local news programme which preceded *Nationwide* from the same studio was already going out.

Eventually, a windswept and out of breath Michael Foot arrived together with his stoical press secretary Tom McAffrey. He had been delayed by a meeting with some supporters in a London constituency. I wondered how many people he had talked to – fifty? A hundred at most. Yet he had nearly missed talking to a television audience of ten million. What a daft sense of priorities I thought, admirable but daft. We got Mr. Foot's coat off in the lift and just had time to sit him in next to Sue and fit the earpiece through which he would hear the questions from the regional studios.

An extremely adept and experienced television performer might have coped but Michael Foot looked old, out of breath, and definitely not in charge of the situation. His answers were long, rather discursive, and this led to a sense of frustration from all sides pervading the programme.

Afterwards Michael Foot was as kind, well-mannered, and considerate as he always is. As one of his Shadow Cabinet colleagues said to me, "Lovely man – lousy candidate." I'm afraid it was true and I think Foot knew it but he kept going to the end without panic, anger or despair ever being displayed.

When Mrs. Thatcher had arrived at Lime Grove a week earlier, the Election, still fourteen days away, looked all over, and a large Conservative majority guaranteed. The so-called Falklands' Election had been run quite brilliantly by Tory Central Office. Nothing was left to chance and the preparations were immaculate. A few days before her appearance on our programme an advance party had checked out the studio and talked over the format with us and then had presented her with a detailed brief.

She arrived with her husband and daughter, advisers and

security personnel well before the rehearsal. I noticed that she carried a large file carefully flagged under relevant headings. I suppose it gave her confidence but such is her phenomenal grasp of detail that I expect she knew everything in it backwards. When we left for the studio only Gordon Reece and the police came with her. She was at her most calm and controlled. For someone who later told me she "hates, hates, hates" television interviews she seemed in a remarkably good mood. She sat down next to Sue Lawley and quickly went through the technical rehearsal before departing to make-up. The face that looked back from the mirror was a very different one from that seen in the mirror during the 1975 leadership contest.

Her suit was immaculately designed, her hair blonder and swept up and her teeth more regular than ever. The voice was lower and a fraction more musical.

She came back, sat down on Sue's right and had a few last words with Gordon Reece. I did the same to Sue Lawley, as even the best have terrible butterflies on such occasions. I told her a joke, which I'm usually disastrous at doing, but this time she smiled. I retreated to the control room, Reece to a chair behind the cameras out of sight but next to a monitor.

The programme went very smoothly and Mrs. Thatcher was in commanding form. No one had been able to lay a finger on her in the television interviews she had done, even Robin Day was despairing of the way he had failed to pierce her defences. Today seemed no different. She answered questions on "Victorian values", unemployment, taxation, pensions, the police and the health service. We had selected the questions on the basis of how representative they were of the cards we had been receiving. Those who did want to ask questions were on the whole critical of Mrs. Thatcher. The same situation had applied to the other party leaders.

There had been a number of questions sent in about the Falklands and we selected one on the *Belgrano* which seemed to sum up the concerns expressed. Sue Lawley thanked the Reverend David Horne, a curate from Handsworth Wood in Birmingham who was concerned about the social justice of tax cuts for the rich. Sue then turned to camera.

"Let's go to Mrs. Diana Gould, in our Bristol studio." The next few minutes were generally regarded as the only time that Mrs. Thatcher looked flustered and upset in the whole of the campaign. Mrs. Gould was a grey-haired geography teacher from Cirencester. According to Martin Harrison, "In the British General Election of 1983, no professional interviewer would have challenged a Prime Minister so bluntly and precisely. Because she was answering an ordinary voter, Mrs. Thatcher had to bite back her evident anger."

Diana Gould asked her question. "Mrs. Thatcher, why, when the *Belgrano*, the Argentinian battleship, was outside the exclusion zone and actually sailing away from the Falklands, why did you give the order to sink it?"

Mrs. Thatcher replied that it was not sailing away from the Falklands, but the teacher from Cirencester knew her navigation.

"It was on a bearing of 280° and was already west of the Falklands, so I'm sorry but I cannot see how you can say it was not sailing away from the Falklands when it was sunk." The *Belgrano* was, in fact, sailing away from the islands.

Mrs. Thatcher had to retreat, "When it was sunk it was a danger to our ships," she said.

Having gained the advantage Mrs. Gould did not let up. The Prime Minister found herself being scolded by a member of the public. "That is not good enough, Mrs. Thatcher," said Diana Gould at one point.

(The full exchange is printed as an appendix to this book.)

Sitting upstairs in the gallery I was watching fascinated as these two iron ladies battled it out in what was the most exciting piece of television in the whole campaign. It seemed to me to be democracy in action and I was thrilled.

Downstairs in the Hospitality Room Denis Thatcher and his daughter were appalled. Carol Thatcher described the *Nationwide* "On the Spot" as "An example of the most crass nastiness and discourtesy shown to a Prime Minister on a television election programme." I took the view that we had treated her as a party leader answerable to the public. Denis Thatcher believed his prejudices confirmed that the BBC was "A nest of long-haired Trots and wooftahs".

Back on the studio floor Mrs. Thatcher had regained her poise and was answering the final question, which was about capital punishment, a subject on which she knew she was in tune with the public.

"I believe that a return to capital punishment would deter some people who go out to do violent crime which leads to murder," she said.

The programme ended and I went down to the studio floor expecting a very cool reception. Gordon Reece was reassuring her that she had done very well. Somewhat mollified she followed me down to the hospitality room. As I opened the door I saw Denis Thatcher with a face like thunder. The family and supporters quickly huddled together and I noticed one BBC executive slip out of the room to avoid the trouble that was clearly about to come. Mrs. Thatcher was soon seething. "Only the BBC," she said, "could ask a British Prime Minister why she took action to protect our ships against an enemy ship that was a danger to our boys." I forbore to point out that the question had come from one of the electors not from the BBC. Refusing a drink the Prime Minister left immediately.

The programme made no difference to the election of course. The Conservatives remained miles ahead of Labour and duly won with a large majority. But it confirmed Mrs. Thatcher's view that something must be done about the BBC and before the next election.

There were to be more storms but I would not be in Lime Grove to face them.

When *Nationwide* came to an end that summer I moved two hundred miles away to be Head of the BBC's Network Production Centre in Manchester. I thought that my somewhat controversial days in Current Affairs were over. I looked forward to a professional life of music, sport, drama, and history programmes, but it was all to end in tears – mine.

10

COMING APART

It does rain a great deal in Manchester but for most of the two years and seven months I spent there, I thought the sun shone. The Network Production Centre was one of three in the Corporation, the others were Pebble Mill, in Birmingham, and Bristol, home of the Natural History Unit. Manchester was the largest both in numbers of hours produced and in the levels of staff. After a period of considerable expansion and success in the late seventies under John Ecclestone, it had become rather bogged down in industrial relations problems and some of its output was looking a little jaded. The vast majority of programmes, however, were good and some were excellent. I felt Manchester needed to reposition itself a little in relation to Television Centre in London. It needed to specialise in output a little more, and could do with a small influx of people from outside. The main requirement, however, was restoring confidence and putting some energy and drive in its leadership. This I set out to do. I felt I could offer the NPC considerable experience in network programming, excellent contacts in the BBC in London, and a Northerner's commitment to his own area. Some in Manchester did use the excuse of metropolitan bias to avoid the fact that their ideas weren't good enough. Equally there was prejudice against the regions in London and I hoped that I could help reduce that by remaining constantly in touch and arguing the case.

One of the most difficult people to deal with was Bill Cotton, who was not very fond of those of us who were out of town. He tended to regard regional network production as a burden that the Television Centre in White City had to carry. As he was Managing Director of Television this was a serious matter. I arranged to see him every three months to discuss my Centre's output but the meetings were often postponed. When they occurred Bill was more likely to talk about his father the famous bandleader, or to tell some, admittedly very funny, jokes about the entertainment business, rather than focus on the matter in hand.

I put up various three-year plans to the Centre asking for a Television Service commitment to accept programming in particular areas from Manchester for that period. This would enable me to recruit outstanding people from London and elsewhere in the knowledge that they would have considerable opportunities and resources for that period. For example I suggested making Manchester the travel centre of the BBC, both in television and radio, with the *Holiday* series and *Breakaway* joining the *Travel Show* which was already in situ. In return for such a commitment I was prepared to cut back in other areas. It would be painful but like pruning, healthy. I could not get that commitment. Radio would not agree with Television. No one seemed able to plan in that way, not even Brian Wenham who as Controller of BBC-2 and then Director of Programmes was an enthusiastic supporter of non-metropolitan broadcasting.

Given that negative response, I pushed ahead and simply offered the Controllers who commissioned programmes whatever I thought we could make and they would accept. One of my prime aims was to strengthen the journalism as I believed the over-centralisation of BBC journalism in London was a great danger. It allowed the view of the Centre to become too dominant in what was a divided kingdom. I felt that with *World In Action* at Granada Television and *First Tuesday* at Yorkshire Television, our own *Brass Tacks* current affairs series would form a powerful triumvirate. Add the excellent radio *File on Four*, which also came from the NPC, and I thought it would be possible to retain and expand a pool of fine journalists out of London. In this I think we were successful not least because Colin Cameron left running the BBC's *Heart of the Matter* series and came up to edit *Brass Tacks*. I still remain very bitter about the collapse of *Brass Tacks* after I left Manchester. It happened either by wilful neglect or by unwillingness to have any journalism out of the direct control of the new Directorate of News and Current Affairs in London.

Back in 1983, however, all was light and hope. I was now responsible for over a thousand people and had control over resources and personnel management, as well as over programmes. I was fortunate in the management team I found there. One person in particular was of very high quality. Michael Green was my Head of Network Radio, a job he had occupied for some time. His only drawback for future advancement was that he lacked television experience. He was an immense asset but I spent a lot of my time trying to persuade BBC Management in Broadcasting House in London to give him a senior post as he was one of the most intelligent and capable public service broadcasters I had met.

It says much about the Corporation that they left him in one job so long, but just after I left the North West he was appointed Controller of Radio 4. What a job! I would have loved it but I would not have done it half as well as Michael.

I tried to open up New Broadcasting House in Manchester and to involve the staff in what I was trying to do. We started a local paper, and introduced Manfax, a local version of Ceefax, installing monitors by the lifts and in reception area so that information and announcements could be seen by the staff. Every week I invited twelve people from across the Centre to come and have a drink with me to talk about whatever they wanted.

Then I tried to get out to meet everyone. This was hardly a hardship. I'd pop into the studios and watch recordings, then go to a lunchtime performance by our magnificent orchestra, the BBC Philharmonic, under a quite outstanding conductor Edward Downes. In the evenings I would drive down the motorway to one of our Outside Broadcast Units which would be covering snooker, darts, rugby league or cricket. Nick Hunter, my Head of Sport, had master-minded the growth of TV Snooker from Manchester and was highly regarded throughout the sporting world.

Days spent in New BH were immensely stimulating because of the presence of Colin Adams and David Brown who ran the Features and Children's Departments respectively. Both were blunt Northerners but with a passionate commitment to the BBC.

Colin in particular had one of the most fertile, if hyperactive, minds I had ever met.

I found I enjoyed managing a large organisation and became fascinated by the problems of resources and personnel. I undoubtedly tried to do too much at the beginning, like a child with a new toy, but eventually settled down. I thought we were getting somewhere and I missed being in charge of my own programme hardly at all.

I also enjoyed going to the Weekly Programme Reviews in Television and Radio, and when I was asked by the BBC house magazine, *Ariel*, to write the weekly diary I thought I'd write about those occasions. After a little wobbling *Ariel* printed my thoughts. This is part of it:

I'm not sure what role I should play at Television Programme Review. The resident wit is clearly Jimmy Moir, Head of Comedy, who I am sure employs all his scriptwriters on the understanding that they write his scripts as well.

I could try being the young radical but I fear I'm getting a little old for that and the alternative spokesman is clearly Mike Fentiman of Community Programmes. Well, he has a moustache, wears a leather jacket and rolls his own. He auditions for the role of chief iconoclast as well. Moral concern is well articulated by Colin Morris, so I suppose I'll have to settle for Ambitious, Manchester.

Of course, the other problem with Programme Review is deciding whether and how much of the truth to tell. I have so far avoided the danger of commenting on programmes I haven't seen, though I wonder if this is true of all my colleagues. Can they really watch all they say they do – even those ambitious and balding gentlemen who are clearly desperate to be Controllers?

I fear political calculation is in danger of limiting my honesty.

If I contradict the Controller, will my budget be cut; if I criticise an ally, will he withdraw to his tent? Above all, should I simply defend Manchester's output and let others criticise? Programme makers are notoriously sensitive and hate their boss criticising their life's work in front of vultures. For the moment

I'll stick to the truth. All programmes are excellent, nobody has any worries about DBS and Cable, and I never make mistakes.

Radio Programme Review is quite different. Oh, it's still wildly unrepresentative, like its Television equivalent, being white, predominantly male, middle-aged and middle-class (although, in fairness, a woman does run it, Monica Sims, DPR).

However, whereas all the Television Review Board members clearly live, sleep and certainly drink their job, the member of the Radio equivalent appears to have more important things on his mind. Calm, collected and a little withdrawn, he looks more like an Advisory Council member who has just popped in from his proper job to pass on a few thoughts, demonstrate his intellectual distinction and make a few impenetrable jokes.

The last Radio Review I attended was in the Langham Gallery. As Monica Sims opened the discussion on a programme about Lord Reith, the gaunt Scot (no, not the present DG, the first one) looked down disapprovingly. It is a remarkable portrait which strikes fear even at fifty paces. Did I imagine that his expression became even fiercer when we began to talk of the Rolling Stones and Frankie Goes to Hollywood? Discussing rock in that formal, besuited atmosphere was rather like watching monks in conclave discussing sexual performance.

In fact I might have been advised not to attend so many of these occasions. I found it impossible not to articulate my concerns as the BBC began to come under great pressure from outside, and seemed to have lost its way. I became almost obsessed with making the Corporation address the dilemmas that faced it and I undoubtedly became a pain in the backside to some people. There was nowhere else to voice one's frustrations, however, and the Director General, Alasdair Milne, hardly encouraged debate.

On one occasion while I was Editor in Lime Grove he had invited me and some colleagues for dinner so that we could have a good frank no-holds-barred chat about the world, i.e. the BBC.

We had a pleasant enough meal, and then Alasdair pushed back his chair and invited me to start. "Ask anything you like, old boy." So I asked him about some unsatisfactory part of BBC-1's schedule.

His brow darkened and he leaned forward angrily. "Don't you tell me how to schedule my bloody programmes. I'm the scheduler, not you." There was a stunned silence. Later when someone else asked a fairly innocuous question they were slammed down in the same way. Alasdair seemed incapable of discussing anything objectively, everything was taken personally. When you combined that with a Managing Director of Television, Bill Cotton, who didn't seem to understand the serious nature of the issues in question, then we knew we had a problem.

It was a uniquely difficult time to run the BBC. The Government was hostile and its supporters in the press, particularly Rupert Murdoch, had a commercial interest in the breakup of the Corporation. They were after all moving into participating or owning satellite television companies. More channels were coming on to the air or were promised and the role of the BBC needed to be clarified and fought for as never before.

Alasdair did not seem to have a vision of what the Corporation should be, nor the political skills needed to steer it through particularly troubled waters.

He had the misfortune to work with two weak BBC Chairmen who both died while in office, and with a Board of Governors which was certainly in tune with much of the Government's thinking. His predecessor, Ian Trethowan, had papered over the cracks of a widening chasm between the Management and the Governors. Milne could not do this. Perhaps no one could.

Sadly, however, Alasdair lost the support of his own Management and staff. One of his members of the Board of Management told me this recently, taking no pleasure in it because he liked Alasdair personally, as many of us did.

"What are the responsibilities of the DG?" he asked rhetorically. "First he must be the respected leader of his troops. Alasdair began with that respect but lost it.

"Second he must be respected by his Board of Management. In the end Alasdair wasn't. Ian Trethowan would always support individual members of Management when they presented papers to the Board. If things got hot he would take over. By contrast Alasdair would often leave his Senior Managers to fight their own corner and sit quietly by." My informant also said he thought

Above: Waiting for the Prime Minister, in *On the Spot: Nationwide*, during the General Election of 1983.

Below: Roger Bolton, Sue Lawley, Margaret Thatcher and her broadcasting adviser Gordon Reece in *On the Spot: Nationwide*, General Election Campaign 1983.

Above: This cartoon appeared in the *Guardian* after the INLA interview, *Tonight* 1979. (Courtesy of Bryan McAllister)

Below: The day after Mrs. Thatcher blew her top in the Commons about Carrickmore. (Courtesy of Gibbard of the *Guardian*)

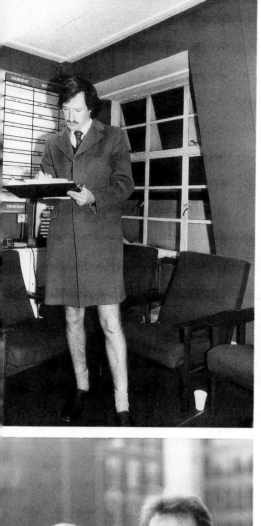

Above left: "As the telecine machines broke down and ran backwards I got so angry I spilt coffee all over my trousers!"

Above right: "No Mrs. Thatcher, I did not mislead you." The author on the phone during the Conservative leadership election campaign of 1975.

Below: Chris Oxley, the producer of *Death on the Rock*, and Roger Bolton on the morning of the publication of *The Windlesham Report*. (Kevin Harvey, *Daily Telegraph*)

Above: Bill Cotton in BBC Network Production Centre in Manchester in 1985 – not telling a joke for a change. (*Manchester Mercury*)

Below: A couple of hours before Alan Stewart was killed by a landmine in South Sudan while filming for *This Week*. From left to right: John Heasman (Sound Recordist), Alan Stewart (Producer – in white shorts), Ian Killiaw (Cameraman) and Peter Gill (Reporter), October 1986.

Above left: Mr. Kenneth Asquez, on his way in a police car to the inquest at the coroner's court in Gibraltar, to give evidence for the second time, 28 September 1989. (Press Association)

Above right: Mrs. Carmen Proetta. (Press Association)

Below: The dead bodies of Mairead Farrell, Sean Savage and Danny McCann. (Douglas Celecia)

Mairead Farrell. (Derek Speirs)

Below left: Sean Savage. (Pacemaker Press)

Below right: Danny McCann. (Pacemaker Press)

Above: Marbella, 9 March 1988. Spanish police move a white Ford Fiesta from a garage after discovering five packages of explosives and a timing device inside it. The car was reported to have been rented by the IRA. (Popperfoto)

Below: A close-up of the timing device, detonators and packages of Semtex high-explosive found in the car. Three days earlier three IRA terrorists had been shot dead by security forces in Gibraltar. Subsequently, British police said that a car bomb was to have been exploded during a changing of the guard ceremony outside the Governor's residence there. (AP Wirephoto)

Overleaf: Published on Thursday 26 January 1989, *The Windlesham Report* cleared Thames Television's *Death on the Rock* documentary of more than twenty criticisms levelled against it. Mrs. Thatcher refused to accept the findings of the report. (Courtesy of the *Independent*)

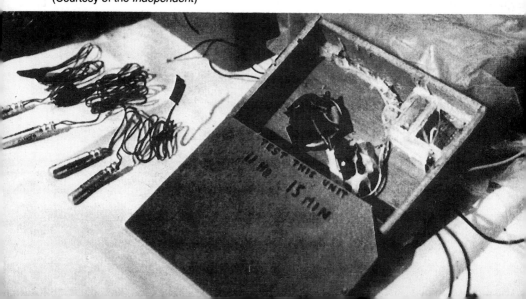

SUMMARY

Telepoint licences granted

THE Government has awarded four licences to operate telepoint, a national mobile telephone service.

The system will allow calls to be made from pocket-sized radio phones costing about £150, fed through thousands of base stations to the public telephone network. .... **Page 22**

£100m drugs case

A London businessman took part in a conspiracy to smuggle £100m worth of Columbian cocaine into Britain while he was in a prison cell, an Old Bailey jury was told. .... **Page 2**

Commons eggs

Eggs which poisoned more than 120 peers and others in the House of Lords came from the Commons kitchen .. **Page 2**

Censorship rating

A new censorship rating, '12', to fall between the present PG and 15 ratings, has been proposed to the film and video industry by the British Board of Film Classification .... **Page 2**

Deaths inquiry

Parents of four boys who fell 450ft to their deaths in Austria are pressing for disciplinary action against teachers, who they have been complacent' **Page 3**

Chalfont accused

Paddy Ashdown, the Democrats' leader, provoked uproar in the Commons by alleging that Lord Chalfont, the new deputy chairman of the IBA, was director of a private intelligence firm with "extremely grubby" connections ...... **Page 8**

Scandal deepens

The French insider-trading scandal took a new turn with

Thames TV documentary on Gibraltar shootings cleared of main criticisms

PM dismisses 'Death on the Rock' report

By Heather Mills and Colin Hughes

MARGARET THATCHER last night utterly rejected the findings of an independent report which exonerated Thames Television's *Death on the Rock* documentary about the shooting in Gibraltar of three IRA terrorists.

The report, published yesterday by Lord Windlesham, a former Conservative Home Office and Northern Ireland minister, and Richard Rampton QC, concluded the programme was not "trial by television" and had the "thoroughly researched" documentary prejudiced the inquest into the SAS killing of the three last March, or contaminated the evidence of the witnesses.

At the end of a three-and-a-half month inquiry, the programme was cleared of more than 20 criticisms and found at fault in only two main areas — in the handling of an unsigned statement of its most controversial witness and in the programme's commentary.

The report was welcomed by the Labour Party, broadcasters, the Independent Broadcasting Authority and Thames TV, which declared that "investigative journalism is alive and well in broadcasting". But no sooner was the much-leaked document released than Mrs Thatcher in effect repeated her statement, made at the time, that the documentary amounted to "trial by television".

The programme, broadcast despite government attempts to stop it and to the admitted fury of Mrs Thatcher, had strengthened her determination to shake up the ITV contractors and the IBA.

Last night, Downing Street issued a statement saying that the

JON JONES

Roger Bolton, the editor of *Death on the Rock*, prepares for an interview on yesterday's report.

The main findings

Among the criticisms of the report rejected were that *Death on the Rock*:
- set out with a preconceived theory;
- misused an interview with the wife of an IRA victim;
- was "trial by television";
- accused the soldiers involved in the shooting of murder;
- broke the IBA's impartiality guidelines;
- was unacceptable for transmission;
- tricked to trick, lead or bully witnesses;
- used a "flawed" witness in Carmen Proetta;
- tried to represent witness opinion as fact;
- was involved in improper behaviour or payment to witnesses;
- distorted or embellished witness evidence;
- failed to find other witnesses;
- gave a false impression of surveillance;
- put undue or indirect pressure on Kenneth Asquez;
- wrongly inferred that Josie Celicia had seen an SAS man pointing a pistol at one of the IRA squad on the ground;
- lacked scrupulousness;
- was in contempt of court;
- could have "coached" or rehearsed witnesses;
- sympathised with the IRA;
- was prejudicial or harmful to the administration of justice;
- and that its makers displayed bad faith or ulterior motives.

The report criticised the programme for:
- being, in a limited extent, "one-sided";
- not fully declaring circumstances surrounding Asquez's statement;
- misstating how many of its four main witnesses were in a position to hear a warning from the soldiers, or see if the IRA terrorists made suspicious movements.

shootings, is also considering the Attorney General's report.

publishing this material.

The inquiry was set up by Thames Television in the face of fierce criticism in the Commons and by sections of the media, after the inquest jury in Gibraltar had decided that the three terrorists, Sean Savage, Mairead Farrell and Daniel McCann, had been lawfully killed.

The documentary, shown four months before the inquest, was the first to cast doubts on the Government's account that the men, though described as unarmed, had made suspicious movements when challenged

shootings, is also considering superseding Andrew Neil, the editor of the *Sunday Times*.

Neil Kinnock, the Labour leader, said Lord Windlesham's report, coming from a former Tory minister, was the most telling indictment of the Prime Minister's attempts to suppress broadcasts she did not like.

The main government submission, released last night, was from Sir Patrick Wright, the Permanent Under-Secretary at the Foreign Office. He told the inquiry that four aspects of the programme were shown by its in-

---

Milne was a bit lazy and didn't read all his papers, thinking he could fly by the seat of his pants. He went on.

"The third thing a DG has to do is to fashion a relationship with the Board of Governors. The Chairman and the DG should be able to carry the Board between them. Whether anyone could have done this in the 1980s is questionable but Alasdair hardly tried to get on with the Governors.

"Fourthly, the DG must be on nodding terms with top people and opinion formers. Alasdair did not want to socialise. Above all a DG must be able to communicate a vision of what he wants the BBC to be and a clear strategy of how he intends to achieve that.

"In the end," said my informant, "Alasdair had lost the respect of every one of those key parts of a DG's relationship."

It is a sad indictment of a decent and honourable man who was fatally unqualified for the job he had wanted all of his life. It was a personal tragedy.

So many of Alasdair's instincts were correct in my view. He saw his responsibilities as being to the licence payer rather than the politicians and he believed in championing the ordinary person against the privileged. He wanted the BBC to reflect all shades of opinion and was very much a publisher. He had real courage in adversity and behind a rudeness which was probably a cover for shyness he was a kind and decent man. If only he had not been made Director General, or had not wanted the job so much.

What was the BBC for? That was the question that needed to be answered particularly in view of the assault that was being mounted on the Corporation. A number of us were concerned that while the BBC was transmitting *The Thorn Birds* ITV was putting out Granada's *Jewel in the Crown*.

In retrospect our concerns were exaggerated as no ITV company has made anything like the *Jewel* since, but the BBC-1 schedule had begun to look no different from ITV. Max Hastings had launched a diatribe against the BBC and its leadership in the *Evening Standard*. "Never has the leadership of the BBC seemed more pitifully inadequate, bankrupt of ideas, lost for a course . . . The BBC has become like a great fat man incapable of seeing over his own back to his toenails . . . Remorseless mediocrity usually prevails in the struggle for promotion."

He continued the argument at the Edinburgh International Television Festival.

"Even five years ago it would have been unthinkable that thoughtful, moderate people in the broadcasting industry should be asking questions about the very rationale of the Corporation's existence. The successes of ITV and Channel 4 make people ask why, if commercial broadcasting is performing so many of the traditional functions of the BBC so well, the British public should continue to be called upon for a licence fee. As technology expands, why should the BBC's appetite for an ever widening range of activities be indulged?"

One of the answers to Max Hastings' question is that ITV is only as it is because BBC-1 sets the benchmark for popular main channel broadcasting. ITV has to follow it up or down. Left to itself, with no BBC to compete with, and no public service requirement, ITV would head downhill fast.

Still Max's concerns hit a chord with many in the Corporation, not just with the Home Office minister who was looking after broadcasting, Douglas Hurd. He was not minded to give the BBC the licence fee increase it was looking for and in a lobby briefing made a few derogatory remarks about *The Thorn Birds*. Later it transpired that it was his wife rather than himself who had watched the programme.

I sat in the audience at Edinburgh with my old friend Peter Ibbotson, then Editor of *Panorama*. He had just lost two editions of *Panorama* which had been replaced by more popular programmes. He was concerned about that and about the general reduction of current affairs in prime time. The debate was an open one, and the BBC had sponsored the Festival, encouraging us to attend. Peter therefore stood up and courageously outlined his concerns about the present BBC-1 schedule. Alasdair Milne was sitting upstairs in the hall, fuming. Typically, he had not chosen to reply to Max himself and to lay down his manifesto. Instead he had dispatched the luckless Brian Wenham to defend the status quo. Brian was not too happy doing so and appeared rather gruff.

I should probably have shut up but I felt Peter deserved support and I was particularly concerned that the BBC reassert its public service values in view of what I regarded as the cynicism being exhibited by one or two of the leaders of ITV, notably John Birt. I had always greatly admired John for his work on *Weekend World*, but here he was commissioning comedy series like *The Bottle Boys*, a new low in situation comedy. He stood up in the body of the hall to explain his new philosophy. "Standards, quality, excellence – what these words mean is programmes that appeal to the middle class." It all seemed a long way from John's earlier philosophy, his "mission to explain".

Jim Moir, the BBC Head of Variety, gave his view of the way forward. "I do see the need for the BBC to become more popular. Yes, an increase in the number of game shows in the autumn."

I stood up to speak, oblivious to Alasdair Milne's eyes in my back. I posed the question as to whether the BBC knew what it meant by public service broadcasting in prime time? We all knew what it meant at off-peak times, and all four channels discharged their duties to minority audiences pretty well. But what about the majority audiences at peak times? Were we in the BBC chasing high audiences with whatever programmes would catch them or were we presenting matters which we considered important even if the audiences weren't so large? Obviously the answer was both but I felt the balance was tipping too far towards the former position – anything for high audiences. "We must put before large audiences programmes that they would not have thought of watching in order that their range of interests might be increased," I said. It was hardly original stuff.

Was I disloyal? To whom? I thought my loyalties were primarily to the television audience and the principles of public service broadcasting and only secondly to any particular institution. Milne did not agree and was almost speechless with anger at what he saw as gross disloyalty. At Edinburgh airport he ran into John Howard Davies, BBC TV's Head of Light Entertainment. John, true to his department, hazarded a joke. "I see Bolton was wearing a flak jacket," he said. Milne's reply was deadly serious, "That won't help him one little bit," he said.

When I returned to Manchester a letter was awaiting me from the Director General. It read,

Dear Roger,
    As you know, I was in Edinburgh yesterday to see how the

[153]

renewed attack on the BBC by Max Hastings was handled. I thought Brian (Wenham) coped very well with what has always been a sterile argument over the screening of *The Thorn Birds*.

I am all for senior programme people expressing their views as strongly as they feel the need within the organisation – and in public too, if they have considered the results. Your contribution was, in my opinion, wholly unhelpful to the BBC at a fairly critical time (you will have seen the hyped up result in this morning's *Telegraph*). If that is the best you can do to help the BBC at this particular time, kindly think again.

I am copying this to Bill (Cotton) and Brian since they too had to sit through your piece.

I felt some sympathy for Alasdair, despite the caning, but I could see we were heading for the rocks and wanted to help steer away from them. Besides there weren't internal forums for debate. When one tried to raise these issues at Programme Review one was quickly shut up. The BBC Management was not very good in coping with the independence of its journalists.

I remembered when I was on *Tonight* at the time of the great football "snatch" when Michael Grade, the Director of Programmes at London Weekend Television, signed an exclusive agreement with the Football League for coverage of soccer. The BBC, and Bill Cotton as Controller of BBC-1, were outraged. Cotton would have a *Match of the Day* with no matches. The story broke in the early evening and we hurriedly tried to put an item together for that night's programme. I dispatched Mike Dutfield to Television Centre to try and persuade Bill Cotton to appear on *Tonight*. Mike was kept waiting while behind locked doors lawyers argued what could be done to avert this seeming catastrophe. At last Mike was ushered into Bill's presence. Cotton explained that he would have liked to appear but the legal advice was that he should not. "However," he went on kindly, "thank you for trying to help us with this problem." A figure loomed languidly out of the darkness, it was Brian Wenham. "They don't want to help Bill, they just think it's a good story." Cotton looked blank.

A few years later when I was editing *Nationwide* we invited Bill

Cotton to be interviewed on the programme and he agreed. On the morning of the interview the BBC's Head of Press and Publicity asked for a list of questions on Bill's behalf. I explained, rather surprised that I needed to do so, that we didn't give a list of questions to anyone, least of all BBC Senior Managers about to be interviewed. The request was repeated during the day and refused once more. The actual interview was tough and thorough. It would be as Sue Lawley was conducting it. Afterwards Bill felt betrayed. "But you are on our side," he said, "do you think that helped the Corporation." I wondered where to start explaining. The BBC was committed to independent journalism, even about itself. Great in theory, very difficult in practice.

Colleagues who produced programmes like *Did You See?* ran into this problem all the time. Aggrieved heads of departments wanted to know how a BBC show could criticise BBC products, albeit one whose sole job was to review programmes. It was "kicking into our own goal".

All this betokened an unwillingness, perhaps an inability, to analyse what the Corporation should be doing and to be self-critical.

This was put much better than I could by Aubrey Singer, Managing Director of BBC Television at his leaving party in 1984. He had been stabbed in the front by the DG so that Bill Cotton, a close friend of Alasdair Milne's, could take his place. Aubrey's views, therefore, were hardly objective but I think they were certainly valid.

"Whilst there can be no doubt that BBC Television is a national asset," he said, "it is not the national asset that it used to be. Three-channel dominance has been exchanged for four-channel parity without the funding to give us primacy among equals that we once had . . ." He went on, "In the end, there has to be an end to expansion within the Organisation." Turning to the then Chairman, Stuart Young, he quoted J. K. Galbraith. "Ageing in an Organisation occurs when excellence is regarded as that which is already there."

There were troubles outside the Corporation as well as within. A hostile Government refused to increase substantially the licence fee and set up the Peacock Report to inquire into the funding of the

BBC. Unity of purpose was essential in order to meet these threats but the Board of Governors was moving to the right, was suspicious of the Management and not very impressed with its efficiency. The events that followed increased the differences between the two groups. Sod's Law had rarely been so actively in operation.

In March 1985 the BBC decided to settle a libel action which a Dr. Gee had brought over an edition of *That's Life*. The case had been in court for many weeks with Dr. Gee, himself, still giving evidence in the witness box. He had a panel of expert witnesses to follow, and the BBC had its own panel to follow them. As Alasdair Milne wrote in his book, *DG: Memoirs of a British Broadcaster*:

"The BBC's counsel came, surrounded by juniors, to tell me personally that the case could go on for months yet, with costs rising to astronomical figures. The Governors were horrified and clearly thought we had bungled." So the BBC settled and got the worst of both worlds, settling too late to stop the prosecution's case being heard, and too early to allow their own defence to be presented. The following year in 1986 the same thing happened with a *Panorama* programme called "Maggie's Militant Tendency". It was made with the assistance of various groups in the Conservative Party who were worried about some of the activities of some right wingers. The evidence was thought to be rock-solid but when the case came to trial some witnesses had faded away as is usual in these matters. The BBC again settled half way through the trial without the defence being heard. This left everyone in the BBC hurt and angry with each other. The lesson was clear: settle early and quietly or fight the case all the way through.

The effect of all this was to demoralise totally the Corporation's legal department, which from then on decided to play safe. For people like myself it was very frustrating. *Brass Tacks*, the television current affairs series in Manchester, was preparing a programme about an underworld figure called Roy Garner, who was also an informer for the Metropolitan Police. We were examining his activities and in particular his relationship with an Inspector called Tony Lundy. This was clearly a hot potato and representations were made to the BBC at the highest level by the Met. I shuffled between Broadcasting House and Television Centre trying to keep the project on the rails. No one wanted to touch it. Eventually the legal department agreed to see the programme and pronounced it untransmittable. "All right," I said, "what do we need to do to make it transmittable? What more research needs doing?"

"It is simply untransmittable, full stop," said the lawyer who refused to discuss it further. This was intolerable. I was quite prepared to alter and amend scripts or fund further shooting but I was not going to have a lawyer tell me I couldn't broadcast something which was clearly in the public interest. He wouldn't budge and the Senior Management used the brief legal opinion to halt the project. I cast around for some way out. I had a couple of journalists fretting at the leash and I didn't want the BBC to be accused of censorship again, or for there to be another front page row.

I decided to get a confidential opinion from a non-BBC barrister and when it arrived we sighed with relief. It did say further work had to be done but that with a few changes the programme certainly was defensible. I set the work in train and armed with the opinion went back and knocked on the door of the BBC's legal department. Although hurt by what I had done they agreed with the opinion and we moved forward to transmission. At which point I was obliged to leave Manchester, in circumstances which I shall explain later, and the programme never appeared – on the BBC. The producer, Vyv Simson, and reporter, Andrew Jennings, left the Corporation, considerably disillusioned, and moved over to Granada's *World In Action*. It later transmitted an improved version of the programme. I thought the BBC, under very heavy fire, had lost the will to publish.

And the fire was extraordinarily heavy and constant, exhausting and damaging. I hope some journalists when they read what they wrote in that period may feel a little ashamed. Is it too much to hope that Paul Johnson will wince when he reads the following? "The BBC not only lies, it lies for the Left. It not only rapes, it rapes for the Revolution." We had grown used to such absurdities as the claim that BBC executives are a "Production Politburo" and that the place "is full of left-wing producers." But the constant restatement of such views can make them generally accepted. Still one shouldn't get too carried away with this. It has happened before. Tony Benn, the former Labour minister, in a section of his diaries headlined "At war with the right-wing BBC", described how "I shamed Hugh Greene with some of my thinking on local broadcasting and my desire to ease the BBC monopoly. I feel no sense of loyalty to him since the BBC is wildly right-wing." Hugh Greene was the notably liberal DG responsible for *That Was the Week That Was*.

At least the BBC had been spared an Irish row. Ireland can usually be depended on to produce something which will greatly disconcert the British but, looking back, the early eighties had been relatively free of major rows.

Broadcasters had somehow negotiated the Hunger Strikes of 1981 in which ten Provisional IRA and INLA prisoners starved themselves to death, but they then had plenty to report on their own doorstep.

On 20 July 1982 the Provisionals bombed the Household Cavalry while they were riding through Hyde Park, and then blew up the Royal Green Jackets Band, in Regent's Park. Eleven died.

On 6 December the INLA, not to be outdone, put a bomb in the "Droppin' Well" pub in Northern Ireland, killing twelve soldiers and five civilians.

The bombers then returned to the mainland a year later and, on 17 December 1983, the Provisionals exploded a car bomb outside the Harrods store, killing eight and injuring eighty.

In this atmosphere no one seems to have proposed interviewing members of terrorist organisations, let alone been turned down. However, support for Provisional Sinn Fein had been growing as it implemented the second part of its strategy of an "Armalite in one hand and ballot box in the other". On 9 June 1983 Gerry Adams, the organisation's President, had been elected to Westminster as MP for West Belfast in the General Election. He didn't take his seat. Two years later Sinn Fein was to take fifty-nine out of five hundred and sixty-six seats in the Northern Ireland local government elections.

The mainland bombings culminated in a strike at the heart of British Government. In the early hours of 12 October 1984, the Provos blew up the Grand Hotel in Brighton where Mrs. Thatcher was staying during the Conservative Party Conference. Five were killed, including the wife of John Wakeham, the Chief Whip. The Prime Minister herself had a miraculous escape as the ceiling fell in on her. Few will forget her courage or coolness in the minutes and hours that followed, nor the bravery of Norman Tebbit as he was slowly pulled out of the rubble. His wife was less fortunate, she was crippled for life, and five years later is still in a wheelchair.

This appalling atrocity must have reinforced Mrs. Thatcher's hatred of terrorism and blank incomprehension of the broadcasters' philosophy. She had lost her closest political friend, Airey Neave, five years before. Now other friends had gone and the terrorists had missed killing her and her husband by a hair's breadth. She and her children faced being guarded for the rest of their lives and she had to attend even public occasions in the knowledge that she was the terrorists' number one target.

Most of the BBC Governors, drawn as they were not from broadcasting but from the Civil Service and the Establishment, agreed with her rather than the broadcasters. The scene was set for the *Real Lives* disaster.

11

REAL LIVES

I stood at the window of my office in Manchester looking out at the grey factories and warehouses sheathed in rain. Tears were forming in my eyes and I wondered if anyone outside the Corporation would understand why. I was surprised at myself. Yet the more I thought about the telex on my desk the more angry and upset I became. I thought the BBC had just lost something very very precious which it might never recover – its reputation, almost alone of national broadcasters, for being independent of the Government.

The telex contained copies of two letters, and read as follows:

FROM THE HOME SECRETARY TO THE CHAIRMAN OF THE BBC: JULY 29, 1985

Dear Stuart,

I was very glad to learn that you and your colleagues are considering whether or not to proceed with the broadcast of the proposed 'Real Lives' programme involving Martin McGuinness and Gregory Campbell. This letter confirms the views which I asked Wilfred Hyde to convey on my behalf to the Corporation this morning.

May I first make it quite clear that I unhesitatingly accept that the decision to broadcast or refrain from broadcasting this programme must rest exclusively with the Corporation. It is no part of my task as the Minister with responsibility for broadcasting policy generally to attempt to impose an act of censorship on what should be broadcast in particular programmes. To do so would rightly be inconsistent with the constitutional independence of the BBC, which is a crucial part of our broadcasting arrangements.

I do, on the other hand, also have a ministerial responsibility for the fight against the ever present threat of terrorism, and I would be failing in my duty if I did not let you and your colleagues have my considered views on the impact of this programme in that context.

It is clear that the 'Real Lives' programme and the *Radio Times* article associated with it will enable McGuinness to advocate or justify the use of violence for political ends, and thus the murder and maiming of innocent people, before a huge public audience. He will, moreover, be doing so not in the course of theoretical debate about terrorism, but as a prominent apologist of an organisation that is proud to have carried out such murders and such maimings and expresses its readiness and intention to carry out more. The BBC would be giving an immensely valuable platform to those who have evinced an ability, readiness and intention to murder indiscriminately its own viewers.

Quite apart from the deep offence that this would give to the overwhelming majority of the population and the profound distress that it would cause to families of the victims of terrorism, it would also in my considered judgement materially assist the terrorist cause. Recent events elsewhere in the world have confirmed only too clearly what has long been understood in this country. That terrorism thrives on the oxygen of publicity. That publicity derives either from the successful carrying out of terrorist acts or, as a second best, from the intimidation of the innocent public and the bolstering of faltering supporters by the well publicised espousal of violence as a justifiable means of securing political ends.

What is at issue is not the overall balance of the programme, or whether its impact on reasonable people is to make such people more hostile to terrorism than they are already. Even if the programme and any surrounding material

[161]

were, as a whole, to present terrorist organisations in a wholly unfavourable light, I would still ask you not to permit it to be broadcast. For the gain that the terrorists would secure by the broadcast would not be the conversion of large numbers of people to their cause, but the opportunity to boost the morale of their supporters and to alarm the innocent majority who have every reason to fear their intentions.

It must be damaging to security and therefore wholly contrary to the public interest to provide a boost to the morale of the terrorists and their apologists in this way. I cannot believe that the BBC would wish to give succour to terrorist organisations: and it is for this reason that I hope that you and your colleagues will agree on reflection that the 'Real Lives' programme should not be broadcast.

THE HOME SECRETARY

FROM THE CHAIRMAN OF THE BBC TO THE HOME SECRETARY

Dear Leon,

In the light of your letter of 29th July, in which you outlined your reservations concerning the BBC programme 'Real Lives: At the Edge of the Union', the Board of Governors met today in special session.

Because of the circumstances arising from your letter, the Governors – quite exceptionally – decided to view the programme before transmission.

We would now wish to discuss with you the profound issues raised in your letter to me. We are anxious that those discussions be conducted in a neutral and dispassionate climate.

Having seen the programme, the Board of Governors believes it would be unwise for this programme in the series 'Real Lives' to be transmitted in its present form: the programme's intention would continue to be misread and misinterpreted.

I look forward to hearing from you.

THE CHAIRMAN OF THE BBC

This was a disaster of the most gigantic proportions and as soon as the letters became public the BBC virtually stopped dead. Had the Governors any idea of the gravity of the situation they had just created? My heart went out to all those in Bush House, the home of the BBC's Overseas Services. All those years of establishing the BBC's reputation for independence wiped away in an afternoon. How had this happened?

Creating a Scoop

It was the "silly season" in Fleet Street. *Sunday Times* journalist Barry Penrose needed a front page story for that week's edition.

He says that "contacts" rang him up about a programme to be shown in the BBC-1 *Real Lives* series of documentaries, two weeks hence. As a result he picked up a copy of the *Radio Times* and read there an extensive feature about the two contrasted figures in the programme, Martin McGuinness and Gregory Campbell: both elected representatives; the former allegedly a past and possibly present member of the IRA committed to the use of the Armalite rifle as well as the ballot box; the latter a hard-line Unionist who advocates the killing of IRA members.

Where was the "story"? McGuinness himself, and his party, had frequently appeared on network television programmes and even more frequently in programmes in Ulster.

At that time the Government had not chosen to ban the party, nor to ban broadcasts which included Sinn Fein representatives (although this was the policy of the Dublin Government).

Penrose, like Leon Brittan, had not seen the programme but those television previewers who had would have told him that it was a low-key, sad and depressing film which revealed the irreconcilability of the two extremes in the North.

It contained no "secret" interviews with hooded men, no secret filming with terrorists. The Security Forces in Ulster were well-informed and had cooperated in the filming.

The one thing going for the story was a general concern, voiced by President Reagan in the wake of the hijack of the airline hostages in Lebanon, that the American media had been manipulated by the hijackers. The US networks, extraordinarily competitive in their news programmes, had been involved in unedifying scrambles at press conferences and had carried extensive interviews with hostages, their families and hijackers. The great media manipulator, Ronald Reagan, found himself being out-manipulated. In a speech to the American Bar Association, Mrs. Thatcher had been quick to join in the complaints that extensive television coverage gave terrorists "The oxygen of publicity".

Penrose checked the *Real Lives* story out and then sought official reaction to the proposed film. He sent hand-delivered letters to the Home Secretary, Leon Brittan, and Bernard Ingham, the Prime Minister's Press Secretary, inviting their comments. He also spoke to the Northern Ireland Secretary, Douglas Hurd, who said he was "alarmed" to hear of the interview.

We were still a long way from a *Sunday Times* scoop. So Penrose began to act as the catalyst, if not the creator of the story.

He got Mark Hosenball, a *Sunday Times* journalist based in the United States, to ask Mrs. Thatcher a hypothetical question about what her reaction would be to a British television company which made a film which featured the alleged Chief of Staff of the IRA. The Prime Minister, caught off guard, gave a typically robust reply. She would "condemn them utterly". She still did not know about the BBC film, and the day before the paper appeared a Downing Street spokesman phoned the paper to stress that Mrs. Thatcher had been speaking hypothetically, not about a particular intended programme. That did not prevent the *Sunday Times* printing a story with the headline: "Thatcher Slams IRA Film".

Then a catastrophic number of balls started rolling quickly downhill.

The Home Secretary, reacting in what some saw as an immature and knee-jerk manner, wrote that letter to the Chairman of the Governors asking him to stop the programme going out and including the following incredible statement: "Even if the programme and any surrounding material were to present terrorist organisations in a wholly unfavourable light, I would still ask you not to permit it to be broadcast."

If any coverage was wrong, why hadn't the Government passed

[164]

the appropriate legislation, banning either Sinn Fein or the broad-casting of interviews with its members? (Eventually in 1988, they were to follow that logic and introduce a partial ban on such interviews.)

Still Mr. Brittan was only playing the politician's game. The BBC's Board of Governors should and could have politely replied that if the Home Secretary wished to he could exercise his legal right and ban the programme, but since the BBC Management, having seen the film, regarded it as suitable for transmission, the programme would go ahead.

The Governors would then review the programme after trans-mission and decide whether the Management's decision was right. If not they would take appropriate measures.

Alas the Governors did not do this. They insisted on seeing the programme themselves before transmission, thus effectively pass-ing a vote of no confidence in the Board of Management and taking direct editorial control themselves. Worse still they then voted 10:1 not to show it. Alasdair Milne was away on holiday in Finland when the Governors and the Board of Management met. His deputy Mike Checkland was standing in for him for the first time and may not have seen the Rubicon he was crossing by not making it clear to the Governors that the Management would be in an impossible position if their decision was countermanded. Some thought he should have threatened to resign and the rest of the Senior Management with him. It didn't happen and the Governors, deeply unhappy with the way the BBC was being managed, watched the film in a fevered atmosphere. There was a break for refreshments and the Governors huddled together in one corner, the Management in another.

Stuart Young, the Chairman, had no journalistic or real political experience himself and tended to defer to his Vice-Chairman, the former Editor of *The Times*. Rees-Mogg was a life-long Tory and Thatcher sympathiser. In fact he was a polemicist rather than a journalist and preferred writing leader columns to anything else. He was not known for his on-the-ground experience in Ulster.

On the resumption of the meeting, Young turned to him first. Rees-Mogg condemned the programme utterly. The men involved were presented as ordinary people and weren't challenged about their involvement in terrorism. Another Governor, Daphne Park,

[165]

called it a "Hitler liked dogs" programme. Stuart Young claimed "It made them out to be nice guys, bouncing babies on their knees. It is a lousy programme." Lord Harewood said, "I hate it, I hate it."

When I finally saw the programme I was baffled by their reaction. Yes it was low-key but it brilliantly illustrated how much these two men had in common and yet how far apart they were across the apparently unbridgeable sectarian divide. And if it was their ordinariness the Governors were worried about, well they lived ordinary lives for most of the time. This was one of the remarkable things about the whole tragedy of Ulster. In any case we couldn't challenge these people as being terrorists since they had not been charged with any offence and were legitimately elected representatives of their people.

I thought it a good if quiet and uncontroversial account of the extremes of Northern Ireland. In other circumstances I cannot believe that the Governors would have banned it. However, the incident gave them the opportunity to show they were in control. Unfortunately, nearly everyone else thought it showed that the Government was in control.

Radio Moscow and Libyan Radio had a field day saying that the BBC's much vaunted independence had been shown to be a sham. Most of the newspapers, including the *Sunday Times*, criticised the Governors' decision. The Board of Management, and the Director General in particular, were left high and dry. The confidence of the staff in the Management and particularly in the Governors was severely dented.

The opponents of public service broadcasting had a field day and many of the staff went on strike.

Three issues were raised which would not go away: first, who ran the BBC? second, were the principles of its journalism to be altered? and third, were the Governors representative of society and were they capable of defending Public Service Broadcasting against party politics, and a frequently hysterical press?

Two reassuring things did happen, however. First, a great many staff were prepared to lose a day's pay by striking, not over wages or conditions, but over the issue of the principle of the independence of the BBC's journalism; second, the Director General immediately authorised a *Panorama* programme about Sinn Fein and the Anglo-Irish Summit for the October of 1985, a programme which would include interviews with Sinn Fein leaders.

I wondered what I could do to help my colleagues in London. After the banning of *Real Lives* I had sent out a notice to all my staff in Manchester expressing support for the Management against the Governors and I passed on to London various petitions which were sent to me. But as the strike got under way I was worried about the absence of any apparent initiative by the Director General. The impasse had to be broken, the programme had to go out. Everything was grinding to a halt.

One day after Programme Review, I persuaded the Controllers of BBC-1 and BBC-2, Michael Grade and Graeme Macdonald, and some Heads of Department, to come with me to meet Alasdair Milne to tell him how serious we felt the situation was and ask what we could do to help. I had in mind the fact that some of us had close contacts with regional Governors, others with people like the former Chairman, Lord Swann. How should we use them, what should be the plan of campaign? There didn't appear to be one. Alasdair said he would make sure the programme went out but we would have to leave it to him. He had thought of resigning but decided that he should see it through. I was impressed by his calm, his dignity and his courage, and I could sympathise with his irritation with me. But there was no strategy, no tactics. I felt both affection and frustration.

At the Edinburgh Television Festival which followed a few days later, there was talk of little else but the banned programme and in the debate about *Real Lives* I said that all Senior Managers, myself included, should resign if it became clear that the film was not to be transmitted in the near future. Was I carried away by the drama and my own part in it? I had thought about what I should say very carefully but I thought it essential that the pressure should be maintained. I was aware it was risky but I thought too much was at stake to fool around. Others, like the *Newsnight* presenter, John Tusa, had gone on strike. The least I could do was add my voice.

Within a few weeks Alasdair managed, with great courage, to get the film transmitted. As usual on these occasions, most viewers wondered what all the fuss was about but some of the Governors never forgave Alasdair, and his fate was sealed.

Alan Protheroe, the Assistant Director General, as usual wrote one of the truest and most witty lines about the whole affair in the *Listener*.

"When the Home Secretary thanked the BBC Governors for banning 'Real Lives: At the Edge of the Union', it resembled nothing more than the White Star line congratulating the iceberg on sinking the Titanic."

Some time after the programme was transmitted a retired Governor was commissioned to review the situation and prepare a report for the two Boards of Management and Governors. He talked in confidence to all the members of both Boards.

He wrote that:

There is a widespread feeling among the Governors that the obligations and responsibilities of their office are viewed less seriously by Senior Management, sometimes to the point of implicit disregard or contempt, than either the Charter or their own understanding of their charge demand . . . The Governors feel themselves often to be inadequately informed and insufficiently forewarned. Too often the first knowledge they have of some development affecting the public position of the BBC is when they read about it in the press . . . They are uncertain how far or how faithfully opinions expressed by the Board are transmitted onward within the BBC. The Governors find it difficult to believe that a crisper administrative style could not be developed which would put paid to charges of slack management.

For their part, the Board of Management are deeply unhappy about the adversarial relationship which seems to have developed between the two Boards. The Governors seem to them chiefly interested in criticism, and they mourn what seems to them the loss of a sense of partnership in a great enterprise, with the friendliness and mutual respect it engendered . . . The Board seems to them to be dismissive of their professional knowledge and experience and mistrustful of their capacity . . . Board proceedings seem to them to be permeated with suspicion.

To his credit Alasdair Milne prints this in his autobiography, *DG: Memoirs of a British Broadcaster*. He then goes on: "His [the ex-

Governor's] description of the Management view was all too painfully accurate; I was, I confess, shocked at the depth of the Governors' antagonism and for that I must take the heavy share of blame."

In fact the relationship was beyond repair. The Governors are the BBC, as they claim, but they cannot run it and are not qualified to do so. The tragedy was that, at that most difficult time for the Corporation, faced as it was by a hostile Government, a hostile Conservative Party, and largely hostile national press, it had neither a strong Chairman nor a strong Director General to guide it through. The storm was not of the BBC's making but the ship's crew were too busy arguing with each other to notice that they were steering further and further into it.

That horrible period was not yet over. The MI5 vetting episode, which followed shortly afterwards, was a cruel kick in the face when the victim was already on the floor.

Since about 1937, the BBC, which was, and in some ways still is, closely modelled on the Civil Service, had a relationship with MI5, mainly to safeguard the system of communications in the event of war. The involvement had clearly grown and quite a large number of staff knew that there was some sort of vetting somewhere.

Programme makers rarely came across it, when they did they generally found it rather absurd, irrelevant and ineffective. I came across it twice in eighteen years in the Corporation. The first time was when I wished to give a year's contract to someone who had been on a temporary short-term one on *Nationwide*. "No," said the administration. "Why?" – "I can't tell you." "Why can't you tell me?" – "Because I can't tell you," and so on, and so on. I thought this was plain daft. I would be supervising the person's work, what damage could the person do? Distort a report on skateboarding ducks? I assume the problem was that the "security risk" had belonged to a communist group at University. That didn't seem to be a barrier to another former member, Denis Healey, becoming Defence Secretary, Chancellor of the Exchequer, and a Privy Councillor, so why not a film director for *Nationwide*? I refused to accept the ruling and eventually the person was offered a one-year contract. Maddeningly the person then decided to go elsewhere. I could have kicked him. All that trouble for nothing!

The second occasion was more serious. I was interviewing for a senior editorial post in Manchester. I had signed the Official Secrets Act since I was responsible, in my job as Head of Network Production Centre, for the communications in the area during a time of national emergency, something I took seriously. Because of my security clearance I was sent a folder marked "Secret" containing details of one of the candidates. That person's main mistake seemed to have been being in possession of the Communist Party's daily paper, and to have socialised with Party members. The accompanying comments by some MI5 person would have been laughable if they hadn't revealed a disturbing ignorance of how journalism and programme-making worked. I wrote to the BBC's Director of Personnel complaining about the file, which could well have done the person concerned great damage without him being aware of it. The Director of Personnel, Christopher Martin, wrote back telling me I was naive.

Feeling a little stung by this I returned to the attack.

As I have often been accused of being a cynical journalist, it makes a change to be charged with naivety.

It is the usual charge made when one questions security arrangements. My memo to you was meant to question:

a) the efficiency of the operation;
b) suggest that a more selective approach would be sensible;
c) raise questions about the criteria being used.

To restate, I do not question whatsoever the need for proper clearance . . . where people have access to information which could be helpful to an enemy.

[But] I question whether the selection, background and training of security personnel enables them to interpret concepts like "subversion" or "bias" in a way which is universally accepted. One man's subversion is another's radicalism. If the approach is now more "relaxed" I assume that the previous method of operation was wrong. Many of my "naive" colleagues still think it is.

He did not bother to reply, perhaps he thought it was pointless. I wrote this in 1984 and then thought little more about it until a few days after the *Real Lives* explosion a year later when two enterprising *Observer* journalists, David Leigh and Paul Lashmar, investigated the issue.

They found some disturbing cases where individual careers had been blocked on security grounds without those concerned knowing anything about it and on the basis of mistaken identity or inaccurate information. Moreover, they named the BBC security man doing the vetting, Brigadier (retired) Ronnie Stonham, and the number of his office in Broadcasting House. He it was who stuck the fabled "Christmas trees" on personnel files to alert personnel officers.

What with *Real Lives* and this, the BBC's much vaunted independence was badly bruised.

However, *Real Lives* eventually went out with nothing cut out, but one or two things added, as agreed by the producer, Paul Hamann. As regards the vetting, I wrote at the time:

> Three things are required: first the reduction of those jobs requiring vetting to a handful, primarily concerned with engineering responsibilities in the event of war; second, the public identification of those jobs which require vetting so that candidates would know they were to be vetted; third, a system of appeal which would allow candidates to discover what was alleged against them and give them the opportunity to challenge what could well be erroneous material.

The BBC announced it was reducing the numbers to be vetted to a bare minimum.

I spent much of the autumn and winter of 1985 debating the reorganisation of the BBC English Regions. Together with many others I argued that we should have Controllers of English regions similar to the Controllers of Scotland, Wales and Northern Ireland, and that one person should be in charge of all the broadcasting: network, regional and local, in radio and television. That way sensible economies could be made and greater cooperation between the different elements could be developed.

Eventually that was agreed, although the new Controllers were to be called "Heads of Broadcasting", for some reason unclear to me. However, I argued that one North should be created from the three areas of the North West, North and North East with the Network Production Centre at its hub. Instead, the Corporation decided to have two areas, divided by the Pennines and to transfer responsibility for my home county of Cumbria to BBC North West in Manchester.

I knew that would cause trouble as Carlisle people in particular felt little affinity with Lancashire. To be honest they didn't feel that much affinity with Tyneside but at least BBC North East had the wonderful Mike Neville presenting its local news and current affairs. I also doubted whether the new region created out of Newcastle and Leeds could work. Both Centres were about the same size, neither would concede primacy to the other, and I doubted that any significant network opportunities would be given to the new North/North East region by London. It would remain a minnow. I think I have been proved largely correct.

Nevertheless, I wanted to be the HOB for the North West as it would be ninety per cent of my old job, with the additional responsibility for my home county. I looked forward to improving the coverage it received, and of continuing to visit my parents regularly. Now I would be able to do so on business.

Perhaps I should have smelt a rat, particularly when together with the other two Heads of Network Production Centres I was summoned to London and told that, as the new jobs were being created out of our present jobs, we would be technically redundant. The implication was that it was all a formality, but we did smile a little nervously at each other.

Readers of this account may think I was a bit bonkers to think I would be, in effect, re-elected, but I thought the Corporation was big enough to take what I thought was the constructive criticism I had put forward, and that anyway the main criteria would be how successfully I had run the Centre's programming. After all the BBC was a broadcaster. I thought I'd done well, certainly the atmosphere had improved remarkably and we'd been successful at the various "offers" meetings. *Brass Tacks* in particular had been getting good reviews. I also thought that I would have been tipped off not to apply if I had been fingered with the "black spot".

There was another straw in the wind. I walked into the Manchester canteen one evening to discover my former Lime Grove colleague, Hugh Williams, sitting there. When I asked what he was doing up here he told me that he was applying for the HOB job and had come to do a recce. I thought it rather strange that he should come up without tipping me off. He had every right to apply for the job, and to come and look around the region, but not to tip me off in advance? Had he been tipped off? Afterwards Hugh told me this had not happened. He had simply wanted the job and thought I might not get it.

Then on the day of the Board itself I was given a list of other applicants. It included Russell Harty. Manchester was his main television base and I had just successfully fixed a new series for him on BBC-2. We had lunched together the previous week and he hadn't mentioned anything about having a crack at "my" job. As I left the interview he was next in. I walked back through the waiting room so he would be bound to see me. He looked rather sheepish but we both grinned. Perhaps I was being childish.

My interview was to take place in the boardroom at Broadcasting House. I reported to Room 518 at 10.25 a.m. on Friday, 4 April and was handed a piece of paper telling me the members of the sub-committee of the Board of Governors who would interview me. It consisted of Lady Parkes, 60, educationist; Chairman of the College Advisory Committee, Malcolm McAlpine, 69, an executive of the building and property company that bears his family name; Bill Cotton; Dick Francis; the Director of Public Affairs, Geraint Stanley Jones, and the Director of Personnel, Christopher Martin, in the Chair.

The interview appeared to go all right, although the Board seemed strangely uninterested and appeared to know little of what I'd done in Manchester. I outlined my proposals for the future and emphasised the need for sustaining vigorous journalism outside London.

After it was over I was told to expect the answer within a few days. I returned to Manchester.

On the following Monday morning I got into the office early before my secretary and was sorting out some papers before the

weekly coffee morning I held for all managers and senior producers, to pass on information and to communicate our plans.

The phone rang – a bit early for callers I thought. It was Geraint.
He came straight to the point. "I'm afraid you haven't got the job.
I'm very sorry." I was shocked. In retrospect I am surprised I was
so shocked but I somehow never thought it would come to an end.
I had so much I wanted to do in the North West.

"What has happened to the other two outgoing HNPCs?" "Oh,
they were appointed to be HOBs." So it was just me who had been
rejected. "Who has got the North West?" "Hugh Williams."

At that moment people began arriving for the coffee morning. I
tended to operate an open-door policy and they walked cheerily
into my office. I said I would ring Geraint back later. I didn't feel I
could tell all the managers and producers there and then. I needed
to get my thoughts together and to tell my Senior Managers first, so
I lied when someone jovially asked me, nudge nudge, if I'd heard
anything yet. I chatted with them all for half an hour outlining the
new programmes we would be doing, then closed the meeting and
asked my Senior Managers to stay behind.

I think they were genuinely surprised and saddened. As I told
them what had happened I felt the power of the job go out of me.
They now had a new boss. Within minutes the BBC Press and
Publicity Office was on the phone. The announcement was to be
made shortly and they wanted to get Hugh up immediately to meet
the local Press. It seemed remarkably, not to say indecently, hasty,
but they were determined. I tried not to lapse into a daze but
arranged to leave for London immediately. It would be better if I
was out of the way. In any case I needed to find out if I had any
future left in the Corporation and what had gone wrong.

Over the next few hours I arranged to host a couple of dinners to
introduce Hugh to his management team, "his" now. Then I set
out on the train for London. We must have passed each other at
Crewe.

Next morning I went to see the Director of Personnel, Christopher Martin. What had I done wrong? He seemed most imprecise.
"It was just sort of a feeling." Getting nowhere I went on to Geraint
Stanley Jones, my immediate boss as Director of Public Affairs. He
was genuinely sympathetic but told me "There was a feeling that

you hadn't made the transition from programme-maker to Senior Manager."

A few years later Alasdair Milne told me that I had "whinged too much at Edinburgh and such like places."

I moved on to Television Centre to see the Managing Director of Television, Bill Cotton. Maybe I was an embarrassment to them all but I was trying to maintain the stiff upper lip and be a very proper Englishman. It wouldn't have done to complain but I wanted to get at the reasons.

I was shown into Bill's office on the sixth floor. He seemed quite brusque. What I meant to ask him was whether there was likely to be anything suitable for me in the Television service. After all I'd edited three of the major BBC-1 programmes; I must have something to offer, didn't I? In the end I thought it too undignified. So I said to Cotton, "What would you do if you were in my position, Bill?" I hoped he would say something like "Well, take some leave. You are a talented programme-maker. We'd like you here though it may take a little time for the right job to come up."

Instead he was much briefer, "I'd leave," he said. So I did.

Dick Francis was also to leave a few weeks later, after a disagreement over the future of local radio (he bought me a fine meal before I went), but he fell on his feet by becoming Director General of the British Council and being given the Knighthood that went with it, an honour denied Alasdair Milne.

Alasdair battled on through the Peacock Report, Duncan Campbell's "Secret Society" series and Norman Tebbit's Libyan assault, but when Stuart Young tragically died and Duke Hussey was appointed in his place it was clear that Alasdair's days were numbered.

Just before Christmas 1986, Milne and his adjutant Alan Protheroe were having a drink in the DG's office. Alasdair was looking out of the window moodily. "You know, DG," said Protheroe, "neither of us could be here by Easter." Milne turned and shrugged his shoulders.

On Thursday, 29 January, 1987, the Director General was walking down the sixth floor corridor to lunch, following a Board meeting, when Patricia Hodgson, the Secretary of the BBC, asked him if he would go and see the Chairman.

Alasdair wrote later, "I thought it odd that she addressed me by my Christian name, everybody else did, but for some reason she had never done so before." In fact she had known for some days what was about to happen but as she had to serve both the Governors and the Management she had not warned the DG. She needed to have ice in her veins.

According to Alasdair, Duke Hussey's lip trembled as he said, "I am afraid this is going to be a very unpleasant interview. We want you to leave immediately. It's a unanimous decision of the Board."

In his memoirs Milne describes his feelings. "I was stunned. What was he talking about? Perhaps I should have seen the plot thickening but I hadn't." Most other people had. I know how he felt.

Five minutes later he had left his office forever. When he reached home there was no one there. His wife was out. Within the hour the hordes of the press and TV cameras were at the front door. Alan Protheroe, ever loyal, was the first to go and see his former boss. He pushed his way through the crowd and was ushered into the hall. As Alasdair shut the door he turned to Protheroe. "I thought you said Easter?"

12

"SWEET THAMES! RUN SOFTLY, TILL I END MY SONG"

I had no reason to get up in the morning. In the midst of the pressures of running the Network Production Centre the promise of a whole delicious morning in bed, with a novel to read, and toast and marmalade to savour, would be intoxicating. Now I could spend every morning that way and I hated it. I had written to various people asking if they were interested in what I had to offer, but I began to wonder what I had got to offer. I quickly understood how the unemployed got depressed and lost confidence.

Lunch was no problem. Friends would entertain me and generously offer advice. A number of people enquired whether I would like to join them in independent production, and I looked round some production houses but I wasn't sure that I wanted to be an entrepreneur just yet. I had been spoilt in the BBC, usually dealing with ideas rather than cash flow. But I had to have a reason for getting up, so I decided to trace my family history. Ours was hardly a distinguished family and there was no lost fortune to discover but I realised how little I knew about my grandparents and their ancestors. I began to haunt the Public Records Office and the Census Office in Holborn, London, and was soon off on a chase which took me past nineteenth-century workhouses, illiterate Irish peasants and ended one glorious early summer day in Uley in Gloucestershire. It was a journey through English social history and if I had any doubts about the remarkable improvements in general living standards in recent years I soon lost them.

Then I had a call from David Elstein who had just been appointed Director of Programmes at Thames. He was determined to bring back the old programme he had edited, *This Week*, together with its stirring music. It would replace *TV Eye* and he wanted someone fresh to become the Editor in place of my old boss, Mike Townson, who had done a remarkable eight year stint. David asked me to lunch in a restaurant in Camden whose walls were completely covered by all sorts and shapes of mirrors. Wherever I looked I seemed to see myself. It was immensely distracting. David is a passionate bridge and chess player and it shows. He had clearly cultivated the technique of remaining largely silent so that other people tend to babble on and reveal more than they intend to do. I held back.

"What do you think of *TV Eye*?" To be honest I hadn't watched that much but I sketched out my thoughts. Mike Townson was always more attracted to the emotional human interest story, I leaned towards the important but less easily accessible. Actually one needed both.

"I've signed up Jonathan Dimbleby," said David. That was good news. Jonathan was an intelligent, immensely energetic journalist, who never stopped thinking about issues, and worrying away at them. We chatted more freely and I thought the lunch was going well but it petered out. David's formidable intelligence does not encourage light-hearted chatter and I'm no expert at it either. He didn't offer me the job immediately but a few days later did so.

I wondered whether I should take it. I'd gathered a decent reputation as an Editor, why risk it all again? And after doing such a big job in Manchester, being responsible for over a thousand people, I would now be in charge of thirty, and have to report not to Elstein but to the Controller of News and Current Affairs, Barrie Sales. My ego had grown a bit. And yet, and yet. It was a chance to get back into programming. A General Election was in the offing and there were forty-one slots a year waiting to be filled with ideas and arguments and good journalism.

When the news of my appointment came out there was a reasonable amount of press attention, some flattering, but one critic accused me of believing I had a licence to bore. "What's the point of *This Week* if it tries to be light-hearted?" I replied a bit pompously. "It is there to address the nation on important matters." The *UK Press Gazette* quoted an admirer of mine saying wryly, "You could take Roger to one of the great, jet-setting places of the world. And as you sat and sipped your cocktail overlooking a sparkling sea, a beautiful girl might walk by. At this point he would lean forward and say earnestly, 'I'm extremely worried about the Government's attitude to CND.'"

Well, I thought I had a sense of humour anyway, and I promised the programme team some fun and a little controversy. What we got was a tragedy.

Alan Stewart was indeed one of the best and the bravest of Current Affairs producers, and the film he was shooting for me with reporter Peter Gill dealt with a subject he felt very strongly about. "Where Hunger is a Weapon" was concerned with the famine and civil war in the Sudan, matters which Alan was determined to bring to the television audience's attention.

He was full of energy and enthusiasm about it, but then so he was about almost all of the projects he was involved in. Alan was rarely quiet, never still. He would allow twelve hours to elapse between projects but not much more, and when he wasn't working he would be charging around a sports field, thundering into tackles, never losing his temper but always wanting to win. He was particularly passionate about soccer and he introduced me to five-a-side football. When he kicked the ball it either ended up breaking the back of the net or in the next borough.

Alan was the sort of person who, seventy years ago, you would have found on an expedition to the South Pole, or who a hundred years ago would have been on an expedition into the dark continent. He was only thirty-five and had spent all his television career with Thames Television, becoming the first *TV Eye/This Week* researcher to be made straight up to producer on the programme. When I arrived as the new Editor, never having worked in ITV before, he took it upon himself to teach me all I needed to know about how things worked and about the history of the company. He also told me how to run the programme, before smiling sheepishly.

He was frequently carried away by his enthusiasm but he could always laugh at himself. He gave me and previous Editors total loyalty and absolute commitment, he knew no other way. He seemed so much more alive than anyone else and was known as the Boy Wonder.

When the news came it was in another early morning call. The phone rang and rang until I dragged myself out of bed into the sitting room and sat on the edge of the couch. It was 6.50 a.m. on Friday, 24 October 1986, and it was still dark. The voice on the other end was faint, but eventually I made out the voice of Eric Gassen of the Red Cross in Geneva. He was the contact point for the *This Week* team filming in the Sudan.

He spoke slowly. "At 7.40 a.m. local time this morning (4.40 a.m. our time) the following message came in via the Red Cross at Lo Kichokio on the Kenyan/Sudanese border. It was from Peter Gill (the Thames reporter)." I started writing on a small pad next to the phone.

"On Thursday at 16.30 the crew vehicle destroyed by a land mine in South Sudan, while returning from Gerang interview. Regret to inform you that Alan Stewart killed." Alan killed? Killed? I asked Eric Gassen to repeat it. "Killed." He went on with Peter Gill's message.

Ian Killian (the cameraman) bruised and shaken but will be fine. John Heasman (the sound recordist) and self are fine. As also *Observer* reporter Shiya Batia and photographer Roger Hutchings. Helen Fielding (the researcher) stayed in Kenya. Please inform next of kin accordingly.

Hope to fly Ian to Nairobi hospital for checks soonest. Then make arrangements for the rest of the crew to return to Nairobi – with Alan.

That was the end of the message from Peter. Eric Gassen then told me the Red Cross were sending aeroplanes in to get everyone out that morning. "We are very very sorry," he said, "they are very brave people." I thanked him and rang off. The sky was beginning to lighten. In London and elsewhere those who loved Alan would be waking up unawares. I'd have to find those closest to him quickly before they heard the news on the radio. I rang Barrie Sales and the programme organiser who both knew Alan from a long way back. We arranged to meet in the office by 7.30.

In the next few hours I learned what it must be like for those policemen and doctors who have to give terrible news. I would telephone a relative or close friend of Alan's and hear the laughter in the background before I spoke, knowing that what I had to say would cast a shadow over their lives that might never lift.

When Peter Gill returned we heard the full story of what had happened.

Only hours before the accident the team had interviewed rebel leader John Gerang at his guerrilla stronghold on the Burma plateau in South Sudan. His forces had prevented food reaching Government-controlled towns in the South. It had been a long and arduous trip but that interview completed the film and Alan, Peter and the team set off triumphantly on the fifteen-hour return journey to the Kenyan border post of Lo Kichokio. They were travelling in two land cruisers, or lorries. The two *Observer* journalists were in the first being driven by Peter Gill. The road was in frequent use by the Red Cross and was considered safe. Ian Killian, the cameraman, and John Heasman, the sound recordist, were in the cab of the second vehicle, a converted Toyota pick-up. Alan Stewart was in the back of the vehicle, together with a rebel soldier.

At about 16.30 Peter turned to Shiya Batia the *Observer* reporter and said "Well, I suppose you've got your story wrapped up?" Batia remembered, "At that moment we heard a dull rumble, like an earthquake. Someone shouted, "It's their petrol tank."

It was in fact a landmine probably buried some time before by rebel forces and forgotten about. Recent heavy rain might have worked away some of the covering soil making detonation more likely. The first vehicle passed over without incident but the second vehicle had detonated the mine.

As Peter Gill looked back he saw black smoke rising and then drifting away. The damaged vehicle had been hurled thirty to forty feet. As they raced back they found Alan Stewart spread-eagled on his back barely conscious. Ian Killian and John Heasman who had been inside the cab were on their feet, badly shaken and bruised but not seriously hurt. The back of the vehicle had taken the major force of the blast, and Alan had been thrown out, sustaining very serious chest and head injuries.

The *Observer* journalist pulled the rebel soldier, Majak, from the wreckage. He had been assigned to the team as a bodyguard. He received leg injuries but survived.

Ian Killian collapsed and was lain in the shelter of the vehicle. John Heasman found a sleeping bag for Alan to be on, and Peter Gill set off in the surviving vehicle to try and get help. "Our main concern was for Alan, who was the most badly injured," said Batia. "Three of us took turns to keep him supplied with water. Around his forehead we tied whatever bandages we could lay our hands on. From my sports shirt we made a makeshift turban to keep the bandages in place. When he stopped breathing we were stunned.

"We closed his eyes, someone mumbled a prayer, and we cried helplessly as we knelt beside him. It was 7.30 p.m. Kenyan time.

"We only realised then how serious was our own predicament, the lucky survivors. If we were to save Killian, who was lying on his side, and Majak, we needed medical help."

Peter returned an hour later with two rebel army jeeps as escorts. He hadn't been able to find a doctor, so the only hope was to drive for the border. Gill is a remarkable man, and in the most awful circumstances he never broke down or lost control. For the next few hours, days and weeks he kept everyone together and did not spare himself.

The survivors placed Alan's body gently at the back of the land cruiser and drove for Lo Kichokio. They arrived at 5.15 a.m. the following morning, slowed down by two punctures, and a leaking radiator. As the others received attention and collapsed into bed Peter wrote out the message with which the Red Cross in Geneva were to ring me. He added a last sentence. "Suggest you start pressing the Foreign Office for Alan's return to London."

The messages of condolence flooded in from Israel, Bangladesh, Canada and throughout the world, and people smiled as they cried. Alan was that sort of person.

The cans of film were badly dented but remarkably the film survived and the programme was transmitted on 6 November. At first it had seemed an irrelevance but not to have transmitted it would have made Alan's death seem even more pointless, and it was essential to publicise what was happening in Sudan, not some natural disaster but a man-made catastrophe.

At the end of the programme Peter Gill said a few words in his quiet understated very English way.

From the moment Alan bounded into Khartoum at the beginning of our work on that film, nothing mattered more to him than getting the story done and done properly. It was always like that with Alan – an energy and enthusiasm for the work in hand that was cheerful, but quite unrelenting.

Even before the accident, our Sudanese trip had proved exceptionally arduous – long journeys through the bush and no comforts at all at the other end. From Alan, of course, not a whisper of complaint. This was all incidental to bringing back a story that he knew as we all knew to be important.

Just a few minutes before the explosion, we stopped to have this group photograph taken with our rebel escorts. Barring another eight hours on the road, the work was done, the filming complete. You can almost see Alan's gaze beginning to search for the next story. He would have wanted to start on that tomorrow morning if at all possible. It is that quality of commitment, that exceptional enthusiasm for the work, which we at Thames have lost.

No one wished to be reminded in this way of the bravery of our crews and journalists. However, it was a salutary reminder to politicians, who so easily criticise our colleagues, of the sacrifices that sometimes have to be made.

Starting Over

Compared with those events any local difficulties we had on *This Week* seemed to be irrelevant. I was steering the programme through an agenda which Jonathan Dimbleby and I agreed on but some of the rest of the team did not. Eventually, I changed direction a little and mixed in more popular subject matter. I also pinched Chris Oxley from *Panorama*, where he wasn't too happy and felt he needed a change. I was glad to assist him. Michael Grade, then BBC Director of Programmes, sent a message to Lyons in France where Chris was filming, asking him not to leave before talking to Michael personally. The legendary Grade talent for persuasion failed however. Mind you, Michael himself left the BBC not long afterwards, after John Birt had arrived. I was delighted to get Chris as I'd had my eyes on him for a while. He was a highly talented and methodical journalist with a real visual flair. Alison Cahn came over at around the same time from the weekly magazine, *Reporting London*. I remembered her from *Nationwide* where I had appointed her as one of our regional researchers. A former editor of *Isis*, the Oxford University magazine, and the daughter of a Professor of Metallurgy, she had been blooded on a newspaper in Birmingham and was ready to take on national and international stories.

Julian Manyon, who I had last worked with on *Tonight*, was almost permanently on a plane for me as he sped from South Africa to Israel to America.

I managed to cover three Irish stories that first year, one about the war of intimidation going on in the streets, a second about increasing emigration from the South and the third about the bloody infighting going on in the Irish National Liberation Army, as INLA Representatives of both factions talked to us and blew the whistle on each other's appalling activities.

Towards the summer of 1987 we really got into our stride, breaking the story of the chaos in Britain's air traffic control and, in "The Secret Missile Trail", detailing the way in which British Intelligence and the CIA had supplied sophisticated anti-aircraft missiles to the Mujahideen. The reporter, Peter Gill, forecast that it would fundamentally change the balance of the war, but at the price of injecting state of the art weaponry into the world's arms black market. One fished in by the IRA.

After the summer break in "Wish you Weren't Here?" we reported on the yobbish behaviour of young Brits in Spain and in the "Battle for the Bottom" chronicled the attempts of the *Daily Star* to plumb new depths in the tabloid war. This moved Philip Purser to write in the *Daily Mail* that "the best ideas in current affairs television just now are all in *This Week*."

Ah well, pride comes before the fall. The magic touch came and then went. One moment I managed to be ahead of the pack and the news, the next I was struggling to keep up.

DEATH ON THE ROCK

Black Thursday

At the beginning of December 1987, we interviewed the Prime Minister again, having talked to her during the June Election Campaign. On the earlier occasion her interview took place on the only real day of the campaign when the Conservatives thought they were in danger of losing. It was a strange campaign. The Tories were always well in the lead, despite the much publicised efforts of the Labour's new publicity director Peter Mandelson, a former LWT producer. He made the best looking commercials but although they heartened his troops they didn't change the voters' minds.

Still there was much doubt, hesitation and unhappiness at No. 10. The Prime Minister and her Party Chairman, Norman Tebbit, didn't see eye to eye on how the campaign should be run and she installed Lord Young, one of her greatest fans, in Central Office as well. Soon it became unclear which of the two really had the PM's ear and there were a number of lover's tiffs. One thing they were all agreed on however: Mrs. Thatcher would not risk a return bout with Mrs. Gould or Sue Lawley. "On the Spot" was out.

Although the polls remained steady the odd one showed Labour closing the gap. Mrs. Thatcher began to consult even more advisers, including those from her previous election triumphs, Cecil Parkinson, Gordon Reece, and Tim Bell. Norman Tebbit accordingly became even more irritated.

Our interview was scheduled for Thursday, 4 June. Tebbit called it "Black Thursday". It was just a week before polling day and that morning Gallup showed that Labour had narrowed the gap to within four points of the Tories. Suddenly it seemed that Labour's slick television campaign was paying off.

According to Michael Cockerell in his book, *Live from Number 10*:

At a series of crisis meetings between Mrs. Thatcher and Norman Tebbit's campaign team, much blood spilled on the carpets at Central Office and Number 10. "She was highly emotional, not at all her usual rational self that day", says one Cabinet minister wearily. The Prime Minister complained bitterly of the Tories' lacklustre campaign and called on Saatchis to rework their advertisement for the final week.

[185]

Waiting for her to arrive at the Thames Studios in Euston Road we knew nothing of this, nor of the raging toothache she had endured for some days. Her schedule was so packed she couldn't, or wouldn't, take time off to see a dentist.

First the dogs came to sniff for explosives, followed by the security men who had examined the studios and surrounding areas some days previously. Finally Mrs. Thatcher arrived, distinctly on edge, and with acolytes like Harvey Thomas, her television organiser, distinctly nervous. When she arrived on the set she demanded that a table, placed between her and Jonathan Dimbleby, be removed. I had anticipated something like this and had decided my own set of guidelines. I would not add anything to the set at the behest of the Prime Minister or her advisers. No flowers, no soft subdued lighting. All the leaders would have to appear in the same *This Week* setting and the same lighting, but I decided to let the table be removed, as it didn't seem to me up to the stuff of principles.

I thought we were in for a bad-tempered unhappy few minutes but as the opening titles rolled the Prime Minister took a deep breath, composed herself, and delivered one of her best performances. Often she turned the question back at her persistent interviewer, never losing her control or mastery of the facts at issue. Afterwards her sycophants surrounded her like footballers congratulating a striker who has scored, except of course that no one dared kiss her.

As she left the studio I asked her whether she enjoyed doing such interviews. She looked at me very directly. "I hate them, I hate them, I hate them," she said. I thought I had heard that somewhere before.

I led the way into the hospitality room and poured her the usual whisky. She sat down, suddenly totally relaxed, and set about reorganising independent television. The satellites would change everything, she said. I couldn't resist probing what I thought was the contradiction between the Tories' espousal of the free market and their desire to control what we all view. "You do know, Prime Minister, that some of the satellite channels in Europe are transmitting pornography? Will your freedom extend to that?" I asked. "No," came the firm reply accompanied by the sharp closing click of her handbag.

[186]

DEATH ON THE ROCK

Just before our interview with Mrs. Thatcher in December 1987, she had met Mr. Gorbachev and was clearly fascinated by him. After the interview she stayed a full hour in hospitality telling us what he was planning to do, what she had told him to do, and how this was the most exciting time in Europe since 1945. As she went on, and on, I stood back to look at her and try and sort out my complex reaction to the person who had been Prime Minister for eight years and with whom I seemed fated to come into conflict.

She is not very tall nor very beautiful but she is quite extraordinarily alive and vivacious. Every piece of her skin seems to glow with energy, the eyes are piercingly lit up and flashing. She is never withdrawn or detached in conversation, always in it up to her neck. She seems to see life as a continual argument which she is determined to win every minute of the day. Are there any moments of quiet repose? Does she ever sleep? She has a formidable grasp of detail, can exhaust any of the men around her and still make breakfast for her husband before running the country. Above all she is a very attractive woman, knows it, and uses that attraction.

Yet at the same time as I admired her determination and courage I found her certainties too final for me, and despite the breadth of knowledge there was a certain narrowness about her, a lack of sympathy for human frailty. She seemed to dare all around to come into the ring with her.

By New Year 1988 I had got on top of *This Week* again with an hour long report on the lessons of the Hungerford shooting and a couple of films by Jonathan Dimbleby from Ethiopia, about whose famine in the early 1970s he had been the first to warn the world.

Then Lorraine Heggessey and Annie Burns took a home video camera to Latvia, posing as tourists, and made a film about the first rumblings of nationalist awakening there. I was sure nationalistic fever would break out everywhere as a result of Glasnost.

By early March I was bothered that we hadn't done much about industry and in particular the Japanese involvement in Britain. Then British Aerospace announced that it was negotiating a co-production deal with Japan. I thought it would be a good idea to follow it through, and in particular to go with a trade mission to Japan the following week. Chris Oxley and Julian Manyon were free so I commissioned them to do it. Poor Chris was rather tired having just made "Beating the Palestinians" on the West Bank. I allowed him three hours off. We would meet after the weekend for a final briefing, but that Sunday there were some shootings in Gibraltar.

13

THE ROAD TO THE ROCK

6.30 a.m. Monday, 7 March 1988. I switched on Radio 4 and
listened eagerly to the BBC's *Today* programme for the latest details
of the shootings that had taken place the previous afternoon in
Gibraltar. The information Sunday night had been confused and I
thought that by this morning there would be a much clearer picture. Peter Donaldson was reading the news in his usual calm
professional way.

"It's now known that the three people shot and killed by
Security Forces in Gibraltar yesterday were members of the Provisional IRA. It's thought they were challenged while trying to
leave Gibraltar after planting a huge car bomb in the centre of the
colony."

After the news the presenter Peter Hobday talked to Joe Paley
the BBC's correspondent in Gibraltar. He had been briefed by the
authorities in there.

HOBDAY: Tell me about the bomb which was finally defused.
What sort of damage would it have done, had it gone
off during the parade on Tuesday?

PALEY: It would have done an enormous amount of damage.
It was something like five hundred pounds of
explosives, packed with bits of metal, shrapnel and so
on.

After a few more questions Hobday turned to the BBC's Irish

[189]

Affairs correspondent, David Capper, in Belfast. The IRA had issued a statement admitting that three of its members had been killed "on active service", and naming them as Sean Savage, Daniel McCann and Mairead Farrell. Capper had further information.

HOBDAY: Do we know where they got the material for the bomb, or anything about that?

CAPPER: Well I've been told that the explosive found in the car is called Goma 2 . . . everything points to ETA (the Basque terrorist organisation) as being the people that supplied them with the explosive.

That all seemed pretty definite and later on the Minister for the Armed Forces, Ian Stewart, stepped into the BBC's radio car to talk to the *Today* programme. He congratulated the Gibraltar Government and went on, "Military personnel were involved. There was a car bomb found, which has been defused."

All the daily newspapers had basically the same story. Some mentioned a shoot-out, all confirmed that a bomb had been found, and that the IRA members were armed. ITN said that "A fierce gun battle broke out" and that "Army explosives experts used a robot to defuse the bomb." The *Daily Mail* agreed about the bomb saying "RAF disposal men defused it later," although the *Daily Mirror* reported that "A controlled explosion failed to set off the bomb."

It didn't seem to me that there was much in it for us. The news organisations would mop it all up, and there wasn't much fuss from either side when such shoot-outs occurred. The British military and the IRA regarded themselves as soldiers at war with each other. Most people would think the terrorists deserved what they got. I didn't disagree.

I shrugged, more wasted lives, pushed the papers away and went down to the cutting rooms to sort out that week's film, an examination of the illegal dumping of nuclear waste in Germany. As usual it took a few hours to sort out the structure and get an opening to the programme which would arrest people's attention. So I had a late lunch and when I came back to the office sat down with Julian Manyon and Chris Oxley to discuss the Japanese project. They thought me somewhat preoccupied with Ireland so, rather playfully, asked me if I was going to do anything about the shootings. "No, there's nothing left to say."

Almost at that moment Oracle updated its report on Gibraltar quoting the Foreign Secretary's statement to the House of Commons.

Sir Geoffrey Howe described the deaths of the IRA members:

On their way to the Border, they were challenged by the Security Forces. When challenged, they made movements which led the military personnel, operating in support of the Gibraltar police, to conclude that their own lives and the lives of others were under threat. In the light of this response, they were shot. Those killed were subsequently found not to have been carrying arms.

Sir Geoffrey then revealed there was no bomb in the car, or anywhere else.

I drew in my breath. Well, that put a very different perspective on the whole matter.

It seemed to me that this incident was now certain to become extremely controversial and be used by all sides in the Irish Question to their own advantage. It would clearly be seen by many people as an example of the alleged "shoot to kill policy" operated by the British Government, and it took no great insight to realise that within a few days a madonna-like painting of Mairead Farrell would adorn the sides of houses in West Belfast, or that a Roman Catholic priest would refer to her as a martyr. The incident also appeared to indicate, despite the absence of a bomb, that the IRA had conveniently forgotten about what its political arm, Sinn Fein, had called "the disaster" of Enniskillen.

I had to make a quick decision, should I pursue the story and if so who should I send to do it? Julian Manyon and Chris Oxley were not filming yet, but were due to set off on the Japanese project in forty-eight hours. Pulling them off one certain story for another speculative one that might come to nothing was risky.

As Editor of *This Week* I had six producers, five reporters, and five researchers at my disposal. All were occupied with other stories or were on leave. For this sort of project Julian and Chris were probably the best team available. Julian was immensely experienced at home and abroad, and had been working on Thames weekly current affairs programmes for nearly ten years. He was extremely bright and incisive, extraordinarily tenacious, and once launched on a project, obsessive. Nothing else mattered. It was pointless locking the door to him, he would walk right through it.

Chris Oxley was equally tenacious and experienced but much more laid back. He would gently circumnavigate a story until he was absolutely sure he had understood everything before making up his mind. He too was remarkably stubborn. Together Julian and Chris were as good, in fact probably better, than any other television current affairs pairing. I left them in the office and walked up and down the corridor for a couple of minutes. I didn't want to give up Japan but yes this was too important and yes they were the best possible team.

I decided to switch them to the Gibraltar story. I didn't give a lot of thought to the political repercussions. I knew it would be difficult and possibly controversial but I had decided long ago that I had to judge a story by its importance, not by the political fall-out one might face.

If I didn't do that I would have to quit. Of course one had to be aware of political sensitivities and find ways of minimising them but not by turning away from something so important. How could we report at home with different standards than we used abroad?

The journalists were not very enthusiastic. Chris in particular was sceptical about our ability to find something fresh, but of course they would go and have a look.

The following day Chris flew to Gibraltar to check out matters there, and Julian flew to Spain to see what information he could discover about the joint Spanish/British surveillance operation that had so successfully identified and followed the three IRA members. I also sent a young Irish researcher from the heart of the Mountains of Mourne in County Down, Eamon Hardy, to Belfast to see what he could discover there.

We planned to meet up in a few days to compare notes, reflect on other media coverage, and decide whether to move on to the next stage, that is to start filming.

As the team set off I went to see Barrie Sales, my immediate boss, and Deputy Director of Programmes, to discuss the project with him. We both thought that the basic unresolved question at the heart of Sir Geoffrey Howe's statement was why three unarmed terrorists, when challenged by armed security personnel, should make suspicious movements, which gave the impression they were a threat? (At this stage one assumed the implication was that the soldiers thought the terrorists were going for their guns.) It did not make sense; there was no logic to it.

Within a week, official sources, presumably the MoD, had leaked to the *Sunday Telegraph* and the *Sunday Times* an apparently more convincing account. This was the "button job" or remote-controlled bomb theory. According to this version of events the soldiers thought the terrorists were about to detonate a remote-controlled bomb, which they had been led to believe had been planted in the white Renault. In its essentials that was the explanation soldiers A, B, C and D were to subsequently give at the Inquest.

However, the "button-job" explanation did not resolve the problem; the basic puzzle still remained. First why try to detonate a non-existent bomb? Secondly, why should the terrorists give the impression (Farrell going for her handbag, McCann going for his pocket) they were about to activate a remote-control device they did not possess? Again none of it quite added up.

Barrie was to tell the subsequent Windlesham/Rampton Inquiry,

There was a further puzzle in my mind and that was why the Security Services should have been so convinced they were dealing with a remote-controlled bomb. On the balance of probabilities it seemed an odd conclusion to reach. Although I am not particularly knowledgeable about such matters, I was aware that remote-controlled bombs are usually detonated by line of sight and also over relatively short distances. A built-up area like Gibraltar did not seem the most obvious place for such a bomb.

There was also the problem of the getaway. If you detonate a remote-controlled bomb inside Gibraltar how do you escape? With only one road in or out it would have been exceedingly risky. In all these circumstances a remote-controlled bomb did not seem an obvious choice; a timer would have been more logical. It was surprising therefore that the Security Services should have apparently reached such a firm conclusion.

Something else nagged at the back of my mind. I knew that in Northern Ireland when the Security Forces thought there was a bomb in a car they evacuated the area immediately. This had not been done in Gibraltar and indeed there seemed to have been a wait of around at least twenty minutes after the shootings before the car was searched. Still, would we be in danger of helping the IRA gain a propaganda victory?

I was well aware of the cynical use of publicity by the IRA but I was particularly struck by an editorial in that Tuesday's *Daily Telegraph*. It read in part,

It is very rarely that we find ourselves less satisfied with the Government's account of events than the Labour Front Bench in the House of Commons. But Mr. George Robertson's Opposition applause for Sunday's shooting in Gibraltar seems to demand some qualification . . . The Government must tell why it gave a succession of contradictory accounts to the world about Sunday's events. Unless it wishes Britain's enemies to enjoy a propaganda bonanza it should explain why it was necessary to shoot dead all three terrorists on the street rather than apprehend them with the considerable force of police and SAS which appears to have been deployed in the locality.

The editorial went on,

It is an essential aspect of any successful anti-terrorist policy to maintain the principles of civilised restraint which obtain in a democratic society. A failure to do so, argues that terrorism is succeeding in one of its critical aims: the brutalisation of the society under attack.

The *Independent* had something in a similar vein. I was clearly not the only person who felt important issues were involved.

Gibraltar 8–11 March

When Chris arrived in Gibraltar he made repeated visits to the Glacis and Laguna Estates, which surround and overlook the petrol station where McCann and Farrell died. He spoke to around fifty people who live in the area. Chris made contact with Josie Celecia and Stephen Bullock, who later appeared in the film. He also met two further people who said they were eyewitnesses to the shootings at the petrol station, Derek Luise and another man who would not give his name. When Chris left Gibraltar, he had established several leads which needed following up.

He had heard from a lady in the Glacis Estate that her father had witnessed the shootings of Farrell and McCann and that Farrell had put her hands in the air before being shot.

He had heard that a woman who lived much of the time in Spain, had seen the shootings at the petrol station also.

Chris had made the acquaintance of some of the reporters from the London tabloids too. All of them were convinced this was a straightforward "shoot to kill" operation. Chris was more cautious; there was too much to check out before one could jump to conclusions like that. Still, he wondered why they were not writing in this vein instead of following the official line. "It doesn't matter what we write," one said, "our editors will change it. You have to give them what they want."

The need to fill space and provide what Head Office wanted was behind the Evelyn Glenholmes story. There had been a fourth person involved in the IRA operation. John McEntee, the *Irish Press* columnist, asked a colourful colleague if he believed the theory of the Fourth Man. "Oh, it's a woman and we are saying it's Evelyn Glenholmes," this crazy veteran explained. Why on earth, I wondered aloud, was he saying it was Glenholmes? "Because," he replied, "we have a nice picture of her and she won't sue."

On hearing the hacks boast of this Chris's eyes opened wide. He made his excuses and left.

Chris was also rather concerned by the behaviour of the Gibraltar Police. It had always seemed odd that they, who had played a major role in the operation, should in effect investigate themselves. Chris discovered what he thought were shortcomings in the police investigation.

According to witnesses, the scene of the incident had not been preserved nor had potential evidence. Numerous on and off duty policemen and ambulancemen had been over the area near the bodies, no one could remember photographs being taken of the bodies in position or of the cartridges on the ground and indeed, shortly after the incident, the bodies and the cartridges were removed from the scene. Chris was also told that the plain-clothed soldiers involved had been driven from the scene without being interviewed there and they did not seem to have been subject to any forensic examination.

These witness accounts of possible shortcomings in police procedure seemed to be confirmed by examining the amateur video film taken shortly after the incident, which was broadcast by Gibraltar television. This video showed that the scene was cleared in a haphazard way.

In fact, with hindsight, we know our initial belief that the police investigation was inadequate is correct. The Police Commissioner said in evidence at the Inquest that he was not suspicious when the three unarmed terrorists were killed. And the coroner said, "Regrettably scenes of crime procedures appear to have been forgotten. No proper identification was made of the exact places where the newspaper was found or where the book ended up on the ground or the spent cartridges . . . spent cartridges could have helped give some idea as to the position of the shooters."

There were other "oversights". Chris was told the soldiers had been allowed to leave Gibraltar that same evening, although no investigating officer was said to have interviewed them. Chris found that few residents in the flats overlooking the incident involving McCann and Farrell seemed to have been approached for information by the police.

Spain 8–15 March

While Chris Oxley was searching for witnesses Julian Manyon was trying to find out more about the surveillance of the terrorists before they reached the Rock.

DEATH ON THE ROCK

The Gibraltar operation which the British Security Services now called "Operation Flavius" began not on 6 March 1988 but in November the previous year when the first members of the IRA "Active Service Unit" arrived at Malaga in Spain.

In the words of a communiqué issued by the Spanish Interior Ministry on 9 March, "for more than five months members of the Spanish and British police have kept close watch on the terrorists who died last Sunday in Gibraltar."

The nature of that surveillance operation, conducted on the Costa Del Sol, in Gibraltar, and apparently in Northern Ireland is central to any understanding of what took place in Gibraltar on 6 March. For the account of events provided by Spanish briefing officers to Thames Television and several British newspapers raises fundamental questions about the decisions and actions of the British Security Forces on the final Sunday of the operation.

Julian arrived in Malaga on 8 March and went on to Madrid on 11 March. There he secured the services of the respected correspondent of *The Times*, Harry Debelius, as consultant and interpreter.

One result of this work was a sequence we included in the first half of *Death on the Rock*. This showed two Spanish police drivers following a white Renault car (driven for the purpose of the film by Chris Oxley) down the coast road between Marbella and Gibraltar. The sequence also included shots of the white Renault taken from above by a helicopter (hired by ourselves).

The purpose of this filming was to provide a partial reconstruction of what Spanish officials had told us about the surveillance, carried out by Spanish police, of the white Renault car driven by the IRA terrorist Sean Savage to Gibraltar on the morning of 6 March.

Julian Manyon's commentary over the above sequence stated,

The first IRA car was a white Renault 5 driven by Sean Savage. Later police reported the red Ford with Farrell and McCann. Each car was expertly tailed with a system the Spanish Police demonstrated for us on the same road that the terrorists took that Sunday. Up to four police drivers follow each suspect, constantly interchanging in order to avoid suspicion.

I am told by the Spanish Security Police that a constant flow of

[197]

information about the terrorists' movements was radioed directly to British officials in Gibraltar. A police helicopter made sure the watchers made no mistake.

The tempting target, symbol for the IRA of British imperialism, had become a carefully prepared trap.

The information included in the film sequence and accompanying commentary came from a series of meetings with Spanish officials, including one formal briefing. The facility of two police drivers was provided by the Malaga police following a letter written by Harry Debelius and Julian Manyon and delivered by Harry to Police Headquarters in Madrid on 15 March 1988. This letter asked the Spanish authorities for help "to reconstruct the operation with exactitude" and requested details of the "critical phase when the Spanish surveillance steam followed the [IRA] commando to the border with Gibraltar".

The letter was addressed to *Sr*. Manuel Jimanez Cuevas, spokesman for the Spanish Police, who had discussed the case with Harry and Julian the day before and asked them to put the request in writing.

On his return to Spain after briefing me Julian went with Harry to the Interior Ministry in Madrid on 21 March for a briefing with *Sr*. Augustin Valladolid, spokesman for the Security Services which began at 6 p.m. and ended at 7.20 p.m. *Sr*. Valladolid provided a wide ranging account of the operation and, above all, confirmed that the white Renault, which later came under suspicion as a car bomb, was under Spanish surveillance all the way down the coast road to its arrival in Gibraltar. (It had begun its journey earlier that morning in Torremolinos where Savage and McCann had spent Saturday night at the Hotel Escandinava). Harry Debelius' notes of the meeting read as follows:

a. Four or five police cars (unmarked – our note) 'leap-frogged' each other on the road while trailing the terrorists so as not to arouse suspicion.

b. A helicopter spotted car during part of the route.

c. The police agents were in constant contact with their headquarters by radio.

d. Observations by agents at fixed observation points along the road. *Sr.* Valladolid further said that the Spanish Police sent minute by minute details of the car's movements direct to the British in Gibraltar. He confirmed that the British were aware of the car's arrival at the border and permitted it to enter Gibraltar.

Sr. Valladolid also stated that the first tip-off which led to the detection of the IRA team in Spain the previous November had come from Britain; that at an early stage the British and Spanish Security Services came to an agreement on how the terrorists would be handled.

Spain accepted a commitment to keep the British informed of the terrorists' movements, and in particular, of the danger of any bomb attack; that Farrell and McCann had arrived in Malaga on 4 March and that Farrell's arrival had gone undetected by the Spanish – it was a warning from the British at midday on 5 March that alerted the Spanish to her presence on the Costa Del Sol; that British Security men allowed the white Renault 5 to enter Gibraltar on 6 March because they thought it might lead them to the bomb which, according to one theory, was hidden somewhere on the Rock; that a radio-controlled bomb was not thought by the Spanish to be the most likely option for the terrorists because it would have required the car to carry an aerial two to three feet high, with the detonator being operated in line of sight. Spanish Security believed a timing device was less problematical.

The other details of the surveillance operation given in a subsequent film were drawn from the Valladolid briefing, conversations with *Sr.* Cuevas, the official communique referred to above, further unattributable conversations with Spanish officials, and our own investigations on the spot. At no stage did any Spanish official ever suggest that contact with the two male terrorists, McCann and Savage, had been lost in the forty-eight hours prior to their arrival at the Gibraltar border. On the contrary, the account given was of a successful surveillance operation.

In *Death on the Rock* we made no reference to any British version of the surveillance operation. This is because, prior to the transmission of the film on 28 April, the only British on-the-record account containing any detail was that given by the Foreign Secretary, Sir Geoffrey Howe, to the House of Commons on the afternoon of 7 March. In his statement Sir Geoffrey said that he was "Confident that the House will wish me to extend our gratitude to the Spanish authorities, without whose invaluable assistance the outcome might have been very different. This co-operation underlines once again the importance of the international collaboration in the fight against terrorism."

Shortly after Sir Geoffrey's statement, it was reported that Prime Minister, Margaret Thatcher, had sent a personal message of thanks to the Spanish Prime Minister *Sr*. Felipe Gonzalez. However, as far as Thames Television was concerned, repeated efforts to secure an on-the-record statement from a qualified British official, met with failure. No attempt was made by any such official to put a point of view conflicting with the Spanish one, the outlines of which had already been published in the British Press.

In the period from the incident to the start of the Inquest virtually all the quality British newspapers reported that Spanish surveillance had been fully effective on the morning of 6 March.

The Times of 8 March reported that, "Spanish security forces kept track of three cars used by the IRA squad and passed on the information to the British. On the Rock, the SAS team watched on Sunday afternoon as a terrorist went across the border in a white Renault 5."

On 4 July *The Times* again reported, "The Spanish police co-operated with British intelligence in the build-up to the killing, tracking the terrorists from their base on the Costa Del Sol to the frontier."

Other newspapers had gone into greater detail in reporting the surveillance operation. On 8 March, the *Daily Telegraph* reported that "The Spanish police tailed the vehicle right up to the gate; on the other side the Gibraltarians took up the tail . . . Once all three were inside, the border was sealed. They did not know it yet but they had walked into a trap of their own making. From now on there could be no escape."

On 8 and 10 March the *Independent* quoted a Spanish police source as saying "We followed their steps right up to Gibraltar's gate." On 14 May a front page story in the *Independent* quoted a briefing by the spokesman of Spain's State Security Directorate, *Sr.* Augustin Valladolid:

> He revealed yesterday that Mairead Farrell, a key member of the IRA gang, had slipped through the police surveillance network, which had included electronic bugging. She had been detected only on the day of the killings. The two other terrorists shot dead were Sean Savage and Daniel McCann. *Sr.* Valladolid said: "We had complete proof that the two Irishmen were going to plant a bomb. We heard them say so."

Also worth noting is the 12 March issue of the Gibraltar weekly *VOX*, which had apparently been comprehensively briefed by a source on the Rock. At the bottom of the second column on the back page, *VOX* reported:

> Three weeks ago, however, the terrorists were lost to the shadows in Almoralla, Valencia. All surrounding Security officers were alerted and subsequently they were found again in Malaga when they were kept under close watch up to and until they crossed into Gibraltar last Sunday where, thanks to the co-operation of the Spanish Security Service with their British counterparts, they were awaited.

The importance of all this was clear. The Spanish believed the British knew there was no bomb in the car and that the British knew exactly when the terrorists were coming. No one was caught offguard.

So there were a number of questions demanding to be answered. If the British knew there was no bomb in the car why did they shoot the terrorists? And if the British also knew exactly when and where the terrorists were arriving why didn't they simply arrest them at the border?

If, however, the British thought there was a bomb on board, why on earth let it be taken into a highly built-up and populated area, where it was many more times as dangerous?

There was only one way into Gibraltar. Everyone had to come through a narrow isthmus, and across the Gibraltar airfield before entering the town. There was one road for cars and one entry for people on foot. Everyone had to stop to be checked.

So when Julian and Chris came back to the office on 15 March we had no real doubts about the nature of the surveillance operation, but reservations about the effectiveness of the Gibraltar Police investigative abilities in this case.

I decided to start filming and told Barrie Sales of my decision. This did not mean we were committed to a programme but I felt it worthwhile to put what we had on film. Remembering my earlier problems at the BBC I made sure that the project was put down on the forward planning sheet I sent to the Director of Programmes, David Elstein, and others.

Before returning to Gibraltar, however, we decided to film the funeral of the three terrorists, which was to take place the following day in Belfast. Chris and Julian, together with Eamon Hardy, followed the procession on a dull and dismal day through the city to the Milltown cemetery where so many young men and women killed in the Troubles lie, and where many more will follow them.

The cortège had come from Dublin via Meath and Louth, and been stoned by groups of Protestants over the border from the edge of the motorway. At a requiem mass for Mairead Farrell in Belfast the night before Father Raymond Murray had said that she had died "a violent death like Jesus . . . she was barbarously assassinated by a gunman as she walked in public on a sunny Sunday afternoon".

They then set up the camera to film the speeches and the lowering of the coffins into the earth. Suddenly at about 1.15 p.m. there was an explosion, and shooting. The distraught relatives and friends, already in a highly emotional state, threw themselves onto the earth, behind the gravestones. Eamon Hardy was badly shaken and dazed by the blast. Far to the right a man with a gun was coming towards the funeral party. He was shooting indiscriminately and lobbing grenades.

Martin McGuinness and some others betrayed their paramilitary training and revealed their courage as, unarmed, they chased the gunman who turned and fled. He kept turning to fire at his pursuers, crying, "Come on, you Fenian fuckers" and "Have some of this, you IRA bastards." The Security Forces had stayed away from the funeral in order to avoid contributing to any disturbance or rioting. By the time they arrived and arrested the Loyalist gunman, three men lay dead on the grass of the cemetery, another two people were critically wounded and sixty-six were hurt. The gunman had been beaten unconscious.

Three days later, on 19 March, two British soldiers apparently blundered into the funeral procession of one of the victims of the attack in the Milltown cemetery. The soldiers were attacked, hauled from their car, beaten by the crowd, and then taken away and shot by the IRA. "We have got two Brits," shouted the crowd. No one who saw the television pictures of the assault, or the photographs of the dead men stripped of their clothes, will ever forget that ghastly day. As Corporals Derek Wood and David Howes of the Royal Corps of Signals lay bloody and beaten a kneeling priest administered the last rites.

Five people had died, partly as a consequence of the Gibraltar shootings. There were now even more compelling reasons to continue the story.

14

MAKING DEATH ON THE ROCK

Lots of concerns were running through my mind after I had given the go-ahead to start filming but legal problems did not loom large among them. Would we prejudice the Inquest? I couldn't see how, and neither could the lawyers we consulted. We were outside Gibraltar's jurisdiction, and in any case, newspapers were carrying dozens of reports about the incident including quite extensive articles in the *Sunday Telegraph* and the *Sunday Times*. Many of those newspapers are delivered to and read in Gibraltar, yet at no time, to my knowledge, did the authorities on the Rock criticise or try to interfere with any of these publications. Besides Government ministers had given their accounts in Parliament and even on the BBC's *Question Time* and the Ministry of Defence was leaking information to selected correspondents, though it looked to us rather more like "planting" stories. In any case, no one questioned the right of television or newspapers to mount investigations following the Zeebrugge Ferry disaster, the Kings Cross tragedy and the Piper Alpha fire, all events which led to several deaths and the possibility of criminal charges. Why was Gibraltar different? And there was another reason for feeling confident about the project.

On his first visit to the Rock, Chris Oxley had spoken to the Gibraltar coroner, Felix Pizzarello, who told my producer that he would welcome journalistic inquiries and the tracing of witnesses for the Inquest.

What I was concerned about was that we should find every witness to the shootings and that no shoe leather should be spared in doing so. I decided to add another researcher, Alison Cahn, to the team. I could have sent Eamon Hardy to Gibraltar but I didn't think that a young Irishman with a broad accent would be able to open many doors on the Rock. Better to deploy him in Ireland and instead to send a sympathetic young Englishwoman of great stamina to Gibraltar. She was as thorough a researcher as I had ever come across. I called her into the office. "I've got a very boring job for you. I want you to go to Gibraltar for about five days to go round all the flats overlooking the site of the shootings and find all the witnesses and get them to do interviews in front of camera, whatever they say." Easier said than done, and Alison was to be there much longer than five days. At that stage I didn't realise that she was to be married in five weeks' time, *This Week* willing.

I made it clear to Alison and to the other members of the team that we must not pay anyone for their interview. It was not the usual practice on *This Week* anyway but the charge of "buying" witnesses would have undermined their credibility and would have led to charges of us contaminating witnesses.

After the awful events of Milltown cemetery Chris wondered whether we should change the focus of our film to the consequences of those events in Ireland. I argued we shouldn't as the news programmes would be bound to do that, whereas they might well now neglect the events in Gibraltar and anyway they did not have the time or resources to do a detailed investigation there.

March 18–31, Gibraltar

Consequently, Chris and Julian flew straight to the Rock with Alison and on 19 March interviewed two key witnesses, Stephen Bullock a barrister, and Josie Celecia, and her husband. Both Bullock and Celecia had already given detailed accounts of what they had seen to the police, the Gibraltar Broadcasting Corporation, and English newspapers.

While they were filming at the Celecias' home there was an anonymous phone call. "It will be the IRA next." There was also a series of mysterious phone calls when Alison was interviewing other people. Someone would just phone up and put the phone down. It was rather unsettling, which was probably what was intended.

Following the leads which Chris Oxley had established, Alison contacted Derek Luise and wrote down his story in her notes. He said that following the sound of a police siren, he saw two gunmen fire on the terrorists on the petrol station side of the road. He said he saw a police car do a U-turn around the metal barrier in the middle of Winston Churchill Avenue and head toward the petrol station. Luise was visited several times and became increasingly reluctant to talk about what he had seen. When asked if he would give a television interview, he declined and subsequently, did not appear at the Inquest.

In the case of the second lead – a man who had reportedly seen Farrell with her hands in the air – Alison indirectly received further details of what he claimed to have seen. But this man categorically refused to meet her or to make a statement about the matter to a lawyer. Alison gave the family an undertaking that we would not name him. Neither he nor his "evidence" played any part in our film.

The third lead – a woman who had reportedly seen the shootings, but lived most of the time in Spain – was resolved by accident when the woman's mother fell into conversation with the *This Week* crew while they were filming at the petrol station. She explained in Spanish that her daughter had seen what happened. Alison followed this up and discovered the existence of the woman who was to find her face on the front pages of every English newspaper and to be widely libelled for her pains.

One man, a taxi driver who did not want to be identified, claimed to have a horrific account which he was only prepared to reveal if it was made worth his while. Alison checked with Chris Oxley who confirmed that no payment should be made. The team had no further dealings with the man.

In addition, Alison went door to door through all the blocks of flats that overlook the site of the shootings. On the first day she did so someone called the police saying that "a young Irish girl was going round the flats asking suspicious questions" (so much for my sympathetic young Englishwoman). This was despite the fact that Alison had shown people her Thames Identity Badge and given them her card. The police went up to the Rock Hotel, where she was staying, to check her out but were told she had left with the rest of the crew. A few weeks later a man in a pub handed her card back to her. He was a policeman.

Alison visited around a hundred and fifty flats, in some cases returning several times if the occupants were out. It was immediately clear that most people were reluctant to discuss the events of 6 March. The impression Alison formed was that ordinary Gibraltarians were frightened by what had happened and by the possible consequences of speaking out. As one of them put it, "With the SAS on one side and the IRA on the other what would you do?"

As a result, our door to door survey produced only limited results, the most useful being one witness, Brian Delaney, who had heard the shooting from inside his flat and had seen its immediate aftermath. His value was an extremely clear recollection of what the SAS men had been wearing and where they were positioned, which proved to be valuable material for cross-checking with other witnesses.

It is worth noting that Alison found and contacted an off-duty policeman, PC Parody, who testified at the Inquest, but he declined at the time to discuss the incidents.

At the end of March, Alison heard of a young woman who had apparently seen something of the shooting of Savage. After several days investigation Alison traced her, resulting in the interview with Dianne Treacey. The team had to talk through the door to her for ten to fifteen minutes before they were let in. Her father, who was there, was a former policeman and he was very disturbed by his daughter's account. The story she told, in quiet hushed tones, was dramatic. A man had rushed towards and past her, followed by another with a gun. She turned round and saw the first man, Sean Savage, shot in the back.

In summary, we spoke to ten of the sixteen independent eye witnesses to the shootings who later appeared at the Inquest. (Three of the witnesses we failed to contact were in fact holidaymakers resident in Britain.)

It was a hard slog but Alison didn't complain. Not the best way

either to prepare for the wedding and honeymoon that were creep-
ing closer. She must have wondered if she would ever get off the
Rock.

She too was struck by how little investigating the Gibraltar police
were doing. If witnesses hadn't gone to speak to the police off their
own bat there seemed little interest in finding them. The police
were interested in Alison however and she was followed on a
number of occasions, a friendly local journalist tipping her off. She
continued to knock on doors but the two most controversial
witnesses were found almost by chance.

Looking for Mr. Asquez

In 1987 Bob Randall walked proudly through the gates of
Buckingham Palace and received from Her Majesty the Queen the
MBE in recognition of his military services. He had served for thirty
years in the Gibraltar Regiment, rising through the ranks to
Quartermaster and retiring with the rank of Major in September
1986. In March 1988 he was employed by a construction company
on the Rock. On the afternoon of 6 March he was at home in Nelson
House on the Laguna estate. One of his sons told him what had
happened and he went out to see for himself, then returned to pick
up his video-camera to record the scene. Later that day he was told
that the GBC, Gibraltar Broadcasting Corporation, had not managed to get any film of the aftermath of the shootings so he gave
them his tape. Extracts from it were subsequently shown by the
BBC, ITN, and many other world TV organisations.

This Week wanted to obtain a copy of the original tape so on the
evening of Tuesday, 22 March, Alison Cahn went to Major
Randall's home. She asked him, as she was asking everyone she
met, if he knew of anyone who had witnessed the shootings. He
said he knew a couple of people who had seen the shooting of Sean
Savage, who had been shot some distance from his two colleagues.

Major Randall then proceeded to tell Alison the account he had
heard from a young man who he said was in a car nearby the
shooting. He mentioned this young man had seen a gunman fire

into Savage's body, then put a foot on Savage as he lay on the ground and put another shot in his head to finish him off. The soldier had then put on his black beret and shown his identity card.

Major Randall would not give Alison the young man's name because he thought the young man might not want to be approached by her. She did gather that the young man worked in a bank and also that one of the other people in the car was a police-man's son. According to Randall he would certainly not speak to Alison, as his father had instructed him not "to get involved": a phrase Alison got heartily sick of hearing in Gibraltar.

Alison asked Major Randall to contact the young man for her and to see if he would do an interview or at least meet her to discuss what he had seen.

The following day Alison phoned Major Randall. Randall said the boy was scared and did not want to get involved but had told Randall what he had seen, with the message that Randall was to pass this account on to Alison. Alison explained to Major Randall that we needed the young man's account in his own words. She asked Major Randall to see if the young man would write out his account for her.

The young man was of course Kenneth Asquez who worked in the Algemene Bank as a clerk. He was then nineteen years old and had played in football matches refereed by Bob Randall, who also knew his parents. He gave Major Randall a hand-written statement the next day. There was no great significance attached to the fact that Asquez had not signed the hand-written statement, as the team knew Asquez did not want to reveal his identity.

When Major Randall handed Alison the statement, he reiterated that the young man was happy for us to use the information in it on our programme, but that the young man did not want to be identified or to get involved. Alison then gave the statement to Julian Manyon.

Major Randall's involvement with Asquez on our behalf effectively ended when the hand-written statement was given to Alison.

Alison never suggested to Major Randall that he offer money to Asquez. She never agreed to pay Asquez money nor said that

Thames would do so. Asquez never asked for any money. Major Randall was not paid for his help concerning Asquez and he never asked for any payment. The only money he received was for the use of his video and he was paid at the going rate with all the negotiations done by *This Week*'s film researcher in London.

Alison eventually discovered Asquez's name and where he lived.

The team felt that Asquez's statement was potentially significant but did not feel it could be used without verification that it was indeed written by Asquez, and with some further checks on its contents.

On Wednesday, 30 March, while Julian and Chris were filming outside the court house in Gibraltar, Alison visited Christopher Finch, a lawyer who we had retained to advise the production team on matters of Gibraltar law and the collection of evidence, and to take statements from witnesses.

We were aware, in selecting Mr. Finch, that he was one of the leading lawyers in Gibraltar. He had worked as Crown Counsel in the Attorney-General's Chambers, had acted for the Ministry of Defence in serious criminal and public law cases, and had a deep knowledge of the colony. He had, at this stage, no connection with Mr. Paddy McGrory or the families of the IRA terrorists.

On that day, Alison told him she was trying to contact Kenneth Asquez who had written an account for us of how he had seen Savage shot on the ground. She did not give Finch any more details about the content of the statement and did not show him the statement.

Finch knew the Asquez family and phoned the young man's home to discover which bank he worked in. Finch then telephoned Asquez in Alison's presence. Finch told Asquez that he was working for Thames Television and that he wished to discuss what Asquez had seen. He suggested Asquez come to see him in the lunch hour. Asquez agreed.

Finch did not want the *This Week* team to be present when he interviewed Asquez. He felt that Asquez was very nervous and would not be relaxed with us there. Finch agreed to take a detailed statement from Asquez and to ask him if he would do an interview. He suggested we wait round the corner at the Holiday Inn.

Asquez did visit Finch, who later joined us at the Holiday Inn and told us that Asquez had given a detailed account of what he saw but had absolutely refused to do an interview. Finch told us that Asquez was frightened and had refused to sign anything for fear of being identified and perhaps called as a witness. Again we were told that Asquez was happy for us to use his account as long as we did not identify him.

We asked Finch about the value of the details he had taken and the statement he was drafting. He told us its value was that it was a statement made to a reputable lawyer who Asquez knew was representing Thames Television, that he believed Asquez was telling the truth and that he was prepared to testify to that in court. Finch's notes were used to make a draft affidavit which Alison collected from his office the next morning and took to London.

Alison returned to Gibraltar the next week, after returning to brief me, and ensure she still had a fiancée. Even though Asquez had told Finch he would not sign anything, we felt that we should attempt to ask him to sign the draft affidavit. Alison asked Finch to approach Asquez, but Finch felt that Alison should make the initial approach. Alison went to Asquez's house twice to try to get him to sign the statement or at least get some further explanation of why he was so frightened. Both times she was told he was not there. After the second visit, Alison was at Major Randall's flat when Asquez rang to speak to him.

Asquez was angry that she had been to his house and told Randall to tell her that she should not go back. She wanted to speak to Asquez on the phone but he refused to talk to her. Far from encouraging Alison to pressurise Asquez, Randall advised her not to approach him again.

At no time did Kenneth Asquez tell Randall, Finch or Alison that Thames should not use either of his two accounts of the shooting of Savage. Nor did he, at any time before transmission of the programme, either retract his statements or make any suggestion that they were untrue. At no time did any member of the Thames team offer money, or suggest that money would be available, in exchange for Asquez's statements.

How to use Asquez's statement was something to be decided in the cutting rooms back in London. Meanwhile another very important witness had surfaced almost by accident.

Enter the Dark Lady

Since our first week of investigation had produced no official explanation of either the IRA's planned bomb attack or the shootings, we began to approach experts outside government for professional advice.

Eamon Hardy entered into contact with Lt-Col. George Styles, the man responsible for setting up bomb disposal operations in Northern Ireland, and the author of a publication entitled *Bombs Have No Pity*. Apart from his expertise with explosives, Lt-Col. Styles has pursued throughout his career an interest in weapons and ballistics.

Lt-Col. Styles flew to Gibraltar, at our invitation, on Friday, 23 March, and in our company he visited the spot where the IRA had apparently planned to detonate their car bomb, walked through the town on one of the routes the terrorists might have taken, and talked personally to a number of the witnesses we had identified.

It was while the team were filming with Lt-Col. Styles at the petrol station where the shootings occurred, that an elderly woman came up to Alison Cahn and spoke to her.

"I didn't actually understand what the woman was saying," says Alison. "I just felt I had to follow and try and find out. She was speaking Spanish, and my Spanish isn't any good. I followed the woman over to Rodney House and she called up at the window. Carmen Proetta put her head out." The elderly woman had been her mother. "I spent about five or ten minutes with Carmen up there at the window and me on the ground, and finally she agreed to let me in. She was fairly reluctant at first. So I went up and chatted to her. It was the first time I'd talked to someone who said they'd seen the start of the shooting." She was a new witness and no one else had approached her, perhaps because she was only in Gibraltar at weekends.

By now the crew had returned to the hotel. Alison phoned them there and got them to come to the flat.

"She was reluctant," said Alison, "and I talked briefly I think about the possibility of doing it back to camera, but when she decided she would do it, she said she'd do it full face."

When the *This Week* team arrived they could not help being

struck by what a striking and attractive woman she was. She talked fluently and would clearly make a considerable impact. They did not rehearse the interview but went straight in.

The team had brought with them our consultant Lt-Col. George Styles, and he listened to the interview as it was recorded and afterwards examined the view from Carmen's flat and talked to her about what she had seen.

George Styles was particularly struck by Carmen Proetta's description of the SAS men getting out of a police car, jumping over the metal railings in the middle of Winston Churchill Avenue and opening fire. Indeed when the filmed interview was over George turned to Julian and Chris with a triumphant expression and said, "QED".

The reason for this was that when Lt-Col. Styles had earlier examined the bullet marks in two petrol pumps in the Shell station, he had declared unequivocally that the shots in question had been fired from a position slightly ahead of the two terrorists next to the metal railings in the middle of the road. At the time we put it to George that this was, on the face of it, an unusual scenario. Lt-Col. Styles replied, "Facts are facts, and you can't argue with them." He regarded Carmen Proetta's account as vindication of his point of view.

The following morning, at the Rock Hotel, we interviewed George Styles himself.

JULIAN MANYON: Now George you sat in with the interview with Carmen Proetta, who says she witnessed the events of the first two shootings through her window. What was your opinion about the accuracy of her account. Did it reflect what she genuinely saw and heard?

GEORGE STYLES: Oh, I think so, yes. Exactly. And she was very coherent about it all too, and shocked.

JULIAN MANYON: What gives you particular reason to believe in terms of the detail that she gave out, that this was what she actually saw?

GEORGE STYLES: Well, we had walked the course before, hadn't we? We'd seen the marks on the petrol pumps, we'd heard the descriptions of other people, about people jumping over the railings, and it all fits into the general impression that we formed at the time, you know. And her evidence was just corroboration really.

Colonel Styles was firmly convinced that Carmen Proetta was a truthful and credible witness. We placed particular weight on Styles's opinion because his work in bomb disposal had, by his own account, included long experience of assessing eye-witness accounts of explosions in order to extract useful technical information about how the bombs were made.

In addition, the first published accounts of the shootings included descriptions by anonymous eye-witnesses of the gunmen jumping out of a car and opening fire.

The Times of 7 March reported "Witnesses say that police in plain clothes jumped out of a car and shot a man and woman dead."

The *Daily Telegraph*, *Independent* and *Irish Times* had similar reports. Shortly after interviewing Carmen Proetta we asked her if she or her husband could possibly have been the eye-witnesses quoted in these press reports. She replied that this was impossible as neither she nor her husband had spoken to the British or Irish Press.

We were also impressed by the facts that a number of apparently minor details mentioned in Carmen Proetta's interview and later affidavit tallied with those mentioned by other witnesses we had spoken to. Mrs. Proetta was the only person we found who claimed to have seen the start of the incident involving Farrell and McCann at the petrol station. Other witnesses claimed only to have seen the latter part of the incident, but their accounts contained enough similarities to give credibility to Mrs. Proetta's account.

This Week also took several further steps in an attempt to check the likely veracity of Carmen Proetta's interview.

The team asked Mrs. Proetta if she would swear a detailed affidavit on her evidence, and she agreed to do so, although she became worried that the programme might be seen to be anti-British. Julian and Alison had to reassure her that all they were interested in was a factual account of what she saw, and that the programme was certainly not anti-British. On 29 March Alison Cahn drove Mr. Christopher Finch, the lawyer we had retained, to Spain where Mr. Finch took notes of a lengthy conversation with Mrs. Proetta. In the course of that conversation, Alison raised, at Julian Manyon's request, Lt-Col. Styles's theory that Carmen's perception of the hands being in the air, had been caused by bullets striking the two deceased in the chest.

In spite of the factor of distance mentioned by George Styles, Carmen Proetta emphatically rejected this explanation. She said that the terrorists had their hands in the air for the "couple of seconds or so" it took for the soldiers to take up their positions. She appeared to be describing a sequence of events, not a reaction. Nevertheless, we reported Lt-Col. Styles's theory in the programme.

As in the case of Asquez, Mr. Finch was asked to form a view on Carmen Proetta's credibility as a witness. He told us that before he interviewed Carmen in Spain he was mildly sceptical, but returned convinced that the wealth of detail in her statement indicated a genuine recollection of what she had seen.

He was particularly struck by two details. First, her description of the Gibraltar police constable who, by her account, had driven the car in which the gunmen arrived. "I remember," her affidavit reads, "that he was wearing a flat cap, and this fell off his head and on to the ground in the rush."

At the time he took the affidavit Mr. Finch found this an intriguing part of her description. However, neither he nor the *This Week* team were then aware that some element of confirmation, at least of the police constable's dress, even then resided in the hands of the Gibraltar police. This was in the shape of a number of photographs taken immediately after the shooting by Mr. Douglas Celecia from the window of his flat across the road.

Shortly after the shooting Mr. Celecia had handed his unprocessed film to a Gibraltar policeman, who requested it to help with their enquiries. The police then refused to give it back, and it was only returned after the Inquest following legal action initiated by Mr. Celecia and paid for by Thames Television. The photographs, finally available with the faces of the SAS men blanked out, clearly show that the soldiers standing around the bodies are accompanied by one Gibraltar policeman wearing a flat cap.

The second detail which Mr. Finch remarked upon was the description given by Carmen Proetta of how a blond gunman had fired on the terrorists as they lay on the ground. "He appeared to be aiming at their heads, and the blood squirted out like water from a broken pipe."

The precise circumstances of the deaths of the terrorists Farrell and McCann remain contested in spite of the Inquest verdict. Farrell, it is certain, was shot in the head, but what struck Mr. Finch when he prepared Carmen Proetta's original affidavit was the description of the blood squirting. This was also remarked on by Lt-Col. George Styles who told us that it was a further powerful factor arguing for the credibility of her statement. He said that only those who have actually seen the horrifying effect of bullets striking the human body, and the torrent of blood that can result, can describe the event so accurately.

It was immediately clear to Julian and Chris that the contents of the interview with Carmen Proetta were highly controversial, and the decision as to how much weight to put on them must depend, in part, on an assessment of her character. On the day following the interview Julian Manyon discussed this question with Alison Cahn and Chris Oxley. He expressed the view that Carmen Proetta's background must be investigated, first to see if it could have influenced her account and then to see if anything in her past could be used in a smear campaign against her which would be a likely result of her appearance on television. Alison and Chris agreed.

Alison Cahn then spent some time in Gibraltar and Spain investigating Carmen's job, her family and her reputation. It emerged at once that her husband was facing drug-related charges in Spain, a fact which Carmen herself volunteered before Alison asked her about it. After some consideration of this we came to the opinion that we had interviewed Carmen Proetta, not her husband, and that Mr. Proetta's legal difficulties in Spain did not appear to constitute a motive for his wife inventing or exaggerating a story about the British security forces. Indeed, Carmen expressed her concern to us that her appearance in our programme might prejudice his position.

As far as Carmen herself was concerned, Alison's work revealed that she was a legal translator working for a law firm in the courts on the Costa Del Sol. Her employers liked and trusted her, and her family appeared normal, and well looked after.

Was There a Bomb?

Following his conversations with the witnesses and examination of the terrain, George Styles expressed his views on the damage an IRA bombing would have caused, and drew up a diagram of how he believed the shootings had taken place. This drawing was accompanied by a description of the sequence of events as George Styles saw it. He believed the shootings to be a deliberate ambush set in motion by the signal of a police siren.

We respected the professional knowledge that had gone into the construction of this argument but felt there was not enough solid evidence to endorse it in our film. We felt it would have been a step too far.

But in the programme we did quote George Styles's view that a "rapid technical examination" of the white Renault parked next to Ince's Hall would have shown that there was no significant bomb in the car. While George Styles was in Gibraltar, we put to him several of the counter arguments which later emerged at the Inquest. We asked him both about the idea of artificially supporting the springs of the car and about whether the weight of explosive could be distributed to avoid detection. George Styles insisted that his view was correct. He pointed out that he had dealt with car bombs in Northern Ireland and knew what he was talking about.

We also quoted George Styles's view that it was unlikely that the terrorists could have detonated a remote control explosion next to Ince's Hall where the car was left, from the position where they were shot. We undertook further research into remote control explosions, as used tactically by the IRA, before we took the decision to include George Styles's statement in the film.

We talked to a wide range of experts including Dr. Kieran Drake, a lecturer at London University; Dr. Michael Scott, Lecturer at NIHE, Dublin and Professor Mike Howes. In addition, we received from the Belfast journalist, Ed Moloney, detailed notes of his own interviews with a number of experts in the field. These included Lt-Col. Hugh Heap, currently serving at British Army Headquarters, Lisburn, who had given a detailed briefing shortly after the Enniskillen bombing.

From all these sources, two points emerged.

a)   No expert could recall any attempt by the IRA to detonate a remote control bomb beyond line of sight over the distance it would supposedly have happened in Gibraltar. It was emphasised that the IRA use remote control bombs against targets they have under visual observation. In an attempt to check this point, a question about this was included in a letter to the Ministry of Defence, dated 21 April. The Ministry declined to answer on the ground of the forthcoming Inquest.

b)   While there was a dispute among the experts over whether a detonation at such a distance, in an urban environment, would be theoretically feasible, those who accepted the possibility believed it would require a substantial aerial to be mounted on the car. Pursuing this line of reasoning, we contacted AVIS of Torremolinos, owners of the white Renault 5, and asked them to describe the aerial with which the car was equipped. They described it as a normal car aerial mounted at an angle in the front centre of the roof, "the cheapest on the market", said the AVIS Floor Manager. His description was proved accurate at the Inquest.

15

A VERY SILENT GOVERNMENT

While the team was away on location I was continuing to edit the other editions of the programme, an interview with Neil Kinnock, a report on private health care, and another on the anti-Semitism in Austria which had come to the fore again during the row over Kurt Waldheim's activities in Yugoslavia in World War II. There was no Easter break for the programme and when I decided to give the *Death on the Rock* team more time and more resources it imposed considerable strains.

Jonathan Dimbleby came to the rescue. He agreed to film over the Easter weekend in West Belfast, giving an impressionistic account of the community which had responded so violently to the incursion of the two British soldiers who had blundered into the funeral procession. Many on the mainland wondered how on earth people could behave like that. Well, we set out to understand and Jonathan produced what I thought was a powerful but compassionate film, which some red ink letter writers saw as being soft on the Republicans.

Danny Morrison, Sinn Fein's National Director of Publicity, didn't see it that way. Shortly after the programme he sent the following telex from the Belfast Republican Press Centre 51-53 Falls Road, Belfast:

Dear Mr. Dimbleby,

You did the British public and the people of West Belfast a major disservice in your recent programme which was wholly without analysis.

[219]

DEATH ON THE ROCK

I regret having made your acquaintance and should you ever return to Belfast please don't look me up. Next to John Ware's [a reference to a *World In Action* programme about Gerry Adams] the *This Week* documentary was the most appalling programme on Ireland I have ever seen.

Jonathan sent him a pungent reply. Eamon Hardy had been the researcher on that programme, temporarily seconded from the Gibraltar team. When he went to keep an appointment at the Republic Press Centre with Danny Morrison a few days later he was led outside to a piece of waste land in front of the Clonnard monastery. Two tall burly figures came up to him. They were wearing flak jackets, the collars of which came up to their noses, so that they could not be recognised. Eamon noticed one had a large ugly scar by his eye. They told Eamon to get out of town fast. He did. It was an extremely frightening experience.

No wonder most television journalists prefer to leave Northern Ireland alone.

By this time the *Death on the Rock* team had established that the IRA were planning to bomb Gibraltar even before the atrocity at Enniskillen, where on Remembrance Day, 8 November 1987, the Provisional IRA had planted a bomb as a parade was due to take place. Eleven people were killed and sixty-three injured. It struck me that it was particularly hypocritical of Sinn Fein to deplore what Gerry Adams called "the disaster of Enniskillen", while its military wing was planning what was intended to be another similar disaster.

It would be important to demonstrate in our film just what the IRA had intended to do. I had no doubt about their intention. The IRA themselves had made a major propaganda mistake by saying, immediately after the shootings, that their three members were "on active service". Had they said nothing until after Sir Geoffrey Howe's remarkable statement in the Commons, they could have severely embarrassed the British Government as their members were unarmed, there was no bomb in the car, and indeed the explosive wasn't found until some days later, and then in a car park in Spain.

I conceived the idea of blowing up a car with the same amount of explosive the terrorists had intended to use. It would be expensive, but we'd use a clapped out vehicle. The resulting explosion, prefaced by scenes of a crowded Gibraltar, would bring home more vividly than anything else what was intended to happen.

I rang the MoD and asked for help and advice. They would see. A short time later they rang back and said sorry they could not help in any way. "This one is being run from No. 10," they said, "and we are not allowed to co-operate in any way."

A contact at No. 10 told me some months later, "Look, I'm bound to say that there was utter disbelief when we were told, when we heard that the MoD had been asked whether it would sanction the explosion of a car. We just didn't believe it. I mean first of all we knew damn well what happens when a car blows up – it's blown apart. I mean it's the preoccupation with the picture you see." I tried to explain how vividly it would convey the terrorists' intention but it was no good.

The contact went on. "We have no faith, we do not trust you." Eventually I found a private contractor who agreed to carry out the explosion for us, but a day or so later withdrew. He had been got at by the Ministry.

We had never attempted to disguise what we were doing from the Government. Far from it. As soon as Chris Oxley had first arrived in Gibraltar he pursued the official sources trying to get their version of events.

In the first few days Chris spoke to both the Governor's assistant, Mr. R. Sindon, and the Gibraltar police spokesman, Inspector Glen Viagas in an attempt to clarify what had happened. They declined to provide any information relevant to the shootings, either on or off the record. They would not even answer the simplest question such as: what time did the incident happen? This apparently could prejudice the Inquest. At least it disproved the old saying, "If you want to know the time ask a policeman".

Chris also had the first of two background conversations with the coroner, Mr. Felix Pizzarello, who expressed his reservations over the Government's announcement that the Inquest would be the only inquiry into the shootings. The coroner indicated that journalistic investigation might play a helpful role.

After she arrived, Alison once again contacted both Mr. Sindon and Inspector Viagas. Neither would help with any details concerning the shootings. Alison later wrote directly to both the Governor and Commissioner of police requesting interviews. Both requests were declined.

On 8 April, Alison Cahn managed to see the Attorney-General of Gibraltar, Mr. Eric Thistlethwaite. He said that he had appealed for witnesses and was anxious for people to come forward. Later he agreed to meet Julian Manyon for an unattributable background conversation which took place on Monday, 18 April. Also present were DCI Emmanuel Correa and Alison Cahn. Waiting in an outer office was a Thames TV film crew in case the Attorney-General should agree to give an interview.

In this conversation Mr. Thistlethwaite and DCI Correa declined to provide concrete details about the shootings. All Thistlethwaite seemed interested in was pumping the *This Week* team for information about what they were going to report and trying to get them to name names. Julian promised all help - after the programme went out. The Attorney-General turned down an invitation to do a television interview or make an on the record statement.

While the team were in Gibraltar and Spain, I was repeatedly in contact with Martin Sands at the Ministry of Defence in London. I asked for an on-camera interview with a Government spokesman, or failing that, help with finding someone who could unofficially put forward the Government's point of view. I also asked for a briefing, either on or off the record, and requested permission to use a Ministry firing range in connection with our filming. All these requests were denied.

We kept up our requests to the bitter end. A week before transmission on 21 April, Julian Manyon had an off the record meeting with two senior officials at the Ministry of Defence. In the course of this conversation, Julian asked the two officials to amplify what the Foreign Secretary, Sir Geoffrey Howe, had told the House of Commons about the shootings. The two Ministry officials declined to supply a detailed account on the grounds of the forthcoming Inquest.

On the same day, Julian Manyon had written to Mr. Martin Sands at the MoD asking for guidance on a series of points. The

Ministry replied in writing that they were unable to comment because of the forthcoming Inquest.

(Despite the reluctance of the MoD to brief *us* on the shootings, a lengthy story detailing their version of events and quoting "military sources", appeared in the *Sunday Times* newspaper on 8 May shortly after the transmission of *Death on the Rock*.)

I learned from my own sources at Westminster that a special Cabinet sub-committee had supervised the Gibraltar operation and, supplemented, had overseen the handling of the fall-out and propaganda offensive up to and during the Inquest. Our activities had been reported to them at regular intervals.

For the first time ever in my experience of programmes covering an issue which involved Government we had no cooperation from them at all. It was most peculiar.

Frustrated in my attempt to have a car exploded I decided that we needed to begin the programme with a sequence about Enniskillen and the appalling casualties that had resulted. I sent Eamon Hardy off to fix that.

He arranged for us to film a sequence with Ronnie Hill who, until he was incapacitated by the bombing, had been the much-loved Headmaster of the local high school. As Julian Manyon wrote in his commentary:

Some wounds heal. Others last long after the memory of the atrocity has begun to fade. . . . Today his [Ronnie Hill's] wife, Noreen, keeps watch as he lives on in a deep coma that, sadly, may prove irreversible. The coma began during emergency surgery to save Mr. Hill's life, after the blast had badly damaged his lungs.

As Julian pointed out, the Enniskillen atrocity was caused by a much smaller bomb than the one intended for Gibraltar.

Internal Politics

After three weeks of research and filming it was clear to me that we were not going to be able to encompass our findings in a standard length *This Week*, which is around twenty-six minutes. So on 31 March I went to see Thames's Director of Programmes. I told David Elstein we now had the makings of an important film but that it was clearly going to be controversial and that it was essential that we put the investigation in context. David, as an ex-Editor of *This Week*, quickly took the point and agreed to try and get us a longer slot. At the Network Programme Controllers' meeting it was agreed that the programme should run for forty-four minutes and transmission should move from 8.30 p.m. to 9 p.m. There was a catch, however. The film had to make that transmission slot because it was the only one with an extended duration. Had the programme remained at a standard length it could have been put back or brought forward almost at will.

While continuing to update Barrie Sales regularly on what was happening I decided we should give the IBA early warning. They are the "publishers" of *This Week* and would clearly need to see it before transmission.

Two days before I talked to David Elstein I had been at an IBA dinner for Arab ambassadors. I took the opportunity to tell my regular contact at the Authority, Peter Ashforth, about the project and that I thought it would be a "sensitive one". I confirmed that there were no plans for secret filming, or for interviews with members of proscribed organisations. I would have needed the Authority's prior permission for that. When I had a definite transmission date and a better idea of how the programme would turn out I would get back to them. Peter said that the IBA would definitely want to preview the programme.

At the Network Controllers Group on 11 April a senior member of the IBA was present when David Elstein outlined the programme and a transmission date was fixed, so they knew it was coming. To all of us concerned at Thames and the IBA it seemed a perfectly proper thing to be doing.

Hoping that I was playing the internal politics correctly, and in between editing the other editions of the programme and commissioning future work, I turned back to the film.

I now knew how we would start the film (with Enniskillen) but how were we going to end it? The normal way would have been to put the evidence we had accumulated to a Government minister, but that didn't look as if it was going to happen.

One of the several people we went to was Mr. Enoch Powell who expressed the view that the SAS must remain within the law. In war, he said, the commission of "crimes" can be justifiable. But it cannot be said that the Army was operating under war conditions in Gibraltar, since it has never been accepted that the IRA is "a state at war". He expressed the opinion that a citizen is not entitled to kill someone on the basis that he knows that person is about to commit murder at a future time.

We raised these issues with a former SAS officer, contacted by Chris Oxley on a non-attributable background basis. He explained that at one stage some elements within the SAS had believed that the Unit should be immune from prosecution because of their unique responsibilities. There had, he said, been debate within the Army, the Ministry of Defence and the Home Office. By this account, it was finally accepted that the SAS should remain under the rule of law, like all other soldiers. "The SAS," said this officer, "are not licensed to kill."

Since neither of the above gentlemen would appear in our programme we approached George Carman, QC, who agreed to address some of the legal issues in an interview. Aware that we had collected eye witness statements that were in apparent conflict with the account given by Sir Geoffrey Howe in the House of Commons, George Carman said on film:

> What is important on the one hand is that Her Majesty's Government take all proper effective steps to stamp out the scourge of terrorism, and I imagine that's beyond dispute. Equally, on the other hand, it is important that the measures that are taken, however extreme and necessary they are, fall within the rule of law, which governs us all. Because even the activities of soldiers or police officers who have to face the awful problem of terrorism, have to be conducted within the framework of the rule of law. So of course it is desirable that there should be a full examination of what actually occurred.

George Carman, QC, went on to make a statement which we regarded as the most important in the film and which we deliberately placed at the end. He said that it seemed to him desirable that some senior judicial power, such as a High Court judge, be appointed to preside over an Inquiry of the kind taking place in Gibraltar.

> Clearly from everything you say, the programme indicates that there are serious important public issues involved, and speaking as a lawyer, one is always anxious that where there is contest on the facts in such important areas, they should be properly and efficiently investigated.

Thus, the last words of our report made no judgement on any of the statements reported earlier but referred instead to "contest on the facts" and the need for an efficient investigation.

We now had nearly all the elements of the film and Chris Oxley started to put it together in the cutting rooms. Julian and I still carried on trying to get some reaction from the Government, with no luck. We had to discard some material due to the usual time constraints, i.e. whatever the length of the programme it is never long enough.

The *This Week* team had filmed a second victim of the Enniskillen blast but decided that such was the power of the sequence with the Hill family it could stand alone to represent the horror of terrorism. At an early stage of our filming, immediately after the shootings at the Milltown cemetery we had interviewed Gerry Adams, the President of Sinn Fein, about the events in Enniskillen and Gibraltar, but he was evasive and we decided to stick with the public statements his organisation had already made.

I first saw the rough cut of the film about a week before transmission. Alison Cahn wasn't with us. Normally I always insisted that researchers should sit in on viewings and check and recheck the scripts. On a sensitive programme like this one it was more than ever necessary but I didn't have the heart to ask Alison to postpone her long planned wedding and honeymoon. A few things are more important than television. We missed her.

Julian and Chris finally gave Alison the go-ahead to leave Gibraltar on the evening of Monday, 18 April (five days before her wedding). She phoned Gibraltar airways to be told that there were no places on any flights till late Wednesday evening. "I went to the

GB airways office, begging for an earlier seat," said Alison. "Eventually, on Wednesday morning, a kind woman in the GB airways office said she had got me a cancellation on the midday flight. I rushed through Gibraltar's terrible traffic to get my flight. I made it on time only to be told by the rude woman on the checking in desk that there was not a seat on the flight and that my later reservation had been cancelled and re-allocated. She said there were no seats out till Friday. I had visions of myself taking a dreadful train journey from Gibraltar to London to arrive on the morning of the wedding. Bill, [Wigmore, her fiancé] hadn't even been able to get the wedding ring because he didn't have my ring size (like a good romantic I didn't wear a ring on the appropriate finger). I just burst into tears and wailed: 'But I'm getting married on Saturday'. The dreadful woman told me to sit down and wait to see if someone cancelled. Someone did and I love them forever.

"I left Gibraltar with wedding gifts from Bob Randall and Carmen, little realising the havoc that speaking to me was about to wreak on their lives.

"Bill did wonder if I'd ever get back. He threatened to break Chris Oxley's legs if I didn't."

The *This Week* editorial meetings in the weeks just before Alison's wedding hardly discussed programmes at all, but whether a stand-in would have to be found for her wedding. Annie Burns, Alison's best friend and also a researcher on the programme said, "They've found one woman to marry Bill Wigmore, how on earth can they find another." He was, after all, a famous Thames bachelor.

I didn't have many reservations about the rough cut of the film but argued that we needed to summarise, towards the end, the evidence we had gathered. That probably added to the furore because when the evidence was put together in that way it did make the Government's official version of events look very questionable. Julian wondered if we were overdoing it. Shouldn't we let the audience do its own summary? I disagreed.

I was sure that the programme was not trial by television. We had raised troubling questions and suggested that the inquest was unlikely to get to the bottom of things, but we had held back on giving a verdict ourselves because we didn't think we had the evidence to give one. Any number of things could have happened at Gibraltar, but we were pretty sure that much of the official version was questionable.

On Monday, three days before transmission I showed the film with a completed picture and an outline commentary to Barrie Sales and the Thames Legal Adviser, Louise Hayman. They made a few constructive remarks but left it largely untouched. Now for the IBA.

I had offered them a preview later that Monday at Thames but when the day came I was informed that the IBA staff preferred to see the programme complete at its own headquarters at Brompton Road, the usual practice. It wasn't the policy of the IBA to preview partly-completed programmes. The Authority seeks to avoid getting drawn into the editorial process, its responsibility being "to see whether a programme as offered for transmission meets the requirements both of the IBA and of the Statutes."

At about 6.00 p.m. on Tuesday, two days before transmission, a copy of the script was dispatched, with a cassette of the undubbed programme later in the evening. The dubbing of the commentary did not begin until the Wednesday and was completed on the morning of transmission, the normal practice. The IBA staff saw the film on Wednesday, 27 April and Peter Ashforth rang me back shortly afterwards, complimenting me on the programme, but asking for three changes to be made in the commentary. Senior staff in the Programme Division, together with the IBA's officer for Northern Ireland, felt that the programme's summing up suggested too strongly that the coroner's Inquest would be unable to establish the truth, and that the Gibraltar police evidence would be unreliable. I accepted these two points but the IBA accepted my arguments on the third point which concerned the Prime Minister's prior knowledge of the detection of an IRA unit in Spain. I had that myself from unimpeachable sources.

At the same time IBA staff also spoke to a Thames lawyer to check the legal position, particularly in relation to the question of possible contempt of court. They received satisfactory assurances. David Elstein, en route to a sales conference, watched the programme on Wednesday night and he was happy with it as well.

Everything seemed to be coming together. Now all that

remained to be done was to get the introduction to the programme right. Here Jonathan Dimbleby was a great asset. He had covered Northern Ireland frequently himself and since taking over the BBC's *Any Questions* as well as presenting *This Week*, had developed into a fine all-round broadcaster. He watched the film, liked it and we discussed together what needed to be said.

He then typed out his introduction:

The killing by the SAS of three IRA terrorists in Gibraltar has provoked intense debate not only in Britain but throughout the world - and especially in the Republic of Ireland and the United States.

There are perhaps those who wonder what the fuss is about, who ask "Does it really matter when or how they were killed?", who say "They were terrorists, there's a war on, and we got to them before they got to us."

However in the eyes of the law and of the State it is not so simple. The question, which goes to the heart of the issue, is this: did the SAS men have the law on their side when they shot dead Danny McCann, Sean Savage and Mairead Farrell who were unarmed at the time?

Were the soldiers acting in self-defence or were they operating what has become known as a "shoot-to-kill policy" - simply eliminating a group of known terrorists outside the due process of law, without arrest, trial or verdict?

There have been many calls for a public Inquiry to establish the facts, though the Government has insisted that the coroner's Inquiry in Gibraltar is an adequate forum at which to discover the truth.

In either case, we believe that the evidence which *This Week* has uncovered for tonight's special programme is of critical importance for those who wish to find out what really happened in Gibraltar last month. Julian Manyon reports.

I thought that would do admirably and for the first time in many days began to relax. It was almost finished. I might even have lunch. The phone rang. It was the IBA again - just checking once more on our legal advice. I thought that was a bit peculiar. We'd been all through the legal position already to their satisfaction. What was up? "Oh it's alright," said Peter Ashforth, "I'll tell you later."

What I didn't know was that at that very moment Sir Geoffrey Howe, the Foreign Secretary, was trying to persuade Lord Thomson, the Chairman of the IBA, not to let the programme go ahead. We were on the verge of the biggest row between Government and broadcasters since *Real Lives*. In many ways it was to be an even greater crisis. I was in the kitchen again and it was hotting up.

16

STIRRING THE POT

The Government sub-committee responsible for the post-Gibraltar propaganda knew well in advance of the date of transmission of *Death on the Rock*, and at our last attempt to get information out of the Ministry of Defence on 21 April we had indicated the likely shape of the programme.

Sir Geoffrey Howe made his move with two days to go. On the evening of Tuesday, 26 April, he phoned the Chairman of the IBA, Lord Thomson, and asked that the showing of the programme should be postponed until after the Inquest. The Foreign Secretary gave as the principal reason for his request the fear that the broadcast might prejudice the Inquest. Lord Thomson said he would look into it and the IBA consulted the leading Counsel. At Thames we had done the same independently and both Thames and the IBA received the unequivocal opinion that the Inquest would not be prejudiced.

(Just to be on the safe side we had withdrawn the sale of the programme to Spain and Gibraltar and advised Visnews and WTN, who had "news access" to our material, that they should take their own legal advice, but that it would be safer to withhold it from Gibraltar.)

Lord Thomson and the IBA did not tell us at Thames what was going on but kept it to themselves. During Wednesday, 27 April, the film was seen by IBA officials who were satisfied with the final content of the script and who reported to an escalating hierarchy of the Director of Television, Director General, and finally the Chairman, each of whom viewed the programme. Lord Thomson was to write later:

Paradoxically, in the light of the controversy it has aroused, the decision to allow the transmission of Thames Television's programme "Death on the Rock", . . . was not a difficult one. My colleagues and I saw no reason why the IBA should prevent Thames's journalists interviewing those who claimed to be eyewitnesses and investigating the affair exactly as numerous other journalists have done ever since the shootings, provided the criminal record of the terrorists and the enormity of the outrage they planned was made clear and the legal position had been established to our satisfaction.

Lord Thomson added robustly, "Sir Geoffrey Howe did his duty and I did mine, and if you do not like that sort of conflict of duty between Government and broadcaster, then you should not be Chairman of an Independent Broadcasting Authority."

We were indeed fortunate to have such a man in charge of the Authority. Ironically the article from which those quotes were taken (*Daily Telegraph* 28 December 1988) was headed, "It was the year of 'Death on the Rock' and death for the IBA."

On Thursday, 28 April, it was decided that the transmission of the programme should go ahead and the Director of Television, David Glencross, was instructed to telephone Sir Geoffrey Howe's Private Secretary to notify him of the Authority's decision, saying that it had been taken at the highest level and after taking legal advice. Sir Geoffrey was soon back on the phone. At about noon he personally telephoned the IBA, and in the absence of the Chairman, spoke to David Glencross. This time, Sir Geoffrey, a former Solicitor-General, raised the issue of contamination and referred to the Salmon Report. The IBA immediately scrutinised the relevant parts of the Salmon Report and again consulted their advisers.

While they were doing so Sir Geoffrey raised the stakes again. The Foreign and Commonwealth Office held a press conference at which the Foreign Secretary's conversations were made public. It was later put about by Government circles that Thames had leaked the story. This was a straight lie. We didn't have the story to leak.

The first I heard of it was from a press call at about 1.15 p.m. I was more than a little surprised. If anything would draw attention to the programme and increase its audience this would. Why had Sir

Geoffrey done it? I phoned Barrie Sales who was just sitting down to lunch at the White House Hotel nearby, unaware of any crisis. He came back immediately.

Meanwhile the IBA had taken the same view of the dangers of contamination as our lawyer had. The subsequent Windlesham/Rampton Report said that the reasons why the IBA felt Sir Geoffrey's arguments ought not to prevail were:

i) The programme had produced new witnesses for the Inquest who might not otherwise have been available.

ii) The programme did not set itself up as an alternative Inquest or Inquiry. It had volunteered all its information to the Gibraltar coroner.

iii) At the time of the programme, no date for the Inquest had been set.

iv) It was clear that the broadcast of the programme in the United Kingdom would not constitute a contempt under the existing law.

v) The effect of the Salmon Committee's recommendations was that any extension of the law of contempt should be limited to interviews or other material obtained or published with the deliberate intent or obvious likelihood of causing any relevant evidence to be altered, distorted, destroyed or withheld. The IBA's considered view was that the interviews with witnesses in *Death on the Rock* did not fall into that category.

vi) The Salmon Committee's recommendation was made in 1969. Under the Contempt of Court Act 1981, a publication can only incur liability for contempt if it creates "a substantial risk that the course of justice . . . will be seriously impeded or prejudiced." In the IBA's opinion, the programme did not fall within that definition.

vii) Because Gibraltar is a small community, the shootings were already likely to have been the subject of much public comment and discussion, even without the benefit of press and broadcasting coverage. There had been a great deal of local coverage in the Gibraltar Press and on the shootings and the Thames programme. The Gibraltar authorities made no move to prevent this. There had also been extensive coverage in the UK Press, without comment from Government or the law officers.

viii) The programme was a legitimate piece of journalistic activity. It was not designed to usurp the function of the Inquest, nor was it trying to set itself up as a quasi-legal process.

Following the Foreign Office briefing about Sir Geoffrey's intervention, the news wires started humming and the matter was raised in the House of Commons. On these occasions there is always a backbencher who is willing to serve his Government's interests. In this instance it was Jerry Hayes, Conservative MP for Harlow. He had not, of course, seen the programme as it had not yet been transmitted. That was no restraint. He rose to the occasion, and put a question to the Minister present in the Commons Chamber, Tom King, then Secretary of State for Ireland.

He enquired if Mr. King would ask the Irish Foreign Minister whether he was as fed up as Conservative MPs with television companies "Raking through the gutters of Gibraltar, finding people to rubbish the Security Services. Will he ask him if he is as fed up as we are with people who are weeping tears for an active IRA unit which would have been responsible for a major massacre in Gibraltar?"

Mr. King replied "I share his concern about the proposal for a television broadcast." He told Parliament that the programme amounted to "trial by television".

Mrs. Thatcher can always be relied upon to go one better. "Trial by television or guilt by accusation is the day that freedom dies," she told a group of Japanese journalists. Asked if she was furious about the programme she replied that her reaction went "deeper than that". She too had not seen the programme when she made that remark.

While all this was going on I was worried that the programme might not go out in the end because we couldn't get the transmission tape completed. We had to add graphics, maps, names and dates, and replace cutting copies of library film with fine prints. With ten minutes to go we edited on Jonathan Dimbleby's closing link.

> That report [he said] was made, as you may have detected, without the co-operation of the British Government which says that it will make no comment until after the Inquest.
>
> As our film contained much new evidence hitherto unavailable to the coroner, we are sending the transcripts to his court in Gibraltar, where it's been made clear to us that all such evidence is welcomed.
>
> From *This Week*, good night.

The stirring *This Week* music, Sibelius's *Karelia Suite*, rang out and the end credits rolled.

We sat back in the hospitality room and relaxed for the first time in weeks. We had done the best we could, and we thought it was something special. I felt a bout of 'flu coming on but it didn't seem to matter. We poured a drink for everyone and toasted Alison Cahn, safely married and on her honeymoon in Venice, blissfully unaware of the last-minute crisis.

Surely the next morning's newspapers would have to pick up the evidence we had discovered and reopen their investigations into Gibraltar? How naive we were: most of the papers were going to go after us.

We should have remembered the words of Colin Wallace, a former Captain in the British Army who worked in Psychological Operations in Northern Ireland in the seventies. He described the potential of misinformation to influence public opinion. "The important thing is to get saturation coverage for your story as soon after the controversial event as possible. Even when the facts come out the original image is the one that sticks."

We were about to be saturated.

The Gentlemen of the Press

The television reviews of the programme in the serious papers were excellent. William Holmes in *The Times* wrote:

[235]

From where I sit, out of the political firing line, the report seemed a significant, thoroughly responsible and serious examination of a most disturbing case . . . Julian Manyon's script jumped to no conclusions and argued no extreme case with "partial witnesses", nor could it remotely be described as "trial by television" – Tom King's phrases in the House of Commons. It simply raised serious questions and suggested they required deep examination.

Editorials in the *Independent*, the *Guardian*, the *Daily Telegraph* and, later in the day, the London *Evening Standard*, supported the IBA's decision to authorise transmission.

The tabloids were a different story. The *Sun*'s editorial was headed "Blood on Screen – Thames' cheap telly scoop is just IRA propaganda," and it began "Does Thames Television want more innocent men, women and children to be killed by Irish Terrorists?" It argued that our report should have been held back until after the Inquest but did not explain why it had not done the same with its reporting. It attacked the IBA in its usual fair and understated way.

Under the quivering geriatric chairmanship of ex-*Dandy* Editor Lord Thomson, it does not merely lack teeth. It has not a fibre of strength or guts in its entire being. [The editorial went on] But in [*sic*] this truly black day for television, the overwhelming guilt belongs to the Thames company. They are supposed to be a British concern and they derive their income from British advertisers.

Their audience is made up of British men and women. *If that audience is diminished in the next few months by bullets or bombs in Ulster or in the rest of Britain, some of the blood will belong on their hands.*

Once more the *Sun* had represented the authentic voice of ignorance and prejudice. The paper's television reviewer Gary Bushell couldn't resist another insult. He wrote "Maybe next time there's a hijack, Thames TV will even have a whip round for the cause." I'm sure he got a pat on the head from his Editor for that.

The *Star* was a little more muted. Its front page was headed "TV slur on the SAS."

I turned to the *Daily Mail*: it usually had something special on such occasions. The headline read "Fury over SAS 'Trial by TV'" with a large picture of Carmen Proetta. Most of the papers had photos of Carmen prominently displayed. Inside the *Mail*, Geoffrey Levy's review of the programme was headed "A woefully one-sided look at the killings." I was about to read on when I noticed a photo of myself looking rather worried (where did they get that?) above a column by Garry Jenkins entitled "Two men trailed by trouble." It was an attack on Julian Manyon and myself. Carrickmore had reared its head again. Jenkins wrote, "As the then Editor of *Panorama* he let a film crew co-operate with an IRA squad who tipped them off they were setting up a roadblock." I made a mental note to sue (I did so successfully) and then got on with the business of trying to brief journalists.

Julian, Chris and Thames's Press Office were working flat out. The details were so complicated that it was difficult to get our story across. I asked *The Times* whether they would like an article from me explaining what we had been trying to do. The features editor said yes, if he could have it in two hours. I locked the door and wrote a thousand words. The sub put a headline on it "Rock: facts we need to know", and the paper put it on the centre page. I was very grateful.

My 'flu was getting worse and I was getting ready to go home when Channel 4's *Right to Reply* programme came on the phone. Would I appear on that week's programme, to be recorded at 6 p.m? I said I'd ring them back and discussed it with Barrie Sales and Thames's Managing Director Richard Dunn, who had been like a rock himself over the last forty-eight hours. Richard's view was that I shouldn't appear.

He felt we were getting our case across – so why risk being stitched up? I disagreed. No one enjoyed going on a programme to be criticised but I didn't see how we could make tough critical programmes about others and yet refuse to be answerable to the viewer ourselves. *Right to Reply*'s format was to invite ordinary viewers to put their criticism to the programme maker. We had to be accountable. Richard still didn't like it but let me make my own mind up. "Be careful", he said. I thought he was being far too pessimistic.

The car from Channel 4 didn't turn up so I walked down Tottenham Court Road, turning right by Goodge Street tube station to the studios in Charlotte Street. I was taken down a corridor into the hospitality area. Linda Agran, the presenter, was already recording other parts of the programme. I was shivering and kept my coat on. I didn't feel like talking any more. I was exhausted and would have loved a glass of whisky, but not before a recording.

After a couple of minutes I was taken into the studio and met the two "ordinary viewers" who would question me. One was a retired naval commander and the other a young man called Christopher Monckton. He had dark hair and looked as though he had just come in from the City via the Guards. I seemed to have heard the name somewhere before, but couldn't place it, yet it troubled me. The recording began and the former naval officer politely put a number of questions and criticisms to me that I felt I answered adequately. We had so much more information than we could put on the screen that I was able to fill in the background to some of our statements. Monckton was different altogether. He avoided the facts and attacked my motives. He sounded like a *Daily Mail* editorial and I half waited to be called a Communist. I replied rather wearily. If I hadn't been so tired I would have lost my temper. I didn't mind people saying I was wrong but I couldn't stand being accused of being unpatriotic. Who was he to define patriotism? I let it go and tried to get back to the basic points. *Death on the Rock* had not been trial by television, we had not brought in a verdict.

The discussion was coming to an end. Linda gave the two "ordinary viewers" the last word. The former serviceman remained critical but friendly. Then it was Monckton's turn. With the seconds ticking away he seemed to look down at a piece of paper and proceeded to slander me, accusing me of being associated with terrorists again. I tried to come back but the recording was over. It seemed to me a straightforward bit of character assassination.

I was furious and told Monckton and Channel 4 that if that recording went out I would sue. The producers were in a quandary,

DEATH ON THE ROCK

because as a matter of principle they never edited such discussions. "Well," I said, "you had better edit this one." I was not at my most reasonable. Then I suddenly remembered the context in which I had met Christopher Monckton before. It had been at a Conservative Central Office cocktail party, yet he had rung up *Right to Reply* as an 'ordinary viewer' and said he was a journalist. I challenged him about his background. It transpired that not long before he had been a member of Mrs. Thatcher's private office at No. 10 Downing Street. I suggested to the producer that was a relevant piece of information to give the viewer and he agreed.

We were left with the slander. Liz Forgan, the Director of Programmes and Michael Grade, Chief Executive of Channel 4, had been watching the recording on closed circuit. They quickly came down to the studio and we all adjourned to Michael's office where the in-house lawyer joined us.

After protracted haggling in which I changed my mind more than once and Liz Forgan's considerable powers of common sense and diplomacy were fully deployed, I accepted that the discussion should be faded out just before the slanderous remarks and that the audience would be told why this had been done.

I crawled off home and went straight to bed. I have never met Christopher Monckton since, although he was unable to resist writing as follows in his column in the *Evening Standard* when he heard that we were considering making a follow-up programme to *Death on the Rock*. Above the article was a photo of Mr. Monckton wearing a bowler hat and a contented smile. You catch the man in his style.

So now they're planning to make "Death on the Rock II", a new and no doubt still more pro-terrorist, anti-Security Forces pseudo documentary on the Gibraltar killings than the first effort.

No doubt Thames TV has been heartened by winning a top award at BAFTA (known to my friends as LEFTA) . . . Fortunately, the vast majority of the British people have no time for the cringeing, limp-wristed antics of the wet liberal pacifists in the TV establishment.

. . . My father was the Army's youngest General. As Director of Public Relations for the Army he faced exactly the same pink-tinged TV bias against the Forces as is displayed in "Death on the Rock".

Smearing Carmen

I had hoped things would have quietened down a little by the Saturday following the programme. The serious newspapers reported continuing attacks upon us by Sir Geoffrey Howe and the Prime Minister but I regarded these as inevitable. The reporting was fair and balanced.

The tabloids, however, were something else. A smear campaign had been launched against our most prominent eyewitness, Carmen Proetta.

Nigel Bowden, a freelance journalist who supplied copy to the London dailies, was the original source of the stories. He had discovered that Mrs. Proetta was a director of a company called Eve International. He made some assumptions about this and the tabloids made rather more.

Their Saturday headlines included "Shame of the SAS smear girl" (the *Star*), "Trial by TV Carmen is Escort Girl boss" (*Daily Express*) and the appalling "The Tart of Gib" in the *Sun*.

Mr. Murdoch's finest alleged that Carmen used to be a prostitute. It also claimed that Mrs. Proetta had a criminal record in Gibraltar. The *Daily Express*, the *Daily Mail*, and the *Sun* alleged that she and her husband were anti-British. The *Star* went so far as to claim that Carmen Proetta "campaigns for Spanish rule in Gibraltar."

All these charges were rubbish and Mrs. Proetta has successfully sued a number of the papers. The *Sun* apologised to Carmen Proetta on 17 December 1988, sadly long after the Inquest had taken place and the damage had been done. The *Sun*'s solicitor told the court the newspaper "regretted that these untrue allegations about the Plaintiff had been published and apologised for them." The paper accepted that "Mrs. Proetta had given an honest account of what she remembers seeing and that she neither hated the British nor was she guilty or involved in the other misconduct described."

Carmen was paid very substantial damages.

Mrs. Proetta is in fact a court interpreter in Spain and she used her qualifications as a Spanish resident to help two non-Spaniards set up a firm called Eve International, whose purpose is stated on company documents to be "providing escorts and tourist promotion services." Shortly afterwards she renounced her shares and involvement in a legal document dated 14 March 1985, three years before the shootings.

She had no criminal record in Spain or Gibraltar and the "senior police officer" named in the *Sun* story as having confirmed that Mrs. Proetta had a criminal record in Gibraltar denied he said any such thing to the *Sun*.

She has never been a prostitute and she does not have anti-British views. The latter is still the case which is rather surprising considering how the dogs of Fleet Street treated her. We all felt terrible that someone who hadn't wanted to be interviewed in the first place, whom we had persuaded to tell what she had seen, should have been pilloried in this way. My respect for those politicians who attacked us would have been greatly increased if one, just one, had raised a voice against this obscene press behaviour. There was of course silence. To some in Fleet Street it is treason to question the Government about a matter of public importance but perfectly all right to smear someone whose only mistake was to have looked out of her window one day in March 1988 and had the courage to tell what she had seen. The message to other potential witnesses was clear.

Nothing could get worse we thought, but we had not allowed for the *Sun*'s stablemate in the Murdoch Empire, the *Sunday Times*.

Insight?

Mr. Murdoch had no love of the existing television order as the success of his extremely expensive Sky Television service depended in large part on breaking it up. The Editor of the *Sunday*

Times doubled as the Chief Executive of Sky TV and devoted his enormous energies to getting it launched. It was a wonder he could do both those jobs and then spend so many evenings at Tramp nightclub.

Doubtless by coincidence Mr. Murdoch's newspapers, the *Sun*, *Today*, *News of the World*, *The Times*, and the *Sunday Times* all argued for the deregulation of television and the freeing of the skies for satellites. Still, the *Sunday Times* retained some vestiges of its once great investigative tradition even though Andrew Neil was critical of some of the past. He said there were hard left elements involved in the old "Insight" team. This gave great amusement to people like the outstandingly independent columnist Hugo Young who worked on it.

Mr. Neil had called his team together when the *Death on the Rock* row began and told them to take the programme apart and examine every bit of it. The zealous young Features Editor, Robin Morgan, was put in charge of the project. Reporters were dispatched to Gibraltar, to Ireland and throughout the United Kingdom. Their copy was sent back to the Wapping offices of the paper and edited by Robin Morgan.

When I opened the paper on Sunday morning I was devastated. Despite the changes of the last few years the paper was still largely respected and the massive centre spread feature that faced me was a scathing denunciation of *Death on the Rock*.

It was headlined *Inadmissible Evidence?* and claimed " 'Insight' has investigated the documentary's evidence and reports that the picture which emerges actually contradicts many of the programme's claims. Indeed, vital witnesses are now complaining their views were not accurately reported."

There was plenty of unsubstantiated Government public relations in the article such as the following statement, " 'Insight' understands that the Government's lawyers at the Inquest will have evidence that is expected to silence the critics and undermine *This Week*'s evidence. Whitehall sources with access to the official evidence are relishing the prospect. 'Insight' has learnt that the Ministry of Defence believes that it can contradict Carmen Proetta's testimony with incontrovertible evidence . . ."

The article concluded "What started as a 'trial by television' may yet become a trial of television."

Well we could take a lot of this huffing and puffing, but what were really damaging were the quotes attributed to two of our witnesses, Stephen Bullock and Josie Celecia, and to Lt-Col. George Styles. They all appeared to be claiming they were mis-represented. It was very worrying. I had not been to Gibraltar myself during the filming and therefore did not have all the detail needed to refute the allegations. Sitting at home with none of my team with me I momentarily despaired. But then I knew somehow there must be a mistake, a *Sunday Times* mistake. Julian, Chris and Alison were just too straight, too thorough and too experienced to have got it so badly wrong. But how could one explain the *Sunday Times* cocking it up totally? It was to be several months before we knew the answer to that, and it was eye-opening.

In fact when we contacted Stephen Bullock and Josie Celecia they were outraged at the way their comments had been misused by the paper. Mrs. Celecia was quoted by "Insight" as saying that Carmen Proetta's account was ridiculous, and accused *This Week* of missing out this inconvenient testimony. In fact Mrs. Celecia told the *Sunday Tribune* that she was 'quite distressed' by the *Sunday Times* report. "I totally reject suggestions . . . that I described the evidence of Carmen Proetta as ridiculous."

The *Sunday Times* reported a "crucial statement" made by the lawyer Stephen Bullock. He had told them "categorically" that the police car he saw had "Five uniformed officers in it", not plain clothes SAS men. It had pulled up alongside him, perhaps a hundred yards away from the garage, as two SAS men travelling on foot had raced along the pavement to the garage. The volley of shots, he said, rang out as the police car turned on its siren and raced towards the petrol station.

"So Proetta's evidence that the SAS men got out of the car outside the garage and shot the terrorists is contradicted by Bullock." In fact Stephen Bullock and Carmen Proetta were talking about two different cars in two different streets. Carmen said she had seen men in civilian clothes jump out of a car in front of the petrol station and open fire. Bullock had passed a police car with uniformed policemen in it in a different, but adjoining, street. Next to the car were two men in civilian clothes who then ran after Sean Savage. As they did so shots rang out and Bullock turned to see the same shootings as those witnessed by Carmen. He too saw McCann's hands in the air, but did not know whether they were in surrender or not. It was the *Sunday Times* not the witnesses who were confused. Stephen Bullock told the *Sunday Tribune* "I emphatically deny that's what I said [to the *Sunday Times*]."

"Insight" gave what they said was Bullock's account about the terrorists raising their hands; saying that McCann's arms were "Outstretched trying to shield himself," and not, as Proetta claimed, in surrender.

However, Bullock wrote to me to say what a good programme he thought *Death on the Rock* was and how disgraceful he considered the *Sunday Times* article. He rang up the paper to complain and was told there would be an inquiry. He heard nothing back.

The other participant in our programme who was supposed to be complaining was George Styles. He had clearly been told by a number of his friends that the programme was unpatriotic, and was under some pressure. However, he did not withdraw anything he said in the programme and indeed he had more space than anyone else to give his views.

The *Sunday Times* said he was an "angry" man who was writing "a letter of complaint to Thames Television" with "a copy . . . to the Prime Minister." In fact he did no such thing. He wrote to my researcher and did not copy it to anyone.

The newspaper alleged that two of his key views were missing from the programme. Firstly, his disagreement with Carmen Proetta over whether Farrell and McCann had raised their hands in surrender or had done so because of the impact of the bullets. The Colonel thought the latter.

This was a bizarre complaint because as anyone who watched the programme could see the Colonel's opinion on this *was* quoted in the programme. However, we did not include the second "key view".

George Styles was clear that a radio controlled device would not have been practicable in the Square in Gibraltar. That we had reported. However, he had gone on to say that perhaps there could have been a bomb in the car that the terrorists had left over the border in Spain to use for the getaway. Neither Sir Geoffrey Howe's statement in the House of Commons nor any on or off the record statement from the Government, or defence sources or the Spanish police ever referred to this possibility. Accordingly we did not include this section of Styles' interview. Why should the terrorists wish to explode a bomb in a car parked by a Spanish roadside?

The irony of this situation was that George Styles thought the Gibraltar shootings had been a straightforward 'taking out' operation by the Security Forces – something he supported. As he wrote to us, "My reading of the Gibraltar incident was that it was a carefully planned operation to prevent a disaster taking place rather than to catch terrorists after the event."

When Chris Oxley rang up Lt-Col. Styles and said he was sorry if George felt badly about it all, he replied, "You don't have to apologise to me." He went on, "The thing which makes me most cross is the way the Press has gone for Carmen Proetta because, you know, what she said was true."

When Chris told me this I was very much relieved, but also well aware of the long uphill struggle we faced to persuade even our friends that we had got it right. The natural reaction to such disputed evidence is to think it's about fifty/fifty with both sides right and wrong.

With impeccable timing the IRA made our situation even worse. On Sunday, 1 May, the day of the "Insight" attack, the organisation carried out the brutal and callous murder of three off duty British servicemen in Holland. They were returning after a Saturday night out when they were blown up and shot. You can imagine what the tabloids made of that. *Today* had a cartoon of a blown-up car and a *This Week* crew interviewing a bystander. The caption read, "No sign of surrender – seems like the IRA were perfectly within their rights then?"

The *Sun's* editorial screamed abuse at the Chairman of the IBA. It was headlined, "For God's sake go, Thomson." It attacked our programme again saying it was "a piece of IRA propaganda. Its only purpose to discredit our Security Services. Its effect was to spur the IRA into fresh atrocities."

We spent the next week trying to row back the tide, briefing every journalist we could. Bernard Ingham, the Prime Minister's Press Secretary, continuted to damn the programme, and Carmen Proetta's life was made hell as the pack descended on her, offering money up and down the Costa Del Sol to anyone who would say something derogatory about her.

The *Sun's* front page "The Tart of Gib" was plastered on lampposts where Carmen lived and at the border with Spain. Carmen was frequently in tears and almost snapped completely when she discovered that her young daughter was being chased to and from school for some quotes.

If ever there was a danger of "contaminating" witnesses surely this was it. The tabloids ignored the fact that Mrs. Proetta would be giving evidence to the coroner's Inquiry, whose purity Sir Geoffrey Howe was so worried about. They harassed a witness. The Government spoke not a word.

The battle continued. The Prime Minister again attacked the programme in the Commons. I wrote a letter to *The Times* explaining that although I regarded the IRA as murderous terrorists, they had to be understood. Ian Curteis, the playwright, responded in the *Daily Mail* by calling me "notorious" and saying that "The mock dignity of his letter fails to disguise the poverty and weasel-wording of his arguments." My programme was "crookedly tendentious." Later on in his article there were references to Goebbels. The paper carried another article headed, "Advertisers in revolt over IRA deaths film." I wondered if the world was going mad.

Relief came from an unexpected quarter. The BBC Northern Ireland current affairs programme *Spotlight* had done its own investigation into the events in Gibraltar, and intended to transmit it a week after our programme. Sir Geoffrey Howe tried to stop that one too. The new regime in the BBC were in a tight corner. They decided to let the programme go ahead but restricted its transmission to the audience in Northern Ireland, for which it was intended. Usually in such a case the programme, or significant chunks of it, would be repeated on the network. When Alex Thomson, the reporter, pointed out that the issues were clearly of national interest and therefore that the programme should get a network transmission he was told, "Look, you've won one battle, don't push your luck." The preservation of the Institution came before its journalistic duty.

Can anyone imagine a national newspaper not reprinting such a story from one of the regional newspapers in the same group as itself?

Sir Geoffrey Howe called the BBC's decision a tragedy which went against twenty years of high standards. We saw it rather differently. The *Spotlight* film fully confirmed what we had reported and went rather further, if anything.

A number of journalists, notably Heather Mills in the *Independent*, began to pursue the unanswered questions about Gibraltar with great tenacity, and were to be followed by the *Observer*, the *Daily Telegraph* and the *Guardian* who all focused on the events rather than programmes which reported on them.

The Government responded by stepping up its campaign against the "irresponsibility" of the British media. The Prime Minister's Press Secretary, Mr. Bernard Ingham, took the unusual step of speaking out on the record. He told the *Observer* that the standards of the media had declined "to the point of institutionalised hysteria." He was not referring to the *Sun*. The Prime Minister was said to be determined to "remind the media of their responsibilities." Broadcasters were to be told that they operated within society and were obliged to uphold its institutions, notably legal proceedings. The *Observer* reported that "According to Home Office sources . . . the Home Secretary is expected to seek an early meeting with the Chairman of both the BBC and the IBA." By Sunday, 8 May, ten days after *Death on the Rock*, I began to think the tide was turning. The *Observer*'s Ian Jack wrote an extremely shrewd and well informed analysis of the controversy and the paper pointed out that Carmen Proetta was "the victim of a British newspaper campaign to discredit her as a witness".

The paper even quoted Sir Joshua Hassan, Gibraltar's most eminent personage and its former Chief Minister, as describing Mrs. Proetta as "A very intelligent woman," and an old family client of his law firm.

Thames management had stood rock solid behind us with both the Chairman, Sir Ian Trethowan, and the Managing Director, Richard Dunn, going out of their way to be supportive. David Elstein, the Director of Programmes, wrote robust replies to the articles in the *Sunday Telegraph* and the *Sunday Times* which they, to their credit, printed.

The *Sunday Times* however published another detailed "Insight" article on 8 May which was just as critical of us as the first, and repeated some of the same errors. The paper quoted "military sources", something they were to do a great deal of over the next few months. They seemed to have a direct line to the Ministry of Defence. The paper managed to have its cake and eat it however. Having criticised us, its "Comment" column argued that the Government was wrong to have tried to stop the programme going out, using "bogus" legal arguments.

Well that was something but it was clear that the battles were going to continue right up and through the Inquest. But when was that to be held?

17

INQUEST – ON THE SHOOTINGS

When would the Inquest be? First it was thought it would be within a couple of weeks, then it was to be May. Finally the coroner's office announced that it would begin on 27 June. We began to think about whether we should mount a programme at the end of the Inquest, analysing what had been revealed and comparing it with *Death on the Rock*.

But at eleven o'clock on 23 May, Bernard Ingham, press secretary at 10 Downing Street, announced that the Inquest would be indefinitely postponed. He added that the Government had received this news from the coroner, Mr. Pizzarello over the weekend. The postponement was of course Mr. Pizzarello's decision and the Government would not dream of interfering with the coroner's timetable.

Unfortunately, Mr. Pizzarello was unaware of the decision he had just taken. Instead he was at that moment telling Dominic Searle, a reporter on the *Gibraltar Chronicle* and correspondent for the Press Association, that he was considering a postponement, but only considering it. At three o'clock in Gibraltar (two o'clock in Britain) the coroner was still denying that a decision had been made. Ingham appeared at four o'clock and said that the position was not clear. He referred enquiries to the Gibraltar coroner who, at around the same time, was confirming the decision to postpone. This curious *pas de deux* led Labour Shadow Northern Ireland Minister Kevin McNamara to comment "I'm surprised the Government did not announce the verdict as well."

What was the reason for the delay? The only official one given was the fact that the Gibraltar International Festival of Music and the Performing Arts was scheduled to begin on 24 June and four days of it would coincide with the Inquest. This coincidence would, apparently, put too great a strain on police resources.

In the event the Gibraltar arts festival was hardly noticed even by Gibraltarians.

The *Daily Telegraph* reported that the festival "was in full swing yesterday, but it was difficult to spot the difference". An estimated two hundred people had attended events which included a baby competition, rowing race, flower arranging, and painting exhibition. "No one in Gibraltar is convinced that the police force of two hundred and forty was not adequate to watch over both the Inquest and the festival", reported the *Telegraph*. There had not been a single arrest in the festival's four year history.

The Inquest was delayed for a further two and a half months, by which time Parliament had gone on holiday, with the consequence that there could be no difficult questions asked in the House arising from the Inquest. Mrs. Thatcher then went on a visit to Spain, where she discussed a number of issues, including security matters.

In the run-up to the Inquest the *Sunday Times* became required reading if one wanted to see how the Government's case was shaping up.

Before our programme official sources had praised the Spanish authorities for their cooperation over surveillance and no one had contradicted the claim that the terrorists had been identified as they crossed the border. However, our film had raised the obvious question: why on earth allow a car bomb to be taken into the middle of a crowded town? What could justify taking such an appalling risk? Such questions need not be answered, of course, if the Security Forces could be shown to have missed the car at the border. Government sources began to develop the latter case.

The second problem was why shoot the unarmed terrorists rather than arrest them, which was the officially stated plan? It seemed there would be two parts to the Government response to this. First, the soldiers did not know that the IRA members were unarmed. Second, the terrorists made moves which suggested to the soldiers that they were going for their (non-existent) weapons.

There was a considerable problem here though. Why should the terrorists have made such moves, why should Mairead Farrell, for example, have gone to open her handbag? After all, the terrorists knew they weren't armed.

There was a final problem for the Government to face. Why had so many shots been fired into the bodies? After the first few moments the Irish were obviously not going to be able to draw their (non-existent) weapons. The official answer to this, leaked to the *Sunday Times*, was the possibility that the terrorists had radio detonators in their hands, 'buttons' to press. The problem was that they had never used such detonators before out of line of sight, and Lt-Col. George Styles had doubted whether it was at all feasible anyway. The Government would have to find their own expert to contradict this.

What would be of the greatest assistance to the Government case would be if some of the *Death on the Rock* witnesses were discredited, or if they retracted, or simply didn't turn up.

I was not entirely surprised therefore when the *Mail on Sunday* of 29 May 1988 carried a front page headline stating "Carmen says 'No'". This "exclusive" was the work of Chester Stern in Gibraltar and Peter Dobbie in London. "Key Gib witness snubs Inquest", it read. "The controversial key witness to the Gibraltar IRA shootings has told the authorities that she will not give evidence at the Inquest. And she has refused to make a statement to police on the Rock about the deaths she claims she saw."

It was our old friend 'government sources' again. The *Mail on Sunday* confirmed it. "Government sources in London have now revealed that Mrs. Proetta, a court interpreter, is refusing to repeat her story in court."

The *Sun* was nothing if not consistent in its reporting of Gibraltar – consistently wrong. It followed up the story two days later with an editorial headed. "Where is Carmen?" It then libelled her again, referring to her as a "shady lady" with a "lurid past". These were to be expensive mistakes for the tabloid to make, and of course Carmen did make a statement, did turn up at the Inquest, and never said that she would not.

A lesser person might well have crumbled under the pressure.

The PR offensive continued up to the eve of the trial when official sources leaked to ITN details of the statements the SAS would make in court, thus getting their case across early. The official doctrine "no comment until after the Inquest" was clearly for the birds.

Meanwhile I was pursuing a libel action against the *Daily Mail*. Normally such actions can take up to two or three years to get to court. I was anxious to get a settlement quickly before the Inquest began, in the hope that this would prevent more of the sort of reporting we had been subjected to at the time of the programme. We settled out of court and on Saturday, 6 August 1988 the *Mail* put out the following apology:

Mr. Roger Bolton.

On the 29th and 30th April and the 4th May 1988 the Daily Mail published articles on Thames Television's *This Week* programme, edited by Mr. Roger Bolton, entitled *Death on the Rock*.

In the course of those articles reference was made to Mr. Bolton cooperating or having secret dealings with terrorists.

We accept that such suggestions are not true, that Mr. Bolton does not sympathise with or condone terrorism in any form nor has Mr. Bolton offered terrorists a platform for their views and that no such considerations influenced the making of *Death on the Rock*.

We unreservedly apologise to Mr. Bolton for the embarrassment caused.

I had a faint hope that some other newspapers would take notice.

I was in a bit of a quandary about how I should deal with the Inquest. It was clear that we would be on trial in the Government's eyes but only three sides would be represented in court; the British Government, security forces and the families of the dead terrorists.

I did not want us to be associated with the families' legal representative Paddy McGrory; on the other hand it was in our interests that he was as fully briefed as possible about our programme and the witnesses we had uncovered. We had a further possible problem when we discovered that Christopher Finch, the lawyer who had worked with us in Gibraltar, was assisting McGrory. He had every right to do so on the "taxi rank" legal principle and, as he had completed his work for us before taking on this other brief, there was nothing improper involved. In fact, Finch had been so outraged by the ruthlessness of the propaganda onslaught which witnesses like Carmen had to face that he became even more determined to get at the truth. Still, I thought it could prove embarrassing for us.

So, if we couldn't be legally represented, should we be present at all? Initially I thought not, partly because it wasn't strictly our business. We had simply made an honest assessment of the evidence we uncovered during our research and made a programme about it. We weren't accusing anyone. The other reason was financial. I couldn't afford to keep someone in Gibraltar indefinitely or keep Julian, Chris and Alison off the road. They needed to work on other stories. *This Week* had a relatively small team and I could ill afford to reduce it further. On reflection it was silly not to have sent someone even though I still find it difficult to see what they could have done which would have affected the way in which the Inquest operated or the way in which our activities were reported.

The reservations about the remit of the Inquest which we had expressed in our programme seemed to be justified as the hearing got under way.

The role of an Inquest is to ascertain who the deceased was, and how, when and where the deceased died. It does not determine *why* death occurred. The coroner's verdict is not binding on anyone and not admissible as evidence in any subsequent court hearing.

The coroner decides who is called to give evidence and has power to subpoena witnesses within his jurisdiction, but not from outside. Limited cross-examination is allowed but only the coroner may address the jury as to the facts of the case.

In Gibraltar it was of course the question 'why' which was most important. It was not to be asked. And as the Government was determined that this was to be the only hearing into the shootings, with a bit of luck, from their point of view, it would never be asked in a court.

[253]

Paddy McGrory was at another disadvantage. Inquests, unlike trials, do not require the advance disclosure of witnesses' statements, so the families' lawyer had no idea what most witnesses would say before they said it. However, as it was the Crown's inquest, the Crown's counsel, John Laws, QC read the statement of every witness beforehand. Laws, therefore, could think ahead, while McGrory was bound to have a hard time keeping up and had no way of testing evidence he was hearing for the first time against what later witnesses might say.

McGrory had other problems. Public interest immunity certificates had been provided to the Crown Counsel which he invoked whenever the questioning seemed as though it might endanger "national security". The Inquest was therefore to learn little about the events in Gibraltar, Spain, Britain or Northern Ireland before the shootings, nor was it to discover the true extent of the military and police operation on 6 March.

The families' lawyer was also short of money. In fact he had given his services free. Meanwhile the legal authorities in Gibraltar had decided to charge ten times the usual rate for the court's daily transcripts. Four days before the Inquest they raised the price from fifty pence to £5 a page – which amounted to between £400 and £500 a day. McGrory had to rely on longhand notes made by a legal colleague from Belfast.

As McGrory was also the only person in court asking awkward questions about the official account, a great deal of responsibility lay upon his shoulders and it seemed as though he faced an uphill struggle.

When the Inquest finally started in September it was hot and humid in Gibraltar. In the courtroom a large plaster representation of the royal coat of arms was fixed to the wall behind the coroner. The lion and the unicorn were resplendent in red, white, blue and gold. The court was wood-panelled, varnished in brown, with a gallery that looked down on to the eleven members of the jury – all men – who were to bring in the verdict. The windows were double-glazed and the air conditioning had broken down. There were no fans and everyone sweltered. It had been finally agreed that the soldiers and police involved in the shootings would testify, but they would only be identified by letters and would give their testimony hidden behind a screen.

The purpose of the Inquest was to determine, not the guilt or innocence of the soldiers, but whether or not the killings were lawful. The operation had been called "Operation Flavius" and there had been written instructions of engagement given to Officer F, the overall military commander.

Use of Force

You and your men will not use force unless requested to do so by the senior police officer(s) designated by the Gibraltar police commissioner, or unless it is necessary to do so in order to protect life. You and your men are not then to use more force than is necessary in order to protect life . . .

Firing Without Warning

You and your men may fire without warning if the giving of a warning or any delay in firing could lead to death or injury to you or them or any other person, or if the giving of a warning is clearly impracticable.

Warning Before Firing

If the circumstances in [above] paragraph do not apply, a warning is necessary before firing. The warning is to be as clear as possible and is to include a direction to surrender and a clear warning that fire will be opened if the direction is not obeyed.

These were the rules and yet three terrorists were unarmed and there was no bomb in their car when they were filled with many, many holes. Was that possible within the law?

As the events unfolded we felt that the questions we had raised as matters of concern in *Death on the Rock* remained just that.

Surveillance

Prior to the Inquest the Spanish had expressed great pride about the efficiency of their operation against the IRA's active service unit, following them up to the gates of Gibraltar, as we reported. The Government position suddenly became that, though the surveillance was generally good, contact with the terrorists was lost in the few hours before they came to the Rock. The granting of a Public Interest Immunity Certificate made it impossible for Paddy McGrory to probe the surveillance operation in any detail. However an attempt was made by the Government side to introduce what was said to be a statement by a Spanish Police Inspector, Rayo Valenzuela, supporting the official line that the terrorists had been lost. The statement was rejected as evidence by the coroner because the Spanish authorities refused to allow the officer to appear at the court to testify. Nevertheless, much public-relations weight was given to this by Whitehall. This alleged statement puzzled us, as it apparently puzzled sections of the Spanish police who expressed their anger at the suggestion that there had been anything wrong with their surveillance.

(After the Inquest we managed to get hold of a copy of this statement, allegedly made to Detective Inspector Correa of the Gibraltar police. We discovered that the statement was taken unsworn, and that the English translation delivered to the coroner was even unsigned.)

In fact Tim McGirk of the *Independent* was told officially by the Spanish police that their surveillance was so good they actually listened into the IRA Active Service Unit as it was preparing the details of the operation.

Still, the official line was that the terrorists came into Gibraltar unseen, that the authorities were expecting them on Monday evening to prepare for a bombing on the Tuesday. When Sean Savage, using an Irish passport in his known pseudonym of Brendan Coyne, drove his Renault over the border on the Sunday they missed him.

But the official position was dramatically queried, if unintentionally, when the head of Gibraltar's Special Branch, Detective Chief Inspector Joseph Ullger, gave evidence.

He said the authorities "were concerned to gather evidence . . . Members of the (British) security service had said that they don't normally give evidence in court . . . so the [police] commissioner spelled it out that evidence was absolutely vital for the subsequent trial of the terrorists".

McGRORY: You said the only way for the operation to succeed was to allow the terrorists to come in.

ULLGER: We had the police officers who were going to identify these people, SAS people . . . to assist us in the arrest, so I did not see the problems at all. It would have been a problem if we'd told the police officers on duty at the frontier because unfortunately word would have got round . . . and I think there was an absolute need for extreme confidentiality.

McGRORY: But you told the Spanish officers?

ULLGER: Yes . . . the Spaniards were told because we required the technical advantages, facilities, which they had with computers, simply because of that.

McGRORY: But you didn't tell the officers on the Gibraltar side, even to look for a passport in the name of Coyne?

ULLGER: No sir, we did not.

(In fact an officer on the Gibraltar side did state that he had the aliases and passport numbers of the terrorists.)

It seemed to us that only two conclusions were possible from Ullger's testimony, which clearly stated that the IRA team were deliberately allowed into Gibraltar with no attempt to have them arrested at the border. Either the authorities did not think there was a bomb in the car, so there was no risk, or else they did and were prepared to risk the lives of the people of Gibraltar for several hours while they could gather evidence before making the arrests. The Security Service watchers who gave evidence at the trial testified that they saw Savage drive his car into the car park at Ince's Hall, where it was expected, at 12.45 p.m. By 2.10 p.m. at the latest, according to the official account, Savage had been clearly identified. Yet the area was not cleared until two hours later. That ran against all my experience of security procedures.

Countdown

Gibraltar Police Commissioner Canepa must have felt overwhelmed when the aircraft landed from London carrying the SAS and their support team of lawyers, watchers, intelligence and all their technology. He was in charge of policing on the island until the moment when he temporarily signed control of the anti-IRA operation over to officer F at 3.40 p.m. that Sunday. Officer F handed it to officer E, who then devolved control to his men in the field. Nothing dramatic had happened until that moment.

By a remarkable coincidence one minute after control was handed to the military a police siren went off "by accident". It was this which official sources had told selected and sympathetic newspapers before the Inquest was the reason why the shootings had started: the terrorists had turned round and seen the SAS men next to them and made those "suspicious movements". Sure enough, that was the official version given in the court. The man who had set off the siren was Inspector Joseph Revagliatte. Together with three of his men he was making a routine patrol of the colony. He testified that he knew nothing of Operation Flavius. At 3.41 p.m. his car received a call to return urgently to the central police station. The car was stuck in traffic so the driver switched on the siren, with rather fatal results.

Revagliatte was adamant he knew nothing about the operation. He was questioned by Michael Hucker who represented the soldiers of the Special Air Service.

HUCKER: When you came on shift at three o'clock or thereabouts did you know anything about the operation at all?
REVAGLIATTE: Nothing at all.
HUCKER: You thought that life in Gibraltar was totally normal, that what was happening between you and the border was the same as happened any other day of the week?
REVAGLIATTE: Exactly.

And there the matter rested. Sadly the Inquest jury were not given sight of a remarkable official document which we obtained some two months later. It was the secret operational order prepared by Police Commissioner Canepa for Operation Flavius. It was read by certain unnamed police officers at a midnight briefing a few hours before the shootings. This order assigned Revagliatte a crucial role in the operation. He was to be the officer in charge of the two police firearms teams, each containing three armed policemen. One of the teams contained policemen P, Q, and R who were witnesses at the Inquest and who were present at the shooting, forming a circle around the bodies immediately afterwards.

This leads to the interesting conclusion that the authorities expect us to believe that policemen P, Q and R knew about the operation but that their commanding officer put in charge of them did not, or that P, Q and R arrived at the scene of the shootings at precisely the time they occurred entirely by accident, and that Inspector Revagliatte did the same. Gibraltar must be a very small place.

A Warning?

Sir Geoffrey Howe, in his statement to the House of Commons, was quite certain that the terrorists had been warned before they were shot. In our research we could find no one who had heard any challenge, something for which we were much criticised. Surprisingly the soldiers themselves, when testifying, did not maintain that there was a warning in all of the cases.

For example, soldier A who, together with his junior soldier B, shot McCann and Farrell said, "I went to shout 'stop!'. Whether it came out I honestly don't know. I went to shout 'stop!' and the events overtook the warning." He then shot McCann and his colleague shot Mairead Farrell without any words being spoken.

Soldiers C and D went after Sean Savage who had separated from his two companions before the shootings and had turned back to the town centre. Soldier C did claim he shouted "Stop!" before firing. But later Paddy McGrory put it to soldier D:

McGRORY: You didn't even finish the warning.
SOLDIER D: Because we didn't have the time to finish the
            warning.

Two on-duty policemen, who witnessed the shootings and were part of the operation, were adamant, however, that soldiers A and B had uttered warnings. Fortunately for the authorities they were able to produce an 'independent' witness who also said he had heard a warning. He was an off-duty policeman, Constable James Parody, who lives in a block overlooking the garage where the shooting took place, and who just happened to be looking out of the window at the right time.

However, there was an embarrassing moment for Police Constable James Parody when Mr. Hucker, for the SAS, asked him: "What about officer P (one of the policemen on duty who heard a warning) who you probably know?" (The witness then knocked down the wooden 'oath card'.)

PARODY: He was the one who was about twenty yards away.

In fact PC Parody knew officer P very well for he was Police Sergeant Harry Parody – the PC's brother.

Unknown to the jury the most convincing independent witness to the shouted warning was the brother of one of the policemen involved in the operation itself. The two brothers heard almost identical warnings which none of the civilian witnesses heard.

The Killings

The Inquest was unable to discover why the three terrorists made threatening movements which indicated that they were either going for their non-existent guns or their non-existent bomb detonators.

However, when the SAS start to shoot, they certainly do shoot to kill. There was never any intention to shoot to immobilise, something which is regarded as impractical. Soldiers are trained to fire and go on firing until they kill, and in this case it was argued that it was necessary to eliminate totally all signs of life in case there was a dying attempt to press the button.

Paddy McGrory wondered what would have happened if Sean

Savage, in the middle of firing, had shouted "Stop! I surrender." Would Soldier D have carried on killing him?

SOLDIER D: I would have carried on firing until I believed he was no longer a threat.

MCGRORY: Even if words of surrender like that had been uttered like that?

SOLDIER D: He may well have said that and pressed the button at the same time.

The SAS certainly took no chances and when the pathologist, Professor Alan Watson of Glasgow University, gave evidence he had a gruesome story to tell. He had been retained by the Government.

Mairead Farrell had three entry wounds in the back and three exit wounds in the chest. There were five wounds to her face and neck produced by two bullets. The head wounds were superficial; she had been killed by gun shot wounds to the heart and liver. Professor Watson thought that Farrell must either have had "the entire body, or at least the upper part of the body, turned towards the shooter" when she was shot in the face and had then been shot in the back as she was going down. McGrory thought that as she was only 5ft 1in inch tall the upward trajectory of the bullets in her back would mean that the gunman would have to be kneeling, or Farrell would have to be close to the ground. Watson agreed.

"Or on her face?"

"Yes."

Danny McCann had two entry wounds to the back, close together, and two exit wounds in the chest. Again the bullets had been fired in an upward direction. He had a hole without an exit in the lower left jaw and extensive damage to the left side of the brain.

The bullets in McCann's back and the back of his head were lethal. Professor Watson suggested that the wound in the jaw stunned him and the rest were fired at his back and head "when he was down or very far down".

The third IRA member was a mess. He had twenty-nine wounds which the pathologist said suggested "a frenzied attack". Sixteen or eighteen bullets had struck Sean Savage. Cause of death was

[261]

recorded as fractures of the skull and cerebral lacerations, added to by gunshot wounds to the lungs. There were seven wounds to the head, five to the back, five to the chest, three to the abdomen and one to each shoulder, two to the left thigh, two to the right arm, one to the left arm and two to the left hand.

Had Savage been finished off on the ground as the *Death on the Rock* witness, Asquez, had alleged? Paddy McGrory showed Professor Watson a photograph of the strike marks left by the bullets on the ground by Savage. Did it look as though those bullets were fired into his head as he lay there?

Watson replied, "Yes, that would be reasonable."

Professor Watson agreed that after Farrell had been shot in the face she would have been in shock and pain. He also agreed that if it was right that she had been shot at close range, as suggested by ballistic reports, then it was 'reasonable' to assume that at that stage she could have been arrested by someone close by. Later, however, when questioned by Mr. Hucker, he agreed it was possible for someone who had been critically shot to draw a gun or press a button.

But as he talked outside the court the officially appointed pathologist made some disturbing and, from the Government's point of view, damaging statements. Asked if the number of Savage's wounds shocked him the professor said, "Yes it did, actually." He thought there was clear evidence that the terrorist had been shot from above while on the ground. He was asked if he found that disturbing. Professor Watson replied, "Well, I think all these things are disturbing. Shooting from the back and all these things, I think it is all disturbing."

Asked if he believed the killings had been murder he replied, "It has to be, doesn't it?" But he added, "Murder is an emotive word. If it was death by shooting you have got to choose between accidental death and murder or suicide. You have got to keep an open mind. Of the three it has to be homicide. It's just a matter of whether it was justifiable homicide."

The professor had more bad news for the Government. He said he had been denied access to key reports on the shooting. He had not seen a ballistic report, clothing worn by the terrorists, the forensic scientist's report – or even a report on a blood sample he had given to a man in London.

Outside the court he was asked whether he considered this official hindrance. He replied, "No idea, but I was hoping I would have the report long before I came here."

The official pathologist's views were supported by Professor Derek Pounder from the University of Dundee, a witness called by Mr. McGrory. He alleged that Professor Watson was hampered in his investigations. "No photographs were provided of the bodies at the scene, neither was any information provided about the scene of death; the bodies were stripped of clothing prior to his examination and he was not allowed to X-ray the bodies."

All this was too much for the *Sun*. It tried to ensure that its readers had the right opinions before they heard the facts. Next morning its headlines read "Why the Dogs had to Die", "IRA Fiend cut down by Sixteen Bullets", and "Blow his Brains Out". The paper called the SAS killings "a super-smooth awayday mission".

On these occasions a quick quote is always available from a handful of MPs who seem to have opinions about everything. Ealing North Conservative MP Harry Greenaway is an acknowledged master of the instant outraged comment. Referring to Professor Watson's views he said, "This was frenzied conjecture on his part. He wasn't there so how would he know?" Had he paused for thought Mr. Greenaway would have realised that a pathologist is never at the scene of a death when it occurs, but that if such an absence is crucial no pathologist in the country would be able to practise.

Professor Watson appeared in court on 8 September. The forensic scientist, David Pryor of the London Metropolitan Police did not appear in court until 27 September. This separation made it difficult to combine their evidence but Mr. Pryor had also been handicapped. The blood-soaked clothes had been dispatched to him in bags. "The clothing was in such a condition when I received it," said Pryor, "that accurate determination of which was an entry site and which an exit site was very difficult." Such information was essential to discover whether the soldiers were telling the truth about the way in which they attacked the terrorists or whether, for example, Carmen Proetta, and Lt-Col. Styles were correct in stating that shooting had come from the centre of the road.

[263]

What Pryor could say, from powder marks found on Farrell's jacket and Savage's shirt, was that a gun had been fired about three feet from Farrell's back, and about four to six feet from Savage's chest. The evidence of these two pathologists threw doubt on the soldiers' stories of how the shootings occurred.

And something else revealed at the Inquest raised eyebrows. After the shootings the SAS soldiers had not given statements to the Gibraltar police. Their travelling lawyer had accompanied the four soldiers when they went to hand over their guns and their spare ammunition at the Gibraltar police station after the shooting. He had also secured permission, from the colony's deputy Attorney-General, that the unit could leave that night for the United Kingdom without first giving statements to the local police. It was not until nine days later on 15 March, after several sessions with the army lawyer, that the soldiers made statements to British policemen who were acting on behalf of their colleagues in Gibraltar.

The Inquest was not able to resolve one way or the other the conflicts of evidence over the shootings. These conflicts of evidence remain today.

A Bomb in the Car?

The Inquest kept coming back to the question of whether the authorities had believed there was a bomb in the car and whether it could have been detonated by remote control by the terrorists in the split second before they lay dead, which was the justification for shooting. The soldiers' demeanour at the court indicated that they, at least, seemed genuinely to have believed so and to have been briefed to that effect. But had they been deliberately mis-briefed by British intelligence who knew better?

Each side produced experts to argue that it was or was not feasible to detonate a bomb out of line of sight by remote control. Lt-Col. George Styles had argued in our programme that it was too risky to use that technique and had also argued that it would have been obvious that there was no bomb in the car by seeing that the springs were not carrying extra weight. A significant bomb would have pushed the car much closer to the ground than it was. We had also pointed out that the small aerial on the Renault would probably have been inadequate to receive the radio messages.

Alan Ferraday, a scientist from the Royal Armaments Research and Development Establishment, showed the court a remote-control device which he said was a favourite of the IRA, and demonstrated how it would fit in the inside pocket of his suit, making little more of a bulge than his wallet.

However, Mr. Ferraday agreed with Paddy McGrory that he was only aware of the IRA using remote control when they had sight of their target. The Hyde Park bomb, which killed several members of the Royal Horse Guards and their mounts, was triggered by a remote control device which the IRA operated with an uninterrupted view from a distance of about six hundred yards.

And Mr. Ferraday told the court that the bomb that was finally found in Spain after the Gibraltar incident was *not* a remote-control device. It had two time-delay units.

Whatever the truth, as far as the verdict was concerned it would be sufficient for the Government to convince the jury that the soldiers *thought* there was a risk of an explosion. The limitation of the coroner's court was revealed by the fact that it could not hope to go back through the intelligence planning to establish whether the soldiers' superiors knew that there wasn't such a risk.

But as far as 'shoot to kill' was concerned and 'finishing off', perhaps we were all asking the wrong question. A better one would be: should you ever send the SAS in if you want an arrest?

It would be a naive politician who decided to deploy the SAS and did not expect shooting to take place. And when the shooting starts it continues until all signs of human life are totally eradicated. Mrs. Thatcher and the members of the secret Cabinet committee which took the decision to deploy the SAS knew this.

If I had any doubts on this score they were removed when some months after the Inquest I had an off-the-record chat with a former Cabinet colleague of Mrs. Thatcher. I was told, "If you get into SAS country you are saying the end justifies the means. I think the danger of the whole thing is that the SAS was put in with such an unsteady ally as the Spanish police, because their values are different anyway."

"You have to take a long time to make up your mind because you know the SAS are trained to shoot first and ask questions afterwards, because they are at risk themselves, and you are putting them into a wartime situation."

The former Cabinet minister went on. "And if they do their job well, as for example at the Iranian embassy, they will undoubtedly shoot some people who could otherwise have been just quietly captured. But that's because that's what they are." What he was referring to was that after the Iranian siege the freed hostages told tales of having held on to the legs of a young terrorist who was trying to slip away – not to have him arrested, but to prevent the SAS soldiers taking him back inside the Embassy building to finish him off. Critics of the Government would doubtless say that the terrorists were dead from the moment it was decided to put the SAS in.

Getting the Right Verdict

Meanwhile where were the gentlemen of the tabloid press? The details of the terrorists' deaths were most inconvenient. The lads were itching to get at Carmen Proetta and the other *Death on the Rock* witnesses. Until they appeared the hacks were relatively unemployed. They worked very hard in the evenings, however. Ian Jack wrote as follows in an excellent analysis of Gibraltar in the December 1988 edition of the magazine *Granta*.

> Lying half asleep in my room at the Holiday Inn one night I listened to a song I hadn't heard in twenty years. The tune was "Marching through Georgia" but the words did not belong to the American civil war.
>
> > Hello, hello, we are the Billy Boys!
> > Hello, hello, we are the Billy Boys!

> We're up to our knees in Fenian blood,
> Surrender or you'll die,
> For we are the Brigtown Billy Boys.

I went to the window. Members of the British popular press were walking unsteadily towards the hotel. Great drinkers and pranksters, these chaps from the tabloids.

Jack went on to describe mass purchases of water pistols with which to shoot people in the back.

When Carmen Proetta, Stephen Bullock, Dianne Treacey and Josie Celecia gave evidence, much of the press magnified every qualification in their evidence. In fact all these witnesses did stand by what they had told *This Week*, although Carmen now conceded that the terrorists might have had their hands up as a reaction to being shot. However, she still thought it was an act of surrender. The surprising thing was how few witnesses there were. *This Week* appeared to have found nearly all the ones who gave evidence at the Inquest, but the shootings had taken place in broad daylight in a fairly crowded area. Clearly many many people had simply refused to get involved and in view of the way Carmen Proetta had been treated, who would blame them?

Something rather more sinister, however, happened to another witness, Robyn Mordue. In the weeks after the Inquest he disclosed that, before he went to Gibraltar, he had been rung up at his ex-directory number, and at a golf club where he works, by men with upper-class English accents who warned him in threatening tones to keep away from the Inquest. Mr. Mordue's subsequent evidence at the Inquest was somewhat unclear.

Then out of the blue came the Kenneth Asquez retraction and then the retraction of the retraction. The former was enough for most of the press. The siege of *This Week* began and the Inquiry was conceded. Did anyone notice that in his summing up the coroner said that the jury should still consider Asquez's first account of events which he had given to *This Week*?

We had done what we could to rectify the damage. Major Randall had sent an affidavit to the court denying on oath Asquez's allegations of pressure and money being offered, but the affidavit could not be read out in court because Randall was in America and therefore could not be cross-examined about it. On his return from holiday Bob Randall publicly challenged Kenneth Asquez to repeat his allegations outside the privilege of the courtroom. If he did so the major promised to sue.

Asquez refused to take up the challenge, and later wrote to a local Gibraltar newspaper denying he ever said Randall had pressured him into making a false statement!

On the morning of 30 September the coroner summed up the evidence to the members of the jury. He did not behave in the curious way of the British coroner at the 1981 inquest into the deaths of the Iranian Embassy siege terrorists. That gentleman effectively prevented the jury from returning any verdict of unlawful killing by telling them, "I think you must consider the implications to this country if the [unlawful killing] verdicts are recorded if soldiers are sent in to do a specific job." The jury was left with a choice between misadventure and justifiable homicide.

Three possible verdicts were available in Gibraltar but Mr. Pizzarello closed off one of them. He urged the jury to avoid the ambiguity of an open verdict. They should decide whether Savage, Farrell and McCann had been killed lawfully, "that is justifiable homicide", or unlawfully, "that is unlawful homicide". If they were to conclude that any of the three, though only Savage was mentioned by name, had been shot on the ground simply to "finish them off", then that would be murder.

The jury left the court at 11.30 a.m. to consider its verdict and came back at 5.20 p.m. to say that it had been unable to agree a decision. The jury was then told by the coroner that they were "reaching the edge" of a reasonable time to produce one and that he would like to see them at 7.00 p.m. This sounded like a deadline. At 7.15 p.m. the jury returned again, and the foreman rose to say it had reached a verdict of nine to two, the smallest majority allowed.

Although the coroner Mr. Felix Pizzarello had impressed most people by the fairness with which he had conducted what he himself thought was by its very nature an inadequate inquiry into the shootings, he was much criticised for not allowing an 'open verdict'. In its report on the Inquest Amnesty International made this point and another equally fundamental one.

The effect of the observance of the Public Interest Immunity

Certificates was that the inquiry was confined to the shootings themselves and to the events immediately leading up to them. The authorities' information and planning decisions outside this context could not be explored.

The fundamental issue was whether the fatal shootings were caused by what happened in the street, or whether the authorities planned in advance for the three to be shot dead even if that was not necessary to prevent their criminal acts. Once immunity was conferred on the planning of the operation, the fundamental issue could not be squarely addressed by the Inquest.

The Government was not interested in any of this. It had made clear that there would be only one inquiry into the shootings. This was it and they had won. All doubts had been removed. The authorities' case had been proved in all its details, it said. Now for another inquest – on *Death on the Rock*.

18

INQUEST – ON THE PROGRAMME

The microphone was placed in front of me. "Could we just check it is recording? Could you just say a few words?" It sounded like a typical television interview set-up, the sort of thing I'd done hundreds of times before as a young producer, but there was no film crew and no lights. Across the polished wooden table from me were three people, an eminent QC, a former Conservative minister, and a barrister who was just checking the recording machine. I was about to be cross-examined with everything I said being available for publication. It was like a courtroom but with a couple of differences. The examining counsel was also the jury and I had no one to defend me. Come to think about it there were many more differences. It was not clear with what I was being charged, there was no formal chart sheet. I would not meet those who testified against me nor would I know what some of them said, or indeed who some of them were.

This was Kafkaesque but it was the United Kingdom, 1988, and the price we were having to pay for questioning the Government's account of a matter of great public interest. It looked to me like a process of intimidation. The new Government, with a large majority, was telling broadcasters to get into line. They could be free as long as they did not use their freedom. Some things were strictly off-limits.

It seemed to me almost incredible that things had come to this, that, at the instigation of the Government, a programme was to be taken apart, word by word and frame by frame, payments examined, witnesses visited, and that anyone who wished was to be invited to give evidence against us. Would this happen anywhere else in the Western world? It seemed more suitable to the Soviet Union. British newspapers would be appalled if it were to happen to them, which of course it would not.

Could it really be that this had come to pass because a witness, whose views were reported in our programme, had made totally unsubstantiated allegations of pressure being applied to him and money offered? In fact he had already admitted that the 'pressure' amounted to a few telephone calls and that no sum of money was mentioned – nor offered. He had not signed his affidavit but would any newspaper be left on a news-stand if everyone interviewed had to sign an affidavit before his contribution could be used?

The *This Week* team had not been consulted about whether there should be an inquiry into *Death on the Rock*. The IBA and Thames management had decided that. Now that it was going to happen how should we react, should we even participate in this extraordinary trial?

Although Julian Manyon, Chris Oxley, Alison Cahn and myself had threatened not to participate on principle, in reality we had little choice. The inquiry offered the only chance, albeit a slim one, of reversing the apparently irreversible steamroller of Government propaganda and tabloid offensive.

It was not only our own careers or the future of Thames that appeared to be at stake. Nigel Ryan, an experienced and highly respected journalist, wrote this in the *UK Press Gazette* in an article headed "A great deal could founder on 'The Rock'".

If the government has its way *Death on the Rock* may go into history as not so much a programme title, more an epitaph for the ITV system . . . At risk is the future of the IBA, which sanctioned it, as well as the free operation of public service journalism.

He concluded:

If [Thames] is found to have offended against the basic ground rules of impartiality and accuracy it will have dealt a double blow to the good name of broadcast journalism, and to the cause of

Press freedom. It will also have put another nail into the IBA's coffin.

TV Week thought the game was up for the Authority. "Mary Tudor died with Calais engraved upon her heart. The Independent Broadcasting Authority will meet its end with Gibraltar as its epitaph."

The Government was indeed intent on pursuing us. Sir Geoffrey Howe had declined an invitation to appear on *This Week* in a programme analysing the Inquest. The Government now wanted to ask the questions, not answer them. Archie Hamilton, a minister at the MoD told the House of Commons on 20 October 1988:

> The facts as they emerged at the Inquest have amply demonstrated that the television programme, *Death on the Rock*, was manifestly flawed with significant inaccuracies, casting a shameful slur for a number of months on the reputations of the soldiers concerned. The timing of the programme was, moreover, unjustified and prejudicial to potential jury members. I therefore very much welcome Thames Television's inquiry under Lord Windlesham into the making of the programme.

Three weeks before, when the Inquest was concluded, we did not know who would be heading the inquiry, or what would be its remit. How were we going to handle it all?

It became clear that the united front of Thames journalists, management and Board of Directors was beginning to break down, not because of any lack of trust, but because the Board had announced there was to be an inquiry and therefore had to withhold comment until after that inquiry had reported. We were told that we were not to write articles or speak publicly about the issues likewise. This enforced silence would have been fine if the Government and some of their supporters in the press had piped down, but they did not. Never have I felt so frustrated at having my hands tied. The Chairman and Managing Director in particular had been extremely supportive, but they now had to consider the future of the Company, its employees and shareholders, as well as the *This Week* journalists. They also had to avoid in any way interfering with the inquiry. The result of this necessary distancing of senior management from the programme-makers was a depressing sense of isolation among the *This Week* team.

I had taken responsibility for the programme but it was clear that the inquiry would be into all four of us. In the normal running of the programme I, as Editor, would take the key decisions, even if I was in a minority of one, but I felt that this approach was inappropriate for these unique circumstances. It was important to demonstrate my loyalty and belief in my colleagues, but, above all, the four of us had to stick together. I thought the best way of ensuring this was to agree that each one of us had an equal voice, that all major decisions would be referred to all of us with a majority required before a particular course of action could be pursued. It would be frustrating, and occasionally one would have to go along with a decision one violently disagreed with, but it was the necessary price of the essential unity.

It was clear that Julian, Chris and Alison would have to work on the inquiry full time; this was to be the best-researched programme after transmission ever. We attempted to keep Eamon Hardy out of the firing line as it was our work in Gibraltar which was in question. Should I also take leave of absence as Editor to concentrate on the inquiry? I decided not to do so, partly for straight political reasons (once you vacate a chair it's very difficult to get back) and partly because if I did step aside I thought it would be seized upon as a damaging admission of guilt. I also felt that I would go barmy if I was left to think of nothing else but *Death on the Rock*, and anyway I had some good programme ideas up my sleeve for the autumn run of *This Week*. Barrie Sales was a little further from the firing line but he too might fall with the rest of us if it went badly, and he felt torn between his loyalty to the company and to us. He compromised neither of these loyalties.

Our next major decision was concerned with negotiating the best possible terms, conditions and leadership of the inquiry that we could. We wanted it to be independent. If it wasn't who would believe it? We knew it would be a tough negotiating process which could permanently damage relationships within Thames. We decided to turn in our hour of need to the National Union of Journalists, to which we all belonged. They had pulled chestnuts out of the fire for me at the time of Carrickmore, almost ten years before; now I was asking them to do it again.

We met the union's general secretary in a pub round the corner from Thames. Harry Conroy was made for the corner of a 'snug'. A lowland Scot of medium height and jet-black hair, he bears the marks of the writing journalist who eats badly and far too late, but he was a born negotiator and a bonny fighter. He also had a sense of humour. We had become rather humourless.

While he was beginning to negotiate there was some bad news from my old employers, the BBC. *Panorama* had made a programme about the SAS and its activities in Northern Ireland to coincide with the end of the Inquest. It was very timely for it examined how the organisation operated and the inquest system in Northern Ireland. Though clearly a hot potato, it had been seen by seven or eight executives including the Director of News and Current Affairs, Ron Neil, and cleared for transmission.

Then on 1 October, two days before it was scheduled to go out, the film was seen by the overall head of the BBC's journalism, deputy Director General, John Birt, and by the DG himself, Michael Checkland. Afterwards the BBC put out a statement saying, "They [Birt and Checkland] saw the Panorama programme on the SAS. They are happy with the themes the programme addresses, but they feel more work is needed to prepare it for transmission. The BBC plans to transmit the programme in the coming weeks." At the very least it was a rebuff to, if not a vote of no confidence in, the judgement of the seven senior executives below John Birt. The *Daily Telegraph* reported those executives as being, "speechless with anger", and "close to tears". One senior manager was reported as saying "Birt's decision that the film should not go out was in the face of approval from seven senior executives, some newly appointed by him to head decision-making in current affairs . . . Everything had been referred along the line. It was probably the most careful programme ever made." The reporter was one of the BBC's most experienced, Tom Mangold. When the programme was eventually transmitted the changes were minimal. In the view of one concerned, "they could have been made in two hours, rather than two days, let alone two weeks".

Maybe this was a simple, if brutal, display of strength by John

Birt, emphasising who was in charge and that he should have been personally consulted earlier. Another way of looking at it was as follows. The timing of a programme and the release of any important new information it contains is as important, in terms of embarrassing governments and creating controversy, as is the actual content itself.

Once the caravan has moved on, and other stories hog the headlines, what was once front page news becomes 'old hat'. Timing is all, especially for a Corporation trying to ensure its survival under a hostile government. Was the lesson the BBC had drawn from *Death on the Rock* "pull down the shutters"? Certainly a very senior BBC executive said to me, "I don't know how one can do those sorts of programme any more."

Terms and Conditions

The list of names we put forward for consideration did not include any far left-wing figures; rather people like Kenneth Morgan, (Director of the Press Council) and Professor Alastair Hetherington (former Controller of BBC Scotland and ex-Editor of the *Guardian*). Some other names we suggested were Andreas Whittam Smith of the *Independent*, Harold Evans, former Editor of the *Sunday Times*, John Tusa, the broadcaster and the BBC's Managing Director of External Broadcasting, and Robert Kee, author and broadcaster. We were looking for a balanced ticket of highly respected and independent figures with experience of political journalism. The list was politely accepted, read, and rejected by the Chairman and Managing Director. Instead they settled for a Conservative politician and an eminent QC, not quite the 'balanced' ticket we had been thinking of. The names were not floated past us, simply announced. We learned along with everyone else.

"Heard of Lord Windlesham?" Barrie Sales asked me on 5 October. I had vaguely, some time in the past. I raced for *Who's Who*, knocking a chair over and spilling some coffee on to my desk. What was his background? My heart sank. Member of the Tory Reform Group, former junior minister at the Home Office and Northern

Ireland, former Conservative leader of the House of Lords and Privy Councillor. I rang a contact in the Tory party. Slightly better news, Windlesham was a bit of a 'wet', not a Thatcherite, and a Roman Catholic, but then, worse news. He was a close friend of Sir Geoffrey Howe. They had been leading lights in the Tory Reform Group together.

The team and I thought this was hardly the experienced independent journalist we had hoped for. Then a friend at the IBA told me to get hold of a copy of the noble lord's book, *Broadcasting in a Free Society*. We raced to the library and skimmed through it. Now I remembered where I'd heard Windlesham's name before. He was managing director of ATV at the time of another controversial programme *Death of a Princess*. Then he had vigorously defended his team against Saudi Arabian pressure and Foreign Office concern. Windlesham was clearly an establishment figure but he seemed to be sympathetic to the broadcaster's role as well.

Who could balance him? A centre-left figure like Alastair Hetherington, who had previously sat on the Peacock Committee on broadcasting? A few days later on 11 October the second name came out. Richard Rampton, a QC specialising in libel. I rang a legal friend. What were Rampton's politics? Had he any? The information was confused. Some in the profession regarded Rampton as a rather dry, conventional figure who was probably a mild sort of conservative. Others pointed out that he had acted for some television companies in the past and had been seen as a publisher rather than a censor. Not left, not right, perhaps SDP-ish. What all agreed was that Richard Rampton was an outstanding and remorselessly effective interrogator with a real flair for ruthless cross-examination. They started work immediately, with a public invitation being issued to anyone who wished to submit information relevant to the scope of the inquiry. On 17 October, Manuel Barca, a barrister in private practice, joined the inquiry as secretary.

We sat back and tried calmly to evaluate the pairing. What most worried us, apart from the absence of political balance, was that there was no one with experience of what it was like to try and do the sort of difficult investigative journalism we were involved in.

[276]

How much would the two of them know about political dirty tricks departments? I could see that in some ways Sir Ian Trethowan and Richard Dunn might have made a shrewd choice. Still, if we were given a clean sheet by this pair of investigators then we really would be cleared. Nevertheless the odds seemed to be weighted against us yet again, and some of the team thought it looked like a stitch-up. Should we pull out now? How could we pull out? We decided to go on to the next battleground, the terms of the inquiry.

Meanwhile the public relations battle went on. Major Randall had now returned to Gibraltar and personally submitted his affidavit to the coroner, sending us a copy. Barrie Sales took a bit of a risk and revealed its contents. We just had to fight back somehow. He told Harvey Lee in the *UK Press Gazette*, "Major Randall's affidavit totally vindicates us on the issue of pressure and offering money. It makes devastating reading in the light of what Asquez claimed in court. We categorically denied his allegations at the time but most papers ignored us."

The *Gazette* also reported that the NUJ chapel in Thames had met and complained to the union's ethics council about hostile press reaction, although some in the chapel had criticisms of what we had done, based on the *Sunday Times* article. It was very dispiriting. The same issue of the *UK Press Gazette* also reported "John Whitney, IBA director general, has warned that should Thames be found to be at fault, the Authority would take action. Sanctions could include forcing the Company to an apology and an IRA [*sic*] reprimand on issuing a notice of breach of contract." Could it be that the IBA that had so stoutly defended us was losing its nerve as well?

The Ministry of Defence had been quiet for a few days but just over a week after the Inquest we discovered why. It had given its favourite journalistic contact, James Adams, Defence Correspondent of the *Sunday Times*, another 'exclusive'. In the 9 October edition of the paper the following headline appeared, "TV 'Wrong 39 Times' on Gib". Mr. Adams wrote,

A dossier listing 39 alleged inaccuracies in the controversial Thames Television programme *Death on the Rock*, will be sent by the Government to the IBA. The fourteen-page report, which describes the programme as 'badly flawed' and operating to a 'preconceived scenario', will be accompanied by a letter, signed by a senior government minister, saying that the dossier should be made available to the independent inquiry investigating the programme."

An appendix to the report had been prepared against the BBC *Spotlight* programme, but the Corporation was to be tackled after Thames had been successfully dealt with. Ironic, I thought. I was now involved in defending the BBC from attack.

The *Daily Telegraph* carried a similar story three days later. It was obviously getting some of the same briefings as the *Sunday Times*, but the *Telegraph*'s coverage of the issue was rather more complex. It was clearly a conservative paper but its editorials had displayed a robust independence typical of its new Editor Max Hastings. Likewise its media correspondent Jane Thynne, apart from being conspicuously well-informed, was scrupulously fair and always gave us the opportunity to respond to the MoD's claims. However her articles often had headlines which were at variance with the article itself, making one think that the sub-editors were considerably to the right of the paper. For example, one report about the MoD's '39 points' was headed, "Errors uncovered in TV documentaries on SAS shooting" – note the absence of any quotation marks by the paper.

As for the alleged '39 points' they were never submitted to the inquiry. It was the Foreign Office who wrote to Lord Windlesham setting out the Government's concerns, which were much fewer in number. The letter was signed by Sir Patrick Wright, KCMG, the Permanent Under-Secretary of State at the Foreign Office, and not by a Government minister. The letter restated Sir Geoffrey Howe's complaints and included a comparison of *Death on the Rock* with the Inquest evidence and a copy of an extract from the Salmon Committee on the law of contempt. We were not to be allowed to see this letter, of course. Why had the MoD not submitted evidence? It was rumoured that the Foreign Office felt that the defence press department was getting a little 'carried away'. We would not have dissented.

Meanwhile Harry Conroy of the NUJ was still battling away on our behalf on the terms of reference. We thought we should be judged on the progamme and the inquiry team should not adjudicate on the still disputed facts of the Inquest. We thought the inquiry should examine our thoroughness and good faith, and how our reporting compared with that of the national press.

Windlesham and Rampton agreed to take these into consideration. In their report they wrote, "Our terms of reference were to inquire into the making and screening of *Death on the Rock*. That has led us to examine and reach conclusions about the genesis, preparation, content and effect of the programme, and any impact which its broadcast might have had upon the subsequent inquest."

We had almost reached agreement but the NUJ, with our enthusiastic support, wished to:

place on record its firm belief that it sees no need for any inquiry such as the one currently taking place. Such a development is a retrograde step for journalism in this country.

There are procedures and institutions already in existence to deal with any alleged journalistic abuses or mistakes, such as the NUJ's own Ethics Council, the Press Council, or the Broadcasting Complaints Commission.

We believe the inquiry was set up as a result of political pressure and is a method of harassment of journalists who are involved in the type of journalism which poses awkward issues.

It was now nearly two weeks since Lord Windlesham had been appointed and he was impatient to get on with things. He had expected the inquiry to last about a month and it was already clear it would last rather longer than that, but we had hit another problem. All our interviews were to be taped and together with our written submissions were to be made available for publication in the Report. We could tell the inquiry team nothing in confidence, yet much of a journalist's investigations involve the use of confidential sources. How could they understand how thorough we had been if we couldn't indicate what these were – in confidence? Lord Windlesham explained that if he wrote in the Report that they accepted our story because of information they had been given in confidence, they would be laughed out of court. Everything had to be capable of being published. We were also lobbying to have ourselves, or any legal representatives we might have, sit in on any interviews with the Ministry of Defence or other witnesses. It would 'not be practical', said Windlesham. We seemed to be losing on nearly every point, though the inquiry team, who were unfailingly polite, clearly thought they were bending over backwards to be fair. "But we have to get on, get on," said Lord Windlesham.

The final crunch came over whether we could have legal representation. The inquiry team had already made independent arrangements to visit Gibraltar and wanted to interview us before they went. The date of departure was getting closer, and my interview, which was to be the first, had been fixed for 20 October. The *This Week* team had decided that all their written submissions would be carefully vetted by a lawyer funded in part by the NUJ, but what about the interviews themselves – should a lawyer representing us be present? I was against that as I thought it would demonstrate that we had something to hide and I was keen to keep as much good will as we could, because we would certainly need it. Julian Manyon, on the other hand, thought this was typically optimistic, if not naive of me. He would certainly have his lawyer with him. Julian had been genuinely shocked by what he had discovered in Gibraltar and by the official disinformation that was now pouring out. He had thought about nothing but *Death on the Rock* for the last month and if it made him a bit more paranoid than I was it also made him rather shrewder and more far-sighted.

In the middle of our reasonably heated internal arguments there was a message that Lord Windlesham wanted to see me. I walked along the corridor to the Chairman's office which he had vacated for the duration – the ever-lengthening duration – of the inquiry. I knocked and walked in. Three very serious faces looked at me. Lord Windlesham had a particularly severe expression and when he began to talk the only comparable experience I could think of was being invited to the headmaster's study to be told one had let the school down. He read me the Riot Act. They had been more than patient, they had a lot of work to do, they had answered all our concerns and now they must get on. Were we going to cooperate with the inquiry or not? Was I going to be interviewed as they had arranged? He was clearly angry and frustrated and had difficulty in keeping it from showing.

I listened to him with mounting anger on my side, and when I replied I let rip. I was not going to be talked to like a little boy. Didn't they understand that our careers and perhaps the future of Thames, the IBA, and this sort of journalism probably depended on this inquiry? Suddenly we had been confronted by microphones as if in a court of law. We didn't know what the charges were, or who would testify against us. All my resentments rushed out. I tried to keep calm but my cheeks were flushing and I felt I'd been calm too long. Did they not understand the strain?

"Right, that's it," said Windlesham, and he shut his briefcase and made as if to leave. There was nothing more to say. I got up and walked out. It was the last thing I wanted to happen. I was supposed to be the calm Editor keeping everyone together and steering this thing through without damaging internal relationships. Now I'd lost control at a vital moment.

I barged into David Elstein's office. The Director of Progammes was sitting with Barrie Sales. I told them what had happened. What could be done? David was at his most frustratingly calm. Despite the fact that any breakdown in the inquiry would be very bad news for him, he told me that I was quite within my rights not to go ahead with it. It was my decision; he felt it improper to influence me in any way. Why was everyone in Thames being so fair?

I walked disconsolately back down the corridor and by the time I'd reached Julian, Chris and Alison I had decided that I would go ahead and be interviewed without a lawyer. It was vital to give the inquiry our side of the story before they reached Gibraltar. We decided that each of us could decide separately whether we wished to be legally represented. In the event Julian was the only one who was.

We switched on the television for the news. The Home Secretary had just announced his ban preventing broadcasters from transmitting the sound of interviews with members of organisations like Sinn Fein or the UDA, even if they were elected representatives. The freedom to report was being reduced again.

[281]

19

ON TRIAL

I was to give evidence on the afternoon of 20 October. It was *This Week's* transmission day, a programme about the Barlow Clowes affair and the Government's responsibility to small investors who were cheated. I decided to watch the *Death on the Rock* film again as I hadn't looked at it for a few weeks. When I did so I was heartened. Of course it wasn't anything like our detractors said: it was a very good piece of broadcast journalism. I wrote to the other three members of the team that I was proud of it and of them and would be glad to be judged by this programme rather than any other one I had been responsible for. Then I walked into the inquiry and sat down before the microphone.

The interview lasted three hours. It was so relaxed I almost did not realise how deftly they were examining my motivations and the background assumptions that lay behind my decision to go ahead with the programme. Richard Rampton was particularly good at asking apparently innocuous questions, then leading one gently through the apparent contradictions he saw in what I'd said with something I had written elsewhere. It was an intense and exciting experience pitting one's wits against such people. I almost enjoyed it, until I thought that I was being lulled into revelation. But as I had nothing to hide I simply wanted to seize the opportunity to redress the balance of the public argument. They were obviously working off the Government's agenda at this stage. Did I have a preconceived view of what had happened in Gibraltar? What had I really intended to say in the programme?

I had no illusions about the fact that when the transcript of my interview was completed, they would pore over it, compare it for inconsistencies with the accounts of the rest of the team, and with the Government's evidence. Julian and Chris were to be given a very tough time. They promised to have lots of further questions to put to me after their visit to Gibraltar.

I went back to my office drained, but happy, and picked up a copy of *Broadcast*, the TV industry magazine, to see how it had dealt with Gibraltar that week. There was a nice letter about Julian Manyon from a man called Keith Belcher, now the creative director of the Gibb Rose Organisation. He wrote:

> In the many months that I was Julian Manyon's news editor at Independent Radio News, I doubt if we had more than half a dozen conversations which were not, to say the least, agitated.
>
> But when questions of integrity are raised, I can only report to you my personal experience when he was reporting the fall of Saigon. He resisted all efforts to extricate him from Vietnam, and maintained regular transmission in impossible circumstances. To my certain knowledge he endangered his life on three separate occasions.
>
> To a news editor he was a pain in the butt. He argued volubly and violently against all efforts to direct his news gathering and on far too many occasions he was right. He may not be the most pleasant man to work with, but in my experience he is a courageous and unimpeachable journalist who deserves a great deal of admiration.

That was Julian all right, warts and all. He now turned his formidable energy to masterminding our response to Lord Windlesham, and more holes in the official account began to appear.

It was noticeable that a number of the serious newspapers, after a period of reflection, had started to ask questions about the shootings once more. The Inquest had not resolved many contradictions in the evidence. Bob Randall was challenging Asquez to repeat his remarks out of court, and Carmen Proetta was in the process of suing several newspapers for libel. The Spanish police continued to insist on and off the record that they had kept up surveillance until the terrorists had entered the Rock, and *Private*

Eye seemed to be particularly well informed and was an essential read if one wanted to see the holes in the official position. Back at Thames, Barrie Sales was bringing his formidable analytical skills to bear on the transcripts of the Inquest and finding much which supported us.

Could the tide be turning? Any optimism was quashed when we learned that Lord Windlesham had been to see his old friend Sir Geoffrey Howe to explain how he planned to conduct the inquiry. The Government appeared quite content with the inquiry and those who led it. Either the Government or ourselves were going to be very disappointed.

On the Rock

Lord Windlesham arrived in Gibraltar on Sunday, 23 October, for a three-day fact-finding mission in which he intended to see as many people connected with the programme as possible. He told the *Gibraltar Chronicle*:

> We are pursuing our inquiry with an open mind and with a sense of humility that it is the population of Gibraltar that would have suffered so grievously if the IRA had succeeded in exploding a bomb. We are aware that we are visitors but it is the population that would have suffered. And we are approaching the matter with an open mind. But the focus of our inquiry is the television programme and not the incident itself leading to the deaths which was of course investigated so thoroughly by the coroner in the Inquest.

Lord Windlesham paid a courtesy call on Governor Sir Peter Terry and also met Attorney-General Eric Thistlethwaite. Now we were in the hands of 'our' witnesses. Would they see the inquiry team? Why should they after all the trouble they had been through as a result of the programme? In fact Carmen and Maxie Proetta, Stephen Bullock, Major Randall and Christopher Finch, all saw the team and stood by the programme. They had not been badly treated, misinterpreted or taken out of context and they said so. They said very different things about the *Sunday Times*.

Those of us who made *Death on the Rock* will never cease to be grateful for the courage and decency of those witnesses who took part in the programme.

Kenneth Asquez declined to meet Lord Windlesham and conveyed this through his lawyer, Sir Joshua Hassan.

When the Windlesham/Rampton team returned they interviewed Julian, Chris and Alison and then started to sift through transcripts to see if we had distorted anybody's testimony. They checked trailers for the programme and payments. In short they seemed to be examining everything with a fine toothcomb. Not all the programmes I have been connected with would have survived such a scrutiny. The Thames Board had taken a considerable risk allowing them such wide terms of reference. It looked rather more like a fishing expedition to us.

They then settled down to the Asquez question again. Why had we used his statement? We ran through the well-rehearsed litany. He had told other people about what he had seen in the bank the day after the shootings. Therefore, he had not invented it for us. We had his handwritten statement. He had given another statement voluntarily to a solicitor, which the solicitor told us we could use. The statement was remarkably detailed and contained information no one else knew about at that stage (although the information was later to be corroborated at the Inquest). He had never attempted to retract his statement or to stop us using it. He simply did not wish to reveal his name.

There had been no pressure and no offer of money. Even Asquez had now admitted no money was offered and that the 'pressure' amounted to a few phone calls.

Had he told the truth to us in the first place? The coroner was puzzled by Asquez's apparent retraction.

CORONER: The trouble is Mr. Asquez, that this question of the beret, the ID card and the words to the effect, "Stop, it's OK, it's the police" [contained in Asquez's original statement to us] have only to my understanding

ASQUEZ: come out for the first time in this court, subsequent to the time that you made the statement. Can you try to explain that a little further?

ASQUEZ: No. As I said before I'm a bit confused. My thoughts are vague from that time.

If those details are a puzzle, it is even more puzzling that Asquez's account is the only one which is consistent with the pathologist's report or the wounds Sean Savage received. This did not surprise us because we had found a way of checking the damage to the terrorists' bodies while we were making our programme. That was another reason for feeling confident about using Asquez's account.

When Professor Watson, the official pathologist, gave evidence, he described the shooting of Savage as a 'frenzied attack'. He also said Savage had been shot five times in the back and that the four or five wounds to Savage's head must have been fired by a gunman standing above him. He was certain of that because of the entry wounds and the strike marks left on the ground where Savage's head had been. That expert opinion was supported by another pathologist, Professor Pounder, who had been called by the victims' families. He too was certain that the wounds to Savage's head had been inflicted from above while Savage was lying face upwards on the ground.

That is the evidence of two highly regarded and experienced pathologists. The testimonies of Soldiers C and D totally contradicted that evidence. Soldier C said he fired six rounds in rapid succession, within five or possibly ten seconds, from a distance of five or six feet. Soldier D said he fired nine rounds, again rapidly, from a distance of two to three metres. Both soldiers categorically denied firing at Savage while standing over him. Their minimum distance away from him, on their evidence, was five feet.

We have then a direct and irreconcilable conflict of evidence between the pathologists and the two soldiers. Yet Asquez's original statement is remarkably consistent with the pathologists' report. What Asquez told us was that one of the soldiers stood above Savage and fired three or four shots and that is the only eye-witness account, to our knowledge, that corresponds with the objective judgement of the pathologists.

[286]

In any case had Asquez actually retracted his evidence at all, despite the way it had been reported? Consider this exchange between Paddy McGrory and Kenneth Asquez:

MCGRORY:	Is the vital part of that statement that the man with the black beret had his foot on the dying man's throat? "He shouted 'stop' and they then fired a further three or four shots." Do you see that part of the statement? Did you make it up?
ASQUEZ:	Probably.
MCGRORY:	Of all the people now present in this room, only you know whether you made it up or not, and what you are saying. These are eleven of your fellow citizens of Gibraltar. Tell them whether it's true or not?
ASQUEZ:	I can't say "yes" or "no". I was probably still confused.
CORONER:	"I was probably still confused." Is that what he said?
SHORTHAND WRITER	Yes.

It was now the middle of November and the inquiry seemed to be an indefinite one. I concentrated more and more on editing *This Week*, while waiting for the next piece of paper with questions from Windlesham or Rampton. We put out another programme on Northern Ireland, this time about the desperate position of some Protestant farmers in remote rural areas near the border. I expected someone would say it was to curry favour with the inquiry. It wasn't of course but I don't think they would have noticed anyway, they were working all hours. Then we hit a major problem.

We had been arguing for some time that we should be allowed to see the oral evidence provided by the Ministry of Defence, particularly that relating to the claim that they had apparently made that we had a biased approach in making the programme.

However a slight problem arose which delayed the handover of the MoD material. This problem related to the fact that the sections of the MoD's evidence dealing with their allegations of bias made reference to other evidence supplied previously by the Ministry to the inquiry. We discovered this evidence consisted of letters from the Ministry marked confidential. We asked Mr. Rampton to contact the Ministry's legal department in an attempt to get the relevant sections of these letters placed on the record.

This latest information was a considerable source of concern. First, the news that the inquiry had been receiving evidence in confidence from the Ministry of Defence ran contrary to our previous understanding of how the inquiry would be conducted. Second, the question arose as to what reliance the inquiry proposed to place on such evidence, particularly if the Ministry declined to place it on the record. It was our view that confidential letters, such as the ones described, should have no place in the current proceedings.

A compromise was finally reached but those who have a copy of the Windlesham/Rampton report should turn to page 6. There it reveals that two Foreign Office knights gave written evidence. They were Sir Patrick Wright, the Permanent Under-Secretary of State and Sir John Fretwell, Deputy to the Permanent Under-Secretary of State and Political Director. K. C. Macdonald, second Permanent Under-Secretary of State at the MoD, did the same but a number of unidentified MoD personnel were interviewed in person by the inquiry team. The Report says, "An Assistant Under-Secretary of State, accompanied by the Director of Public Relations, Army, a Legal Adviser, and a member of the General Staff Secretariat, gave oral evidence to the inquiry supplementing written submissions." Who were those unidentified people? I think we should be told.

It was now December, the days were closing in, but for us the skies were brightening. In the middle of the month the *Sun* made a full apology and an award of damages of over fifty thousand pounds to Carmen Proetta. Other settlements were to follow.

Her lawyer, Oscar Bueselink, appearing in the High Court of Justice, Queen's Bench, said that Mrs. Proetta had been the subject of highly defamatory material. The comments made on the front page and other stories published by the *Sun* and its journalists, Kelvin Mackenzie, Michael Fielder, and Martin Smith, were "*untrue* and meant, and were understood to mean, that the plaintiff was at that time or had been a party to criminal activities involving drugs and that she so hated the British that she fabricated her claim to have seen the shooting of two IRA terrorists in Gibraltar." He continued, "In so far as the shooting incident is concerned Mrs. Proetta was a wholly independent person who has at all times given an honest account of what she remembers seeing. As soon as she was approached by the Gibraltar police she gave a statement freely and voluntarily. At the subsequent Inquest she gave evidence which was consistent both with her statements given to police and her earlier statement given to a Thames TV interviewer. At no time have her statements or evidence been seriously challenged or contradicted either on behalf of the three IRA personnel or the security services."

Lawyers for the *Sun* confirmed 'all' that Mr. Bueselink said and said they regretted they had ever published these untrue statements. They recognised her sincerity in giving the accounts of 6 March that she had.

This was justice, but justice delayed until the Inquest was over and the damage done.

Carmen was asked why she thought such things had been said about her. "You don't have to be a genius to know I was a risk, wasn't I?" she said. "It's all politics."

By Christmas the inquiry was still going on, several weeks after Lord Windlesham, Richard Rampton and presumably the Thames finance director had hoped it would be finished. The strain on the *This Week* team had been intense and we were weary. At least on Christmas Day I thought I'd be able to get away from it. I drove the four or so miles from my home to the small church next to my sister's house in Petersham, near Richmond, Surrey. Inside it had retained all its Georgian fittings, with box pews and a gallery where a small orchestra accompanies the singing. The fine Tudor memorial had been newly painted and holly and ivy were everywhere. It was an idyllic scene. As I stood up to sing the first hymn I noticed a familiar figure two pews away on my right. As we left at the end of the service he turned to me with a half-smile and said, "I hope I haven't spoiled your Christmas." It was Richard Rampton. I was stuck for a reply so I said nothing and he left. I decided not to tell my family.

However, there was a wonderful Christmas present awaiting us in the 2 January edition of the *UK Press Gazette*. It was a letter from the *Sunday Times* journalist Rosie Waterhouse who had been sent to Gibraltar, in her words, "to find the witnesses interviewed by Thames, show them the film and establish whether their interviews were accurately reflected on the programme or whether they were unfairly edited, misinterpreted or used in a selective and misleading way. I was also to take them through what they saw or heard of the shootings." We had never met Rosie Waterhouse and so the letter was a complete surprise. It read:

Sir

Now that I have resigned from the *Sunday Times* I would like to set the record straight, belatedly, about my involvement in the "Insight" investigation into the Thames TV documentary *Death on the Rock*.

After the programme I interviewed two witnesses to the shootings of the three IRA terrorists in Gibraltar who appeared on the programme – Josie Celecia and Stephen Bullock.

Their account of my interviews with them was inaccurate in the *Sunday Times* and had the effect of discrediting parts of the documentary and the evidence of another witness, Carmen Proetta.

In brief, Josie Celecia did not dismiss all of Proetta's evidence as 'ridiculous', only one aspect of it. Stephen Bullock has only one quarrel with his interview on Thames – that he was portrayed as saying no warnings were given before the SAS fired, when in fact he said he told the reporters that he was not in a position to hear if a warning was given. However, Bullock stressed to me, and I quoted him as saying: 'Nothing I saw was inconsistent with what Carmen Proetta said she saw."

After the story appeared I complained to Robin Morgan, Focus editor, who compiled the story, that my interviews had been inaccurately represented in the paper, and gave him a full transcript of my interviews with Celecia and Bullock, so the mistakes would not be repeated. I also apologised to Celecia and Bullock for the errors, saying they probably occurred because of the speed with which the story had been put together. But some of the mistakes appeared again the following week.

I came very close to resigning then, but my mortgage got the better of me. I did however send a very detailed memo to Morgan and the features editor who is in charge of "Insight", listing my complaints. Two other reporters took similar action regarding complaints about how their copy was used.

No further action was taken and I was advised that if I took the matter further I was unlikely to win in any confrontation between an "Insight" reporter and the Focus editor.

I was and still am deeply unhappy that my copy was used to discredit another piece of investigative journalism. A copy of this letter has been sent to Thames TV and Lord Windlesham who is conducting the enquiry into the making of *Death on the Rock*.

I resigned over another, unconnected matter.

ROSIE WATERHOUSE

Her internal memo to Robin Morgan was even more damaging. It was written in May 1988. She wrote that the *Sunday Times* story

left the ST wide open to accusations that we had set out to prove one point of view and misrepresented and misquoted interviews to fit – the very accusations we were levelling at Thames . . . I believe the criticisms of the ST in the *Observer* story and by David Elstein in the *Sunday Times* on Sunday were well founded and I now find myself in the untenable position that if I was asked to stand by certain parts of both stories of 1st May and 8th May which involved my research, I could not.

She then detailed nine specific errors Morgan's article had made. She went on,

You were not interested in any information I obtained which contradicted your apparent premise – that the Thames documentary was wrong, and the official version was right . . . It became almost impossible to make any point which

[291]

contradicted the official line. . . . You then gave me a lecture on how "Insight" did not have to be like a provincial newspaper and present both sides, that Harry Evans had told you how "Insight" had to make a judgement. I said this whole story revolved around conflicting evidence which should be left to a jury to decide.

She then listed six more errors made in the second *Sunday Times* article.

We then discovered that another journalist had written a three page note complaining that the paper had not published evidence he had collected. He complained about 'double standards in the evidence'. And on 10 May 1988 Barrie Penrose, a senior journalist on the paper for nearly ten years, had written to Robin Morgan.

In recent weeks I have expressed strong reservations about our coverage. In a nutshell, I have seen how facts and witnesses are misused to launch the attack on *This Week*.

Last week I urged you to be more sceptical and to listen to what the reporters were saying on the ground, but to no avail. You then included my by-line on Sunday, knowing I wanted nothing to do with what you were preparing, and after I had asked that my name be kept off the piece.

Robin Morgan wrote to the *UK Press Gazette* and the *Guardian* defending himself. This gave us the opportunity to launch our attack. We had been silent for long enough. Chris Oxley wrote a detailed and devastating analysis of the errors in Morgan's letters. The effect was remarkable. Some of our friends and former colleagues in the BBC rang up Chris and said, "Why didn't you tell us this before?" Despite our protestations at the time of the inquest and after the *Sunday Times* attacks some colleagues still thought there must be something in the paper's offensive. No one could have imagined what had been going on inside its editorial offices. The *Sunday Times* NUJ chapel asked for an inquiry into the paper's reporting.

Nine months later there was an interesting postcript to the Robin Morgan saga. The *UK Press Gazette* of 9 October 1989 carried this article about Tony Bambridge who had worked with Morgan at the *Sunday Times* and co-authored a book on the SAS with him. (Robin Morgan had become the new editor of the *Sunday Express* and wanted Bambridge to join him.)

Tony Bambridge claims his change of heart over the deputy editorship of the *Sunday Express* was because he found the 'hyped news stories' under new editor Robin Morgan unacceptable.

Although Bambridge, managing editor (features) of the *Sunday Times*, agreed to become deputy editor to former colleague Morgan he later changed his mind.

This led to speculation that he had been offered financial inducements to stay at the *Sunday Times*. But in a frank letter to Morgan, Bambridge attacks the news content of the *Sunday Express*.

In particular he is critical of two front page splashes. One on the interrogation of Khalid Birawi, allegedly suspected of the Lockerbie bombing. The other the paper's report on the Deal bombing.

Bambridge said in his letter that the reason for his change of mind was a simple one: "I don't think my joining you will work and it is better to face that fact now rather than in the future when an unwinding of our relationship would be messy and probably even more damaging.

"I think that many of the things you have done at the *Express* are admirable; what I cannot accept are the hyped news stories.

"The first blatant example was the Birawi story. At the time I voiced my doubts about its veracity. These you dismissed, pointing out that time would demonstrate the strength of the story. The fact that the Italians then let the man go seemed not to worry you one jot. 'The Italians were wrong' was what you said. I really can't accept that as justification for the story.

"Last Sunday's splash (the Deal bombing) left me breathless. I have read that story many times since and nothing that has appeared subsequently has made me change my view that it was a disgraceful piece of journalism."

The *Express* story claimed that the Deal bomb was hidden up to three weeks before the blast under the floorboards of a house.

Bambridge added: "You said that if I came to the *Express* I would be listened to. I believe you meant this at the time and that there would be no more 'Gibraltars'." This was a reference to the "Insight" investigation into the *Death on the Rock* documentary co-ordinated by Morgan when he was at the *Sunday Times*.

Bambridge ends his letter on an upbeat note: "I hope that your plans for the *Sunday Express* transform that paper and that it becomes a success."

The Verdict

Lord Windlesham and Richard Rampton completed and signed their report on 19 January and sent if off to the printers. On the night before publication, Wednesday, 25 January, BBC-2's *Late Show* offered me the opportunity of doing a *What the Papers Say* on *Death on the Rock*. I undertook it with relish, then went home to prepare for the next day. There was bound to be a great deal of publicity and I had agreed to do interviews and discussions with anyone who wanted me. It wasn't simply egotism, I wanted to head off a right–left argument with Conservative MPs arguing with Labour ones. To me this was not a party political issue at all.

Publication day began with a press conference held by Richard Dunn and David Elstein at which Chris Oxley and I sat in the front row. The inquiry Report was almost a complete vindication of our programme, our journalistic methods and our integrity. It was everything we could have hoped for and never dreamed would happen. There were only three points of criticism.

On Asquez, while saying that it was reasonable for us to have placed some reliance on his statement and that it was legitimate to refer to it,

> we think it would have been preferable to have given a fuller account of the circumstances in which such an unusual piece of evidence had been obtained and of the reasons for its inclusion in the programme. If that had been done, the viewer would have

been better equipped to form his own conclusions about the true weight and significance to be attached to what was, as the commentary implicitly recognised, a dramatic account of a deliberate act of murder.

This was fair comment, although if we always explained the background to interviews and statements our programmes would double in length overnight.

The inquiry also found that in two respects a key passage of the commentary was open to criticism. We had said that none of the four key witnesses had heard a warning. We should have pointed out that Stephen Bullock was not in position to hear if a warning had been given. (In fact, as I pointed out earlier, the soldiers who had carried out the shootings of McCann and Farrell were far from certain that they had given a warning.)

We also said that none of the four witnesses had seen the terrorists make threatening movements. We should have said that neither of the two witnesses who were in a position to see if there had been any threatening movements did so.

The Report summarised its findings on these points.

The Ministry of Defence have submitted that these faults demonstrate that 'the degree of scrupulousness displayed by the programme-makers was not commensurate with the gravity of the accusations implied against the soldiers.' We think that goes too far. In the first place, we repeat, we do not consider that the programme, taken as a whole, made accusations against the soldiers. More important, while we have no doubt that the passage in question was inappropriately worded, with the result that it misstated the effect of the evidence in two respects, we are not persuaded that that arose from any lack of scrupulousness. Indeed, when the thoroughness of the research for the programme and the way in which the results were deployed are taken into account, the conclusion to be drawn is that the production team sought to obtain a wider range of evidence and to present it as fairly and accurately as possible.

For the rest it was a clean bill of health. The Report concluded:

The programme-makers were experienced, painstaking and persistent. They did not bribe, bully or misrepresent those who took part. The programme was trenchant and avoided triviality. Those who made it were acting in good faith and without ulterior motives.

The vast majority of the newspapers accepted the Report as an extremely thorough one which vindicated the programme and the programme-makers. Not so the *Sun*, it never lets you down. Its editorial column read as follows:

The Verdict: Still guilty

Thames Television can wriggle like a puff adder.
They can posture like Mick Jagger.
They can hold all the inquiries they wish into the truthfulness of witnesses and the integrity of their journalists.

But they cannot alter basic truths.

Their programme, *Death on the Rock*, was an irresponsible, mischievous, deeply shaming episode.

It should NEVER have been made.

It should NEVER have been broadcast.

There was one more major ordeal to negotiate. The Thames Board, in what one might view as an excessive display of public responsibility and fairness, had decided to transmit a programme about the Report's findings on the evening of publication. It had decided this before it knew what the Report would contain and had given the job to an independent producer, my former colleague, Christopher Capron, who was also notoriously fair-minded. He could do what he wanted, within half an hour. We expected that since the Report vindicated us he would use all the time to spell out the Windlesham/Rampton findings. Not so. He determined to summarise the conclusions but leave well over half the programme for a discussion to be chaired by another non-Thames person, Nick Ross. Lord Windlesham would not get involved in any such discussion; he confined himself to a short statement at the top of the programme suggesting that the Report, now published by Faber, should be read in its entirety. Chris asked me to represent Thames and Lord Thomson, though now retired from the chairmanship of the IBA, to represent the Authority.

Who were the other two to be? I nearly fell out of my chair when he told me they would be Andrew Neil, Editor of the *Sunday Times* and Michael Mates, MP, two of our chief assailants. All right, it might make for an exciting programme but the Report had just rejected nearly all their charges. Why were they to be given another go? Chris Oxley argued vehemently with me that we should pull out, that this was really too much. Chris is normally the calmest of people but he stormed off down the corridor, ablaze with anger. In the end, of course, I had no choice but to appear as an empty chair would have undone all the good work of the past few weeks.

I warned Chris Capron that we retained the right to sue him, his programme, and Neil and Mates if they slandered us. Capron had already had such an eventuality underwritten by Thames and he had retained his own independent lawyers to advise him.

I had a couple of hours free before the recording at 6.30 p.m. and took the opportunity to pop over to the University Hospital in Gower Street nearby to see Alison Cahn.

She had not been at the press conference because two days before publication she had given birth to Daniel, who weighed in at seven pounds. It was a good job we had let her go on her honeymoon some nine and a half months previously. One of our worries during the whole affair was of the danger the stress might cause for her unborn child. To our delight Daniel was as robust and healthy as they come. I began to get the *Death on the Rock* saga in perspective. I walked back over to Euston Road and went into the make-up room to prepare for the programme. A photographer from the *Independent* poked his head around the corner. Would I mind if he took a photograph of me being made up?

I shrugged my shoulders, "All right." I couldn't think the paper would use such a photograph. It did, blown up on the front page.

I left the make-up room and went back up to my office to await a call to go to the studio. I wanted to keep out of the way of Andrew Neil because I didn't know if I could contain my anger with him and his paper. All this time he must, or should, have known what distortions he was printing about our programme. If he had had the decency to correct them we would have been spared so much, and the real issues of Gibraltar could have been more fully addressed.

Andrew arrived in a bad temper in the hospitality room and was in the studio long before I came down. I sat next to George Thomson. Surprisingly I had not seen him since he had cleared *Death on the Rock* for transmission. We owed that brave man a great deal. I clenched my hands together and tried to stay calm. If I attacked Neil and Mates then the audience might feel sympathetic towards them, but if I didn't interrupt and challenge some of their statements, more inaccuracies would go uncorrected. If I did qualify every answer they gave, the audience and the programme might well get lost in a welter of detail and the former might feel irritated with what might be seen as my nit-picking. Andrew in particular was a very skilled television performer. I would need to be careful.

I thought back to the days when I had admired Andrew's work on *Tomorrow's World* and when he had made some appearances for me on *Nationwide*, while working for the *Economist*. He was always a propagandist but then he was a relaxed witty man, if a little prone to wearing cuban heels, and a medallion around his neck. We had lunched together and planned a regular series for him with *Nationwide*, but then the *Sunday Times* came up. We had hardly met since. And now he was to become the Chief Executive of Sky television as well.

The discussion started. I acknowledged our mistakes but pointed out that nearly all the criticism had been decisively rejected and that all wilder charges had been convincingly disproved. Michael Mates had not read the Report in full and though restating his criticisms was a little subdued. Andrew Neil, however, went on to the attack. Perhaps he knows no other way, but he kept getting things wrong and fortunately Nick Ross was able to clarify pieces of the Report. Still, Andrew kept on attacking us and time was running by. Nick Ross tried to wind up this section of the programme.

NICK ROSS: We can't go into too much detail . . . Quickly
               Roger . . .
ROGER BOLTON: There's an easy way of resolving this [the

dispute]. Thames Television has had this
exhaustive inquiry by independent figures.
Why does not Andrew Neil agree to have an
independent inquiry into the reporting of the
Sunday Times on the *Death on the Rock*
programme? After all, if he is telling the truth,
he has nothing to fear. Will he agree to that?
His own journalists have asked him for it.

I turned to Andrew, "Will you now agree to an independent report
into the *Sunday Times* journalism?"

Andrew Neil ducked that one. I pressed him again. His answer
was brutally frank. "Because we are not in the dock, you are."

Nick Ross asked me if I would do the programme again. "Yes I
would, but I'll tell you what I would do. I think I'd have about
twelve times the number of lawyers working for *This Week* than
we've had."

After the recording finished Andrew Neil left the studio
immediately without speaking to me. Upstairs the independent
lawyers were working out what bits of the interview to cut due to
defamation. I had one more programme to do. A car arrived from
the BBC *Newsnight* programme and took me to Television Centre. I
was to take part in a discussion with Conservative MP Ivor
Stanbrook, another vehement critic. This discussion was to be
recorded as well, for legal reasons. It seemed to go reasonably well
and at the end when we had finished Stanbrook said with evident
satisfaction, "Well, Thames won't do that again quickly." I
remarked that I thought that was a cynical remark even for a
politician. "Well," he replied, "politics is a cynical business."

The Government was not a gracious loser. On the afternoon of
the day of publication, John Wakeham, leader of the Commons,
told the House that the Government 'profoundly disagreed' with
the Report, even though he had not read it.

The next morning's headline in the *Independent* was "PM
dismisses *Death on the Rock* report". *The Times* had a similar headline
"Thatcher hits at *Death on the Rock* report". A statement had been
jointly issued by No. 10, the Foreign Office and the Ministry of
Defence making all the old points as if the inquiry had never existed.

The *Independent* stated that the programme had strengthened Mrs. Thatcher's determination to shake up the ITV companies and the IBA.

I turned on the radio to listen to the *Today* programme. Mrs. Thatcher listens to it regularly. Perhaps we both heard Sir Geoffrey Howe dismiss the inquiry, conducted by his old friend, in a carefully prepared statement. He said it was a report "about television, by television, for television". I thought nothing more could surprise me but the ungraciousness of this did so, particularly coming from the mild-mannered Sir Geoffrey.

Lord Windlesham was deeply hurt by his friend's attack and at the Royal Television Society's Television Awards on 23 February 1989 he said:

Since my independence and integrity have been questioned I should like to make it clear that I do not intend to accept payment for my work on the Report during a period of fourteen weeks.

Those who are ready to believe that my judgement has been compromised by my previous experience of broadcasting, despite over six years in the public service since I gave up all connections with televison, could not be slow to point to one more reason why I was unfitted to carry out the task which I took on in good faith and without any preconception. Accordingly, I have informed the Board of Thames that I do not wish to receive any fee for the time spent in carrying out the Inquiry and preparing the report.

Consequences

Death on the Rock went on to win the Broadcasting Press Guild award for best documentary, and a similar award from the British Academy of Film and Television Arts.

Subsequently the Government did publish a broadcasting bill which, when enacted, will result in the disbanding of the IBA and its replacement by a 'lighter touch authority'. At the time of writing the new ITV franchises are to go to the highest bidder and it is uncertain whether Thames will retain its franchise. Whether *Death on the Rock* contributed to this is difficult to say. The Sinn Fein ban was introduced after the programme but I doubt if our programme was the direct reason for it.

On 21 April 1989, almost a year after *Death on the Rock*, the *New Statesman* published an article by two Spanish journalists, José Maria Alegre and Enrique Yeves. They wrote four major articles on the Gibraltar killings for the Spanish weekly magazine, *Interviu*. They talked to a number of the Spanish policemen involved in the surveillance of the three IRA members and they were categoric in their view of the "affidavit" allegedly made by Police Inspector Rayo Valenzuela. "We believe it to be a false statement, fabricated by the British authorities to sustain their version of events. That version has frequently been contradicted not only by ourselves, but by the Spanish authorities too."

Moreover, they had spoken with Valenzuela himself, "who indicated that he is not authorised to make declarations to the press. However, he said he could 'deny emphatically having ever signed a document of this type, not only because I lacked the authority to do so, but also because it's written in English, a language which I neither speak, nor understand, which would make it difficult for me to sign something like that; it's an absolute lie and I don't know where it came from.'"

Amnesty International published a critical report on the Gibraltar Inquest and called for a further inquiry. There will not be one of course.

No one has done a follow up to *Death on the Rock*, but we have not been idle.

20

AFTERMATH

Is that the Editor of *This Week*?
   Yes, who's speaking?
   It's the Anti-Terrorist Branch here. We would like the rushes of your interview with Father Ryan. All the untransmitted material and the transcripts.

Pause. Editor wonders if the conversation is being taped, and experiences that tingle in the spine to which he has become accustomed over the past eleven years.

Well, er, I must consult our legal adviser, but in these circumstances we need a formal written request from you that we can consider, and we usually refuse to release such material [I forgot to say 'if we have it'] without a subpoena.
   [The policeman had his reply ready.]
   We will send a letter round immediately and meanwhile, I suggest that you ask your lawyer to look at Section 18 of the Prevention of Terrorism Act.

I put the phone down. Here we go again, I thought – Ireland once more.
   We had made a *This Week* programme about the Irish Catholic priest Father Patrick Ryan who had been accused in the House of Commons of working for the IRA. The subsequent row about whether he should be extradited from Dublin had damaged Anglo–Irish relations. Our interview with Father Ryan had

[302]

avoided the Home Secretary's ban because he was a candidate for the European Elections which were taking place.

The next morning the letter arrived pointing out that Section 18 of the Prevention of Terrorism (Temporary Provisions) Act 1989 provides for a person to be guilty of an offence against the Act if he has information which he knows, or believes, might be of material assistance in securing the prosecution or conviction of any person for an offence involving the commission, preparation or instigation of an act of terrorism, and that he fails, without reasonable excuse, to disclose that information as soon as reasonably practicable.

The Anti-Terrorist Branch went on to make clear that they were of the opinion that the contents of the interview with Father Ryan might be of material assistance to the prosecution and formally notified us accordingly. They also pointed out that Schedule 7 (2) of the said Act provides for the granting of a warrant to search for such material, but they hoped they wouldn't have to resort to that.

I arranged to talk to Barrie Sales, thinking that we'd have a couple of days to think through the arguments and the conflict of interest and responsibility we faced. On the one hand, journalists are not above the law and, as citizens, must work within it. On the other, we have a responsibility to keep reporting the facts, no matter how unpalatable. If we just handed over the rushes, then certain physically active people might take the view that we were simply extensions of the police force and act accordingly.

We were not given much time however because within twenty-four hours of the phone call, members of the press were mysteriously briefed, with the result that I was bombarded with phone calls. I could see the headlines: "*Death on the Rock* team in new row over terrorism". If a search warrant were issued, I had little doubt that news teams would know exactly when the detectives would arrive at Thames reception. That search warrant could easily be used for a 'fishing expedition'. I didn't want to be done over *à la* Zircon.

However, in this case we convinced ourselves that we could hand over the film with a relatively clear conscience. There was no question of confidentiality involved, and the interview had been done openly on the campaign trail with no pre-condition. Still, we felt uneasy. We'd been pushed another step down a road with an uncertain ending.

Over the last decade the pressures on broadcasters have steadily increased. After the Prevention of Terrorism Act we've had the Home Secretary's Broadcasting Ban and now the new and highly restrictive Official Secrets Act. All have reduced the freedom to report. Where the law hasn't been sufficient straightforward, political and economic pressure has been used against the broadcasting organisations. Post 1992 the viewer will be unlikely to find any prime-time current affairs on ITV, and out of prime time such programmes will have their resources cut and their ability to undertake difficult investigations much reduced.

How much of this was inevitable? As I look back what astonishes me is how relatively insignificant were the causes of some of the great rows I have been involved in. At Carrickmore, for example, some film of an IRA manoeuvre was shot, but nothing was transmitted. Why, therefore, was there so much bother?

One of the reasons is the continual sore of Ireland, insoluble as ever, embarrassing and corrupting. As harsh a test of a civilised society as any, tunnelling away at our tolerance, our system of justice. No broadcasting organisation could operate trouble-free in this area.

Another reason is the importance, perhaps overestimated, that politicians attach to broadcasting. Its journalism is widely perceived to be independent and objective – perhaps that is why it is dangerous.

Above all, however, there is no great demand for freedom of information in this country. Politicians lose no votes by opposing it. The British seem strangely indifferent, confusing it with freedom of speech.

The time is long overdue when a freedom of information act should be introduced so that politicans should have to justify why they are withholding information rather than the public having to demonstrate why they should have access. It would be rather funny if it wasn't so sad that you can now see secret servicemen being interviewed on Soviet television but you can't see British secret servicemen anywhere in the UK.

As the lights go on again in Eastern Europe are they fading over here? Certainly ten years in power has given the Prime Minister, who is not naturally sympathetic to broadcasters and journalists, plenty of opportunity to curtail their activities.

But she is no different from earlier prime ministers like Harold Wilson. She has just had longer at it with rather larger majorities than most. In these circumstances the major broadcasting organisations have to hold the line and not bend, they must not put corporate survival before journalistic responsibility. The Parliamentary opposition will watch what happens and if the organisations do bend, they will demand that they bend back and probably bend over.

In the end there is probably no resolution to the eternal conflict between those who believe they know what Britain's interests are (and think they have a right to define them) and those who believe a responsibility to the facts comes before everything.

Not long after the Windlesham/Rampton Report was published I had lunch with one of our most outspoken critics in Covent Garden. We knew each other quite well and I rather liked him. He was witty, charming and laughed at his own arrogance. Why did we find ourselves on opposite sides of the argument?

"You see, Roger," he said, "you and I come from different cultures. Mine is the army and politics. You are a typical grammar-school boy from the sixties. Of course there was a shoot-to-kill policy in Gibraltar just as we had in the Far East and in Aden. And if they would give me command in Northern Ireland I'd soon sort out the situation and take out the paramilitary leaders. But it's none of your business. There are certain areas of the British national interest that you shouldn't get involved in. *Death on the Rock* just wasn't necessary."

But the truth is always necessary.

I wondered how often my luncheon companion had left clubland and walked down the Falls Road in Belfast and listened to what the people actually said and believed. Sometimes I fear the English and the Irish – separated, but related by blood – are fated never to understand each other.

Could the rows have been avoided by better and more cunning management? Perhaps but I think not. One can always have peace – at a price.

I share the views of Lord Windlesham who told the Royal Television Society:

If the price of harmony is to leave sensitive subjects alone; to ask

no awkward questions; to take no risks incurring official dis-
pleasure on issues of high public importance; then it is a price set
too high. Far from being a symptom that something is wrong in
the body politic, I regard periodic rows between governments of
whatever colour and broadcasters as genuine marks – stigmata
may be the better word – of a free society.

I hope there are more rows to come.

INLA INTERVIEW

conducted by David Lomax for the BBC's
Tonight programme in July 1979

Q: Why did you murder Airey Neave?

MALE: Well I murdered Airey Neave because he was a
       militarist. He was in fact Margaret Thatcher's principal
       adviser on security. He was an advocate of order and
       increased repression against a nationalist people in the
       six counties. And we find it a surprising question why
       people wonder why we executed Neave. The same
       questions aren't asked when ordinary British soldiers
       are shot. Neave was to be the head of the British
       military apparatus in the north. We had done serious
       intelligence work on Roy Mason and obviously during
       the period of the Labour Government, Roy Mason was
       also a prime target for the Irish National Liberation
       Army. We took the decision to do, to switch our
       emphasis to Mr. Neave when it became obvious that
       there would be a Tory Government.

Q: How was the act itself carried out?

MALE: It was carried out by an active service cell of the Irish
       National Liberation Army. We're not prepared to say
       whether that cell was based in Britain or whether it er,
       went from the six counties or the twenty-six counties,
       that is a matter of security for us and it's up to the
       British intelligence agencies to puzzle out how, and who
       it was carried out by for themselves.

Q: But how did they go about it?

MALE: They breached security around the Palace of Westminster, round the House of Commons.

Q: That's what you said in your military communiqué, that you'd breached security at the House of Commons. How did you do that?

MALE: Er, we're not prepared to say how we did it.

Q: Isn't a much more likely explanation that somebody planted a bomb underneath Mr. Airey Neave's car while it was outside his flat?

MALE: I'll just repeat that it was planted inside the security net around the House of Commons.

Q: But how was that done?

MALE: I'm not prepared to say.

Q: But what did the murder of Mr. Neave achieve except widespread revulsion in Britain and a determination that no one should be able to get his way, his own way in our democracy by force?

MALE: We didn't see any examples of that revulsion except from the ruling interests in Britain.

Q: But isn't it true that there's widespread revulsion in Britain over that act?

MALE: We didn't see thousands of British workers marching in the street in mourning for Mr. Neave, we saw no obvious reaction against Neave's assassination. Neave had a record of consistent anti-working class attitudes towards the British people themselves.

Q: What do you think that the murder of Mr. Airey Neave achieved for your organisation?

MALE: We would say that it wasn't a murder first of all. We would say that Airey Neave was assassinated or executed.

Q: Well whatever word you care to use what do you think it achieved for your organisation?

MALE: We think, we see that assassination of Airey Neave in the context of the overall struggle aginst the British occupation source, forces in Ireland.

Q: What do you mean by that?

MALE: The British military. The RUC. The RUC reserve, the UDR.

Q: But what does that murder achieve for you? What difference does . . .

MALE: Because we have a war against the British military occupation forces. Neave had a responsibility for that.

Q: But the British military have been in Northern Ireland for the last ten years. There is absolutely no evidence whatsoever that the British Government is weakening its resolve to stay there.

MALE: That remains to be seen whether the British Government will stay there or not.

Q: Why should anyone in Britain be sympathetic to your cause when you use methods like that?

MALE: We have never directed our military operations against British civilians, or against the working people of Britain.

Q: Wasn't Mr. Neave a British civilian?

MALE: Mr. Neave was not a civilian, did not act, or never acted like a civilian in regard to the Irish people. Mr. Neave was an advocate of torture in Ireland Mr. Neave was an advocate of capital punishment for Irish freedom fighters. The British establishment will have to know that not only their soldiers are at risk, but also the people who direct the actions of those soldiers, and it's up to that establishment to take responsibility for that position, not ours. Mr. Neave was a legitimate target.

Q: But is there any other evidence apart from the grief which people feel for his death that the British establishment as you call it is taking you seriously?

MALE: Well, one had to only view Mrs. Thatcher's reactions in the days after Mr. Neave's assassination, to understand that.

Q: What do you mean by that?

MALE: Pardon?

Q: What do you mean by that?

MALE: We think that had a visible affect on the Tory Cabinet. We think Mr. Neave, who brought Mrs. Thatcher to prominence, who planned her leadership takeover in the Conservative Party, that she relied very much on Mr. Neave, and in that extent it affected the British establishment. We don't think that just by assassinating Airey Neave that you are going to win the struggle, we would see it more as a protracted struggle, but we are determined to let the British people know and the British ruling class establishment, that this struggle in Ireland is going to be a protracted struggle, and that it won't cease until Britain has granted the Irish people the right to self-determination.

David Lomax, in a studio link, then provided evidence to contradict the distasteful allegations made against Mr. Neave. The interview then continued.

Q: How big is the INLA?

MALE: We're not prepared – I'm not interested in disclosing the numbers that are in the Irish National Liberation Army.

Q: It's been reported that it's very small, less than a hundred activists.

MALE: We're not interested in what's reported about the strength of our organisation.

Q: And what is your position in that organisation?

MALE: I'm a spokesperson for the Irish National Liberation Army.

Q: How long have you been in the INLA?

MALE: I'm not prepared to say.

Q: What sort of weapons does the INLA have?

MALE: Not prepared to discuss that.

Q: How's the INLA financed, apart from bank robberies?

MALE: Well, you've stated a position that I'm not accepting. We are self-financing, we do selective expropriations. And we are financed by our supporters in Ireland, and abroad.

Q: What are selective appropriations?

MALE: They are exactly as I've stated. We will expropriate money from the enemy in order to finance our campaign.

Q: Sounds like another word for saying bank robberies.

MALE: It's as simple as that. You can put any interpretation you prefer on it.

Q: But it sounds another way of saying bank robberies.

MALE: I've stated the position that we expropriate money from the enemy.

Q: Why should anyone in Britain take your organisation seriously when you have no political support. North or South of the border?

MALE: First of all I don't accept your assumptions that we have no support. Why should the British people take us seriously? I mean, first of all we don't address ourselves, don't address our politics to all the British people. The British people that we would have an interest in and would have a feeling affinity with, would be the working people in England, Scotland and Wales. We are

a Republican Socialist organisation. Our aims are a
democratic socialist republic in Ireland. We want power
over the wealth that's created for the working people of
Ireland, and we would have a similar view for the
people in England, Scotland and Wales, but that is for
them to work out. We think our politics has a relevance.
We think that if and when the British withdraw from
Ireland, that it is to the benefit of the working people of
England, Scotland and Wales.

Q: You talk about – you talk all the time about British
        Imperialism, and the British Occupation Forces as you
        call them. You have not mentioned at all anything about
        one million Protestants, do you expect to bomb a million
        Protestants into a United Ireland?

MALE: We've bombed Airey Neave. We didn't bomb or haven't
        bombed Protestants. We don't attack people because of
        their religious affiliation.

Q: What can you say to the Protestants in Northern
        Ireland, the vast majority of whom want the British to
        stay?

MALE: That's a question that can't be answered in a couple of
        sentences but I will try and give – try and answer it
        briefly. We have never in any of our public statements
        made any claims to be superior or want to oppress the
        Protestant people. We've seen working class Protestants
        that live in the short Strand, they share many of the
        problems of working class people of the nationalist
        population who live in areas like Ardoyne and
        Andersonstown.

Q: But is the solution to that problem, the killing of say, for
        instance, volunteers in the UDR, men who have families
        and children who live in isolated farmhouses?

MALE: The UDR are a part and are directed by the occupation
        forces. They're part of that machine. They direct their
        energies against the nationalist population, against

[312]

volunteers in the Irish National Liberation Army, and the Irish Republican Army. Therefore they are a legitimate target for attacks by the National Liberation Forces.

Q: How long do you think it wil be before your aim is realised in Northern Ireland?

MALE: Well, the British Government have a large responsibility, and in a sense it's up to the British Government to decide how long this conflict, this war, is going to last. The decision rests with – fairly and squarely with the British Government. The conflict with the British Army could be over tomorrow if the British Army would state its intention of leaving this island on a specified date, and when we say a specified date we don't mean sometime in the next twenty years, we need the earliest specified time.

Q: And the point of view of a million Protestants in Northern Ireland, that's irrelevant in your eyes?

MALE: No. I stated previously that it is not irrelevant and I stated our political position on the whole question of the Protestant population in the six counties. We have never stated that we want the Protestant population to leave Ireland. It has been their home for hundreds of years, Ireland, and we look upon them as Irish people.

Q: What sort of future operations are you planning in Britain?

MALE: We're not going to specify our plans for Britain.

Q: But are you saying that it is your intention to continue what you call military operations in Britain?

MALE: It's our – it's our intention to continue military operations against the British military in six counties. It is our intention to carry out those operations in England, or wherever the opportunity presents itself.

NATIONWIDE "ON THE SPOT"

General Election, 1983

SUE LAWLEY:	Let's go to Mrs. Diana Gould in our Bristol studio. Mrs. Gould, your question, please.
DIANA GOULD:	Mrs. Thatcher, why, when the *Belgrano*, the Argentinian battleship, was outside the exclusion zone and actually sailing away from the Falklands, why did you give the orders to sink it?
MRS. THATCHER:	But it was not sailing away from the Falklands. It was in an area which was a danger to our ships and to our people on them.
DIANA GOULD:	Outside the exclusion zone.
MRS. THATCHER:	But it was in an area which we had warned . . . at the end of April we had given warnings that all ships in those areas, if they represented a danger to our ships, were vulnerable. When it was sunk that ship, which we had found, was a danger to our ships. My duty was to look after our troops, our ships, our navy. And, my goodness me, I lived with many, many anxious days and nights.
DIANA GOULD:	Mrs. Thatcher, you started your answer by

saying it was not sailing away from the Falklands. It was on a bearing of 280° and it was already west of the Falklands, so I'm sorry but I cannot see how you can say it was not sailing away from the Falklands when it was sunk.

MRS. THATCHER: When it was sunk it was a danger to our ships.

DIANA GOULD: No, but you have just said at the beginning of your answer that it was not sailing away from the Falklands, and I'm asking you to correct that statement.

MRS. THATCHER: Yes, but it was in an area outside the exclusion zone, which I think is what you are saying is 'sailing away'.

SUE LAWLEY: We're arguing about which way it was facing at the time.

MRS. THATCHER: It was a danger to our ships.

DIANA GOULD: Mrs. Thatcher, I am saying that it was on a bearing of 280°, which is a bearing just north of west. It was already west of the Falklands and therefore nobody with any imagination can put it sailing other than away from the Falklands.

MRS. THATCHER: Mrs. . . . I'm sorry, I've forgotten your name –

SUE LAWLEY: Mrs. Gould.

MRS. THATCHER: Mrs. Gould, when orders were given to sink it and when it was sunk it was in an area which was a danger to our ships. Now, you accept that, do you?

DIANA GOULD: No, I don't.

MRS. THATCHER: Well, I'm sorry, it was. You must accept that when we gave the order, when we changed the rules which enabled them to sink *Belgrano*, the change of rules had been notified at the end of April. It was all published, that any ships that were a danger to ours within a certain zone, wider than the Falklands, were likely to be sunk.

And again I do say to you my duty – and I'm very proud that we put it this way and adhered to it – was to protect the lives of the people in our ships and the enormous numbers of troops that we had down there waiting for landings. I put that duty first, and when the *Belgrano* was sunk – and I ask you to accept this – she was in a position which was a danger to our navy.

SUE LAWLEY: Mrs. Gould, let me ask you this, Mrs. Gould. What motive are you seeking to attach to Mrs. Thatcher and her government in this? Is it inefficiency? Lack of communication? Or is it a desire for action, a desire for war?

DIANA GOULD: It is a desire for action and a lack of communications, because giving those orders to sink the *Belgrano* when it was actually sailing away from our fleet and away from the Falklands was, in effect, sabotaging any possibility of any peace plan succeeding. And Mrs. Thatcher had fourteen hours in which to consider the Peruvian peace plan that was being put forward to her, in which – those fourteen hours – those orders could have been. . .

MRS. THATCHER: One day all of the facts, in about thirty years' time, will be published.

DIANA GOULD: That is not good enough, Mrs. Thatcher, we need . . .

MRS. THATCHER: Would you please let me answer!

SUE LAWLEY: Let Mrs. Thatcher answer. I think you've put a fair point.

MRS. THATCHER: Would you please let me answer. I lived with the responsibility for a very long time. I answered the question giving the facts – not anyone's opinions, but the facts.

These Peruvian peace proposals, which were only in outline, did not reach London until after the attack on the *Belgrano*. This is fact. I'm sorry, that is fact, and I am going to finish. They did not reach London until after the attack on the *Belgrano*.

Moreover, we went on negotiating for another fortnight after that attack. I think it could only be in Britain that a Prime Minister was accused of sinking an enemy ship that was a danger to our navy when my main motive was to protect the boys in our navy. That was my main motive and I'm very proud of it.

One day all the facts will be revealed, and they will indicate as I have said.

SUE LAWLEY: Mrs. Gould, have you got a new point to make, otherwise I must move on?

DIANA GOULD: Just one point. I understand that the Peruvian peace plans, on a *Nationwide* programme, were discussed at midnight, 1 May. If that outline did not reach London for another fourteen hours, I think there must be something very seriously wrong with our communications and we are living in a nuclear age when we're going to have minutes to make decisions, not hours.

MRS. THATCHER: I have indicated what the facts are. And would you accept that I am in a position to

know exactly when they reached London,
exactly when the attack was made. I repeat:
the job of a Prime Minister is to protect the
lives of our boys on our ships. And I'm proud
of it, because that's what I did.